Taste of Home

Make it!

TAKE IT

TASTE OF HOME BOOKS • RDA ENTHUSIAST BRANDS, LLC • MILWAUKEE, WI

PAGE 26

PAGE 18

PAGE 62

PAGE 108

CONTENTS

PAGE 119

PAGE 217

PAGE 197

PAGE 82

Visit us at **tasteofhome.com** for other
Taste of Home books and products.

Executive Editor: Mark Hagen
Senior Art Director: Raeann Thompson
Senior Editor: Christine Rukavena
Art Director: Maggie Conners
Deputy Editor, Copy Desk: Dulcie Shoener
Copy Editor: Sara Strauss
Contributing Layout Designer: Jennifer Ruetz

Cover:
Photographer: Dan Roberts
Set Stylist: Stacey Genaw
Food Stylist: Shannon Norris

Pictured on front cover:
BBQ Chicken Sandwiches, p. 77
Creamy Cavatappi and Cheese, p. 72
Watermelon Cupcakes, p. 192

Pictured on title page:
Cheese Enchiladas, p. 79

Pictured on back cover:
Caramelized Ham & Swiss Buns, p. 73
Strawberry Cream Floats, p. 231
Ham & Cheddar Brunch Ring, p. 45
Blueberry Lemon Trifle, p. 210

International Standard Book Numbers:
D 978-1-62145-872-2
U 978-1-62145-873-9
International Standard Serial Number:
2166-0522
Component Numbers:
D 118100108H
U 118100110H

Printed in USA
10 9 8 7 6 5 4 3 2 1

More ways to connect with us:

GOOD TIMES ARE ON TAP
TAKE GREAT FOOD ON THE GO WITH OUR BEST RECIPES & TIPS!

Make lasting memories of wonderful get-togethers when you cook with *Make It, Take It.* This edition is packed with hundreds of crowd-pleasing party foods, plus dozens of tips for making recipes in advance, and transporting and serving your dishes with ease.

Savor every moment of party preparation as you consider these reader-submitted recipes and Test Kitchen pointers, all approved by the experts at *Taste of Home.*

Inside, you'll find 248 magnificent new dishes! Also watch for these features:

KIDS' SIMPLE FAVORITES:

I scream, you scream, we all scream for old-fashioned ice cream floats (shown on back cover)! From Hawaiian pizza to hand-pulled taffy, in this special bonus chapter you'll discover 26 ideas sure to delight young partygoers.

MAKE AHEAD recipes have instructions to help you prep the dish ahead and then store it for easy serving later on. Hooray!

BRING IT
These tips sprinkled throughout the book provide insights for organizing the buffet, keeping foods hot or cold, and making sure your dish is a standout contribution.

PACK LIKE A PRO
These tips and tricks will have you hitting the road with confidence.

1 Build a DIY Multilevel Tote

If you have more dishes than hands, reach for a cooling rack with folding legs. Fold out the legs and use the rack to create sturdy, stable levels inside a carrying tote without crushing what's below. Get creative. You can also build layers by propping up a sheet pan with ring molds or cans.

2 Ensure a No-Slip Trip

Place grippy drawer liners or silicone baking mats in the car before loading your food. The lining will keep dishes from sliding and contain any errant spills. An old yoga mat works well for this, too.

3 Keep a Lid on It

Use a bungee cord, painter's tape or thick ribbon to keep the lid for your slow cooker or Dutch oven in place. Secure the cord around the handles and over the top. Now you're ready to transport without risk of a mess.

4 Bring a Salad

Yes, you can serve a crisp, freshly tossed salad when you're far from home. Just bring the fixings in a serving bowl, along with the utensils. Toss the salad at your destination. Voila! Remember to bring a grocery bag to corral the leftovers and dirty dishes.

5 Frosting Is Good Glue

If you're transporting a cake to a special event, make it easier to tote with this little tip. Secure the cake (or cardboard cake circle if you're using one) onto the presentation plate with a dab of frosting. This makes the cake less likely to slide around, even if you have to brake suddenly. And you're the only one who'll know the frosting is there!

6 Pack a Touch-Up Kit

Make a little touch-up kit of decorations and frosting (just in case) to take with your decorated cake. Pack the items with a clean dish towel and offset spatula. Transport the frosting in its pastry bag if you used one.

7 Tailgate Grill Skills

Place the grill on a solid surface, away from any activities so no one bumps into it. Don't set the grill near shrubs, grass, overhangs or fences. Keep coolers away from the grill. Set the coolers out of direct sunlight and replenish the ice if possible.

8 Keep a Tailgate Kit

Store all your tailgate needs (such as linens, serve ware, games and sunblock) in a plastic bin inside a cooler. You'll be ready to go at a moment's notice.

Grilled Glazed
Drummies
page 23

Appetizers & Dips

Dig into pimiento cheese spread, nachos, Buffalo wings and dozens of other party classics. Discover the perfect crowd-sized beverage for the gathering, too. You're sure to find new favorites here.

FETA CHEESE-STUFFED TOMATOES

These tempting cheese-stuffed tomatoes are bursting with fresh flavor. Use the small end of a melon scoop to easily remove the pulp.
—Laura LeRoy, Waxhaw, NC

- -

Takes: 25 min. • **Makes:** 2 dozen

24	firm cherry tomatoes
3	oz. cream cheese, softened
⅓	cup crumbled feta cheese
¼	cup sour cream
1	green onion, finely chopped
¾	tsp. lemon juice
⅛	to ¼ tsp. dried oregano
	Coarsely ground pepper

1. Cut a thin slice off the top of each tomato. Scoop out and discard the pulp. Invert tomatoes onto paper towels to drain.

2. In a small mixing bowl, beat the cream cheese, feta cheese, sour cream, onion, lemon juice and oregano until blended. Pipe mixture into tomatoes. If desired, sprinkle with black pepper. Chill tomatoes until serving.

1 stuffed tomato: 25 cal., 2g fat (1g sat. fat), 6mg chol., 28mg sod., 1g carb. (1g sugars, 0 fiber), 1g pro.

TEST KITCHEN TIP
To save time, you can prep the tomatoes and filling the night before your event, then fill the tomatoes right before serving. If you don't have oregano on hand, substitute dried basil.

CITRUS & WHITE GRAPE PARTY PUNCH

I was looking for a punch that wouldn't stain expensive prom dresses and tuxedos. Everyone loved this! You can mix the first four ingredients ahead of time, refrigerate and add the soda right before serving.
—Karen Ballance, Wolf Lake, IL

- -

Takes: 5 min. • **Makes:** 32 servings (4 qt.)

- 4 **cups white grape juice, chilled**
- 1 **can (12 oz.) frozen lemonade concentrate, thawed**
- 1 **can (12 oz.) frozen orange juice concentrate, thawed**
- 2 **bottles (2 liters each) lemon-lime soda, chilled**
Optional: Lemon slices, orange slices and green grapes

In a punch bowl, combine grape juice, lemonade concentrate and orange juice concentrate. Add soda; serve immediately. If desired, garnish with fruit.
½ cup: 119 cal., 0 fat (0 sat. fat), 0 chol., 17mg sod., 30g carb. (26g sugars, 0 fiber), 0 pro.

BUFFALO CHICKEN WINGS

Hot wings got their start in Buffalo, New York, in the kitchen of a bar. Although there was no game on at the time, today spicy wings and cool sauces are traditional game-day fare. Cayenne, red sauce and spices keep these tangy buffalo chicken wings good and hot, just like the originals.
—Nancy Chapman, Center Harbor, NH

Prep: 10 min. • **Cook:** 10 min./batch
Makes: about 4 dozen

- 5 lbs. chicken wings
  Oil for frying
- 1 cup butter, cubed
- ¼ cup Louisiana-style hot sauce
- ¾ tsp. cayenne pepper
- ¾ tsp. celery salt
- ½ tsp. onion powder
- ½ tsp. garlic powder
  Optional: Celery ribs and ranch or blue cheese salad dressing

1. Cut chicken wings into 3 sections; discard wing tip sections. In an electric skillet, heat 1 in. oil to 375°. Fry the wings in oil, a few at a time, for 3-4 minutes on each side or until the chicken juices run clear. Drain on paper towels.
2. Meanwhile, in a small saucepan, melt butter. Stir in the hot sauce and spices. Place chicken in a large bowl; add sauce and toss to coat. Remove to a serving plate with a slotted spoon. Serve with celery and ranch or blue cheese dressing if desired.
Note: Uncooked chicken wing sections (wingettes) may be substituted for whole chicken wings.
1 piece: 126 cal., 12g fat (4g sat. fat), 25mg chol., 105mg sod., 0 carb. (0 sugars, 0 fiber), 5g pro.

AUNT KAREN'S SHRIMP SALAD

When unexpected company calls during the holidays, this salad is the perfect fit. It's quick to put together, too, leaving you more time to spend with your guests.
—Karen Moore, Jacksonville, FL

Prep: 10 min. • **Cook:** 10 min. + chilling
Makes: 24 servings

- 2 lbs. uncooked shrimp (26-30 per lb.), peeled and deveined and halved
- 1 Tbsp. white vinegar
- 1 Tbsp. lemon juice
- ⅓ cup plus 1 Tbsp. mayonnaise, divided
- ½ tsp. garlic salt
- 2 celery ribs, chopped
- 5 hard-boiled large eggs, chopped
- ¼ cup chopped sweet red pepper
- 24 Bibb lettuce leaves or Boston lettuce leaves
  Sliced green onions, optional

1. In a Dutch oven or large saucepan, bring 6 cups water to a boil. Add shrimp; cook, uncovered, until shrimp turn pink, 3-5 minutes. Drain. Transfer to a large bowl. Add vinegar, lemon juice, 1 Tbsp. mayonnaise and garlic salt; toss to coat. Refrigerate, covered, at least 4 hours or overnight.
2. To serve, stir in the remaining ⅓ cup mayonnaise, celery, eggs and red pepper. Serve in lettuce leaves. If desired, top with green onions.
¼ cup: 74 cal., 4g fat (1g sat. fat), 85mg chol., 120mg sod., 1g carb. (0 sugars, 0 fiber), 8g pro. **Diabetic exchanges:** 1 lean meat, 1 fat.

CHEESE & PIMIENTO SPREAD

This pimiento and cheese spread is a spicy, modern version of my mother's delicious recipe. Serve it stuffed in celery or spread on crackers or a sandwich.
—Elizabeth Hester, Elizabethtown, NC

Takes: 15 min. • **Makes:** 2¾ cups

- 12 oz. sharp white cheddar cheese
- 8 oz. reduced-fat cream cheese, softened
- 2 tsp. Worcestershire sauce
- 2 tsp. white vinegar
- ¼ tsp. white pepper
- ¼ tsp. garlic powder
- ¼ tsp. cayenne pepper
- 1 jar (4 oz.) diced pimientos, undrained
  Assorted crackers and vegetables

Shred the cheddar cheese; transfer to a large bowl. Add the cream cheese, Worcestershire sauce, vinegar, pepper, garlic powder and cayenne; beat on low speed until blended. Drain pimientos, reserving 2 Tbsp. juice. Stir in pimientos and reserved juice. Serve with crackers and vegetables.

2 Tbsp.: 90 cal., 7g fat (4g sat. fat), 23mg chol., 150mg sod., 1g carb. (1g sugars, 0 fiber), 5g pro.

JALAPENO POPPER POCKET

For a fresh take on fried jalapeno poppers, we stuff chicken, cheeses and jalapenos inside puff pastry and bake.
—Sally Sibthorpe, Shelby Township, MI

Prep: 15 min. • **Bake:** 20 min. + standing
Makes: 12 servings

- 2 cups chopped rotisserie chicken (about 10 oz.)
- 1 carton (8 oz.) spreadable chive and onion cream cheese
- 1 cup shredded pepper jack or Monterey Jack cheese
- 1 can (4 oz.) diced jalapeno peppers
- 1 sheet frozen puff pastry, thawed
- 1 large egg, lightly beaten

1. Preheat oven to 425°. In a bowl, mix the chicken, cream cheese, pepper jack cheese and peppers.
2. On a lightly floured surface, unfold puff pastry; roll into a 13-in. square. Place on a parchment-lined baking sheet. Spread half with chicken mixture to within ½ in. of the edges. Fold remaining half over filling; press edges with a fork to seal.
3. Brush lightly with beaten egg. Cut slits in pastry. Bake 20-25 minutes or until golden brown. Let stand 10 minutes before cutting.
1 piece: 237 cal., 15g fat (6g sat. fat), 58mg chol., 252mg sod., 13g carb. (1g sugars, 2g fiber), 12g pro.

QUICK TURKEY NACHOS SNACK

My husband is one of the biggest snackers around. I keep the ingredients on hand so I can whip up a batch of these nachos any time.
—Kathy Faulk, East Hartford, CT

- -

Takes: 30 min. • **Makes:** 8 servings

1	lb. ground turkey
1	pkg. (1¼ oz.) taco seasoning
¾	cup water
1	pkg. (12 oz.) tortilla chips
½	cup shredded Monterey Jack cheese
½	cup shredded cheddar cheese
2	cups shredded lettuce
½	cup sour cream
½	cup salsa
4	green onions, chopped

1. In a large nonstick skillet over medium heat, cook turkey until no longer pink, breaking into crumbles; drain. Add taco seasoning and water. Bring to a boil. Reduce heat; simmer, uncovered until thickened, 8-10 minutes.

2. Arrange tortilla chips on an ungreased baking sheet. Top with turkey and cheese. Broil 4 in. from the heat until cheese is melted, 2-3 minutes. Top with lettuce, sour cream, salsa and onions.

1 serving: 400 cal., 21g fat (7g sat. fat), 54mg chol., 760mg sod., 35g carb. (1g sugars, 2g fiber), 18g pro.

★ ★ ★ ★ ★ **READER REVIEW**

"I have made this many times. We love it for a quick lunch on football Sundays."

WIENER TASTEOFHOME.COM

FESTIVE HOLIDAY SLIDERS

My mini turkey sandwiches with cranberry sauce, horseradish and ginger keep well in the refrigerator. I like to have a batch on hand for holiday get-togethers.
—Pamela Miller, Big Rapids, MI

Takes: 30 min. • **Makes:** 2 dozen

- 1 pkg. (8 oz.) cream cheese, softened
- ½ cup mayonnaise
- ¼ cup Creole mustard
- 2 Tbsp. minced fresh gingerroot
- 1 Tbsp. grated orange zest
- 1½ tsp. prepared horseradish
- 1 cup whole-berry cranberry sauce
- 4 green onions, sliced
- 2 pkg. (12 oz. each) Hawaiian sweet rolls or 24 dinner rolls, split
- 1½ lbs. thinly sliced cooked turkey

1. Beat cream cheese and mayonnaise until smooth. Beat in mustard, ginger, orange zest and horseradish. In another bowl, mix cranberry sauce and green onions.
2. Spread cream cheese mixture onto roll bottoms. Top with turkey, cranberry mixture and roll tops.
1 slider: 231 cal., 10g fat (4g sat. fat), 54mg chol., 221mg sod., 22g carb. (10g sugars, 1g fiber), 13g pro.

SIMPLE GUACAMOLE

Because avocados can brown quickly, it's best to make this guacamole just before serving. If you do have to make it a little in advance, place the avocado pit in the guacamole until serving.
—Heidi Main, Anchorage, AK

Takes: 10 min. • **Makes:** 1½ cups

- 2 medium ripe avocados
- 1 Tbsp. lemon juice
- ¼ cup chunky salsa
- ⅛ to ¼ tsp. salt

Peel and chop avocados; place in a small bowl. Sprinkle with lemon juice. Add salsa and salt; mash coarsely with a fork. Refrigerate until serving.
2 Tbsp.: 53 cal., 5g fat (1g sat. fat), 0 chol., 51mg sod., 3g carb. (0 sugars, 2g fiber), 1g pro.

HAM & SWISS BRAIDS

Satisfy hearty appetites with these golden loaves. Each slice is like a hot sandwich packed with ham, broccoli and Swiss cheese. Hot pepper sauce adds a nice kick, while refrigerated crescent rolls make it extra easy. The braids are perfect for a special occasion lunch or as an appetizer.
—Donna McCord, Fishers, IN

Prep: 30 min. • **Bake:** 20 min.
Makes: 2 loaves (6 servings each)

- ¾ cup mayonnaise
- 2 Tbsp. Dijon mustard
- 2 Tbsp. honey
- ⅛ tsp. hot pepper sauce
- 2 cups chopped fully cooked ham (about 10 oz.)
- 1 cup shredded Swiss cheese or crumbled goat cheese
- 1 cup chopped fresh broccoli florets
- 1 cup chopped fresh spinach
- 2 tubes (8 oz. each) refrigerated crescent rolls
- 1 large egg white, lightly beaten

1. Preheat oven to 375°. For filling, mix the first 4 ingredients; stir in the ham, cheese and vegetables.
2. Unroll 1 tube of crescent dough onto an ungreased baking sheet; seal perforations to form 1 long rectangle. Spoon half of the filling lengthwise down center third of the rectangle. On each long side, cut 1-in. wide strips at an angle to within ½ in. of filling. Starting at 1 end, fold alternating strips at an angle across the filling; seal ends. Brush with egg white. Repeat with remaining dough and filling.
3. Bake 20-25 minutes or until dark golden brown, rotating pans halfway through baking. Cool 5 minutes before slicing.
1 piece: 306 cal., 21g fat (6g sat. fat), 27mg chol., 721mg sod., 20g carb. (7g sugars, 0 fiber), 11g pro.

ANTIPASTO KABOBS

My husband and I met at a cooking class. We have loved creating menus and entertaining ever since. These do-ahead appetizers are a favorite to serve.
—Denise Hazen, Cincinnati, OH

Prep: 35 min. + marinating
Makes: 40 appetizers

- 1 pkg. (9 oz.) refrigerated cheese tortellini
- 40 pimiento-stuffed olives
- 40 large pitted ripe olives
- ¾ cup Italian salad dressing
- 40 thin slices pepperoni
- 20 thin slices hard salami, halved

1. Cook tortellini according to package directions; drain and rinse in cold water. In a large bowl, combine tortellini, olives and salad dressing. Toss to coat; cover and refrigerate for 4 hours or overnight.
2. Drain mixture, discarding marinade. For each appetizer, thread a stuffed olive, a folded pepperoni slice, a tortellini, a folded salami piece and a ripe olive on a toothpick or short skewer.
1 kabob: 66 cal., 5g fat (1g sat. fat), 9mg chol., 315mg sod., 4g carb. (0 sugars, 0 fiber), 2g pro.

STROMBOLI SANDWICH

I've made this stromboli sandwich many times for parties, and it gets terrific reviews. You can add ingredients and spices to suit your taste. The recipe is so good I just had to share it with you!
—Leigh Lauer, Hummelstown, PA

Prep: 20 min. + rising • **Bake:** 30 min.
Makes: 10 servings

2	loaves (1 lb. each) frozen bread dough, thawed
¼	lb. sliced ham
¼	lb. sliced pepperoni
¼	cup chopped onion
¼	cup chopped green pepper
1	jar (14 oz.) pizza sauce, divided
¼	lb. sliced mozzarella cheese
¼	lb. sliced bologna
¼	lb. sliced hard salami
¼	lb. slice Swiss cheese
1	tsp. dried basil
1	tsp. dried oregano
¼	tsp. garlic powder
¼	tsp. pepper
2	Tbsp. butter, melted

Let the dough rise in a warm place until doubled. Punch down. Roll loaves together into one 15x12-in. rectangle. Layer the ham and pepperoni on half of the dough (lengthwise). Sprinkle with onion and green pepper. Top with ¼ cup of pizza sauce. Layer mozzarella, bologna, salami and Swiss cheese over sauce. Sprinkle with basil, oregano, garlic powder and pepper. Spread another ¼ cup of pizza sauce on top. Fold plain half of dough over filling and seal edges well. Place on a greased 15x10x1-in. baking pan. Bake at 375° until golden brown, 30-35 minutes. Brush with melted butter. Heat the remaining pizza sauce and serve with sliced stromboli.

1 piece: 388 cal., 23g fat (10g sat. fat), 60mg chol., 1175mg sod., 28g carb. (5g sugars, 2g fiber), 19g pro.

CARAMEL CHEX MIX

This wonderfully crunchy snack is loaded with cereal, pretzels and nuts—and coated with a not-too-sweet brown sugar mixture. Set out a bowl at your caroling party and watch it disappear by the handful.
—Samantha Moyer, Oskaloosa, IA

Prep: 10 min. • **Bake:** 15 min. + cooling
Makes: 3 qt.

- 2 cups each Rice Chex, Corn Chex and Wheat Chex
- 2 cups miniature pretzels
- 2 cups pecan halves
- 2 cups salted cashews
- ¾ cup butter, cubed
- ¾ cup packed brown sugar

1. In a large bowl, combine the cereal, pretzels and nuts. In a small saucepan, combine butter and brown sugar. Bring to a boil; cook and stir until thickened, about 2 minutes. Pour over cereal mixture; toss to coat.

2. Spread into 2 greased 15x10x1-in. baking pans. Bake at 350° for 8 minutes. Stir; bake for 6 minutes longer. Transfer to waxed paper-lined baking sheets. Cool completely. Store in airtight containers.

¾ cup: 383 cal., 27g fat (8g sat. fat), 23mg chol., 333mg sod., 34g carb. (14g sugars, 3g fiber), 6g pro.

MINI ROSEMARY-ROAST BEEF SANDWICHES

Roast beef sandwiches never last long at a party, especially if you dollop them with mayo, mustard, horseradish and pickled giardiniera relish.
—Susan Hein, Burlington, WI

Prep: 25 min. + chilling
Bake: 50 min. + chilling • **Makes:** 2 dozen

- 1   beef top round roast (3 lbs.)
- 3   tsp. kosher salt
- 2   tsp. crushed dried rosemary
- 2   Tbsp. olive oil, divided
- 2   tsp. pepper
- 2   cups mild giardiniera, drained
- 1   cup reduced-fat mayonnaise
- 2   Tbsp. stone-ground mustard
- 1   to 2 Tbsp. prepared horseradish
- 24   Hawaiian sweet rolls, split

1. Sprinkle roast with salt and rosemary. Cover and refrigerate at least 8 hours or up to 24 hours.
2. Preheat oven to 325°. Uncover roast and pat dry. Rub roast with 1 Tbsp. oil; sprinkle with pepper. In a large cast-iron or other ovenproof skillet, heat remaining 1 Tbsp. oil over medium-high heat. Brown roast on both sides.
3. Transfer to the oven; roast until a thermometer reads 135° for medium-rare, 50-60 minutes. (Temperature of roast will continue to rise about 10° upon standing.) Remove roast from skillet; let stand 1 hour. Refrigerate, covered, at least 2 hours, until roast is cold.
4. Place giardiniera in a food processor; pulse until finely chopped. In a small bowl, mix mayonnaise, mustard and horseradish.
5. To serve, thinly slice the cold beef. Serve on rolls with the mayonnaise mixture and chopped giardiniera.

1 sandwich with about 2 tsp. mayonnaise mixture and 4 tsp. giardiniera: 220 cal., 9g fat (3g sat. fat), 50mg chol., 466mg sod., 18g carb. (7g sugars, 1g fiber), 17g pro.

STRAWBERRY WATERMELON LEMONADE

The nutrition department at my local hospital inspired me to create this refreshing summer sipper. I tweaked their recipe slightly to create this drink full of sweet-tart flavor.
—Dawn Lowenstein, Huntingdon Valley, PA

Takes: 20 min. • **Makes:** 12 servings (3 qt.)

- ¼   cup sugar
- 2   cups boiling water
- ½   lb. fresh strawberries, hulled and quartered (about 2 cups)
- 12   cups cubed watermelon (about 1 medium)
- 1   can (12 oz.) frozen lemonade concentrate, thawed
- 3   Tbsp. lemon juice
     Ice cubes

Dissolve sugar in boiling water. Place the strawberries and watermelon in batches in a blender; cover and process until blended. Pour the blended fruit though a fine-mesh strainer; transfer to a large pitcher. Stir in lemonade concentrate, lemon juice and sugar water. Serve over ice.

1 cup: 119 cal., 0 fat (0 sat. fat), 0 chol., 7mg sod., 34g carb. (30g sugars, 1g fiber), 1g pro.

PANCETTA, PEAR & PECAN PUFFS

I was recently at a wedding reception where the menu was all small bites. Here's my rendition of the pear pastries they served. They're the perfect combo of savory and sweet.
—Arlene Erlbach, Morton Grove, IL

- -

Prep: 25 min. • **Bake:** 10 min. + cooling
Makes: 2 dozen

- 1 sheet frozen puff pastry, thawed
- 6 oz. cream cheese, softened
- 2 Tbsp. honey
- ⅛ tsp. salt
- ⅛ tsp. pepper
- ¼ cup (1 oz.) crumbled
     fresh goat cheese
- 3 Tbsp. crumbled crisp pancetta
     or crumbled cooked bacon
- 3 Tbsp. finely chopped
     peeled ripe pear
- 2 Tbsp. finely chopped pecans, toasted

1. Preheat the oven to 400°. On a lightly floured surface, unfold the pastry dough. Using a 1¾-in. round cookie cutter, cut dough into 24 circles. Transfer to parchment-lined baking sheets. Bake until golden brown, 10-12 minutes. Cool completely on a wire rack.

2. Meanwhile, beat cream cheese, honey, salt and pepper until well blended. Fold in goat cheese, pancetta, pear and pecans.

3. Halve each cooled pastry. Spoon the cream cheese mixture over bottom pastry halves; cover with the top halves. Serve at room temperature.

Note: To toast nuts, bake in a shallow pan in a 350° oven for 5-10 minutes or cook in a skillet over low heat until lightly browned, stirring occasionally.

1 puff: 105 cal., 7g fat (3g sat. fat), 13mg chol., 178mg sod., 8g carb. (2g sugars, 1g fiber), 2g pro.

MAKE AHEAD
GRILLED GLAZED DRUMMIES

My family prefers these mild, slightly sweet chicken wings to the traditional hot wings. They've been a favorite at so many gatherings.
—Laura Mahaffey, Annapolis, MD

- -

Prep: 10 min. + marinating • **Grill:** 15 min.
Makes: about 2 dozen

- 1 cup ketchup
- ⅓ cup reduced-sodium soy sauce
- 4 tsp. honey
- ¾ tsp. ground ginger
- ½ tsp. garlic powder
- 3 lbs. fresh or frozen chicken
     drumettes, thawed
     Optional: Sliced green onions and
     ranch dressing

1. In a small bowl, combine the first 5 ingredients. Pour 1 cup marinade into a large shallow dish. Add the chicken; turn to coat. Cover and refrigerate for at least 4 hours or overnight. Cover and refrigerate remaining marinade for basting.

2. Drain chicken, discarding marinade. Grill, covered, over medium heat until juices run clear, 15-20 minutes, turning and basting occasionally with the reserved marinade. If desired, top with sliced green onions and serve with ranch dressing.

1 serving: 141 cal., 9g fat (2g sat. fat), 43mg chol., 311mg sod., 3g carb. (3g sugars, 0 fiber), 11g pro.

CRANBERRY-LIME SANGRIA

Tart, light and fruity, this party-worthy sangria is a hit any time of the year.
—Katy Joosten, Little Chute, WI

Takes: 20 min.
Makes: 13 servings (about 2½ qt.)

- 2   cups water
- 1   cup fresh or frozen cranberries, thawed
- 1   bottle (750 milliliters) white wine, chilled
- ¾   cup frozen limeade concentrate, thawed
- 1   each medium orange, lime and apple, peeled and diced
- 1   bottle (1 liter) citrus soda, chilled

1. In a small saucepan, combine water and cranberries. Cook over medium heat until berries pop, about 5 minutes. Drain and discard liquid; set cranberries aside.
2. In a pitcher, combine the wine and limeade concentrate. Stir in the diced fruit and reserved cranberries; add the soda. Serve over ice.
¾ cup: 134 cal., 0 fat (0 sat. fat), 0 chol., 12mg sod., 24g carb. (21g sugars, 1g fiber), 0 pro.

BARBECUE & BEER MEATBALLS

This simple meatball recipe relies on time-saving ingredients like frozen meatballs and barbecue sauce. It's the perfect last-minute appetizer!
—*Taste of Home* Test Kitchen

Takes: 30 min. • **Makes:** 20 servings

- 1   pkg. (22 oz.) frozen fully cooked Angus beef meatballs
- 1   cup barbecue sauce
- ⅓   cup beer
  Thinly sliced jalapeno pepper, optional

1. Prepare meatballs according to the package directions.
2. Meanwhile, in a small saucepan, combine barbecue sauce and beer; heat through. Add meatballs; stir to coat. If desired, top with sliced jalapeno.
1 meatball: 106 cal., 6g fat (3g sat. fat), 17mg chol., 338mg sod., 7g carb. (5g sugars, 0 fiber), 4g pro.

FRUIT KABOBS WITH MARGARITA DIP

Your adult guests will love the margarita flavor of this cool and creamy dip. Serve the kabobs as either a snack or a dessert.
—Michelle Zapf, Kingsland, GA

Takes: 25 min.
Makes: 6 kabobs (1½ cups dip)

- 3 oz. cream cheese, softened
- ½ cup sour cream
- ¼ cup confectioners' sugar
- 1 Tbsp. lime juice
- 1 Tbsp. thawed orange juice concentrate
- 1 Tbsp. tequila
- ½ cup heavy whipping cream
- 12 fresh strawberries
- 6 pineapple chunks
- 1 medium mango, peeled and cubed
- 6 seedless red grapes
- 2 slices lb. cake, cubed

In a large bowl, combine first 6 ingredients. Beat in the whipping cream until fluffy. Meanwhile, thread fruits and cake on metal or wooden skewers. Serve with dip.
1 kabob with ¼ cup dip: 273 cal., 18g fat (11g sat. fat), 78mg chol., 97mg sod., 25g carb. (16g sugars, 2g fiber), 3g pro.

CREAMY HAZELNUT DIP

This creamy mousse-style dip with chocolate, hazelnut and vanilla flavors is a have-it-all spread when served with fruit, cookies and biscotti.
—*Taste of Home* Test Kitchen

Takes: 15 min. • **Makes:** about 3 cups

- 6 oz. cream cheese, softened
- ½ cup Nutella
- 1 tsp. vanilla extract
- ½ cup confectioners' sugar
- 1 cup heavy whipping cream, whipped
- ½ cup chopped hazelnuts
  Fresh strawberries, biscotti and Milano cookies

In a small bowl, combine the cream cheese, Nutella and vanilla. Beat in confectioners' sugar until smooth. Fold in whipped cream and hazelnuts. Serve with strawberries, biscotti and cookies.
2 Tbsp.: 79 cal., 6g fat (2g sat. fat), 10mg chol., 14mg sod., 6g carb. (6g sugars, 0 fiber), 1g pro.

DILL DIP

Be prepared—you'll likely need to make a double batch of this delightful dip. One is never enough when we have a get-together. It tastes fantastic with just about any vegetable, so you can use whatever you have on hand as a dipper.
—Kathy Beldorth, Three Oaks, MI

Prep: 10 min. + chilling • **Makes:** 2 cups

- 1 cup mayonnaise
- 1 cup sour cream
- 2 Tbsp. dried parsley flakes
- 1 Tbsp. dried minced onion
- 2 tsp. dill weed
- 1½ tsp. seasoned salt
- 1 tsp. sugar
  Fresh vegetables or potato chips

In a small bowl, combine the first 7 ingredients. Chill for at least 1 hour. Serve with vegetables or potato chips.
2 Tbsp.: 123 cal., 13g fat (3g sat. fat), 5mg chol., 219mg sod., 1g carb. (1g sugars, 0 fiber), 1g pro.

TEST KITCHEN TIP
To make the dip a bit lighter, sub in reduced-fat mayonnaise and sour cream.

GARDEN-FRESH SEAFOOD COCKTAIL

For something cool on a hot day, we mix shrimp and crabmeat with crunchy veggies straight from the garden. Look for adobo seasoning in your grocery's international section.
—Teri Rasey, Cadillac, MI

Prep: 15 min. + chilling • **Makes:** 6 cups

- ¾ lb. peeled and deveined cooked shrimp (31-40 per lb.)
- 1 container (8 oz.) refrigerated jumbo lump crabmeat, drained
- 3 celery ribs, chopped
- 1 medium cucumber, peeled, seeded and chopped
- 1 medium sweet orange pepper, chopped
- 2 plum tomatoes, seeded and chopped
- ½ cup red onion, finely chopped
- 1 to 2 jalapeno peppers, seeded and finely chopped
- ¼ cup minced fresh cilantro
- 3 Tbsp. lime juice
- 1 Tbsp. olive oil
- 2¼ tsp. adobo seasoning

Combine the first 9 ingredients. Whisk together the lime juice, oil and adobo seasoning; drizzle over shrimp mixture and toss gently to coat. Refrigerate at least 1 hour, tossing gently every 20 minutes. Serve shrimp mixture in cocktail glasses.
Note: Wear disposable gloves when cutting hot peppers; the oils can burn skin. Avoid touching your face.
¾ cup: 103 cal., 3g fat (0 sat. fat), 92mg chol., 619mg sod., 5g carb. (2g sugars, 1g fiber), 15g pro.

MINIATURE CORN DOGS

Fun-sized corn dogs add a little wow to any gathering. Kids and adults love them equally, so expect them to disappear fast.
—Deb Perry, Bluffton, IN

Prep: 25 min. • **Cook:** 5 min./batch
Makes: about 3½ dozen

- 1 cup all-purpose flour
- 2 Tbsp. cornmeal
- 1½ tsp. baking powder
- ¼ tsp. salt
  Dash onion powder
- 3 Tbsp. shortening
- ¾ cup 2% milk
- 1 large egg
- 1 pkg. (16 oz.) miniature smoked sausages
  Oil for deep-fat frying
  Spicy ketchup

1. In a small bowl, combine the flour, cornmeal, baking powder, salt and onion powder; cut in shortening until crumbly. Whisk milk and egg; stir into flour mixture just until moistened. Dip sausages into the batter.
2. In a cast-iron or other heavy skillet, heat oil to 375°. Fry sausages, a few at a time, until golden brown, 2-3 minutes. Drain on paper towels. Serve with ketchup.
1 mini corn dog: 68 cal., 6g fat (1g sat. fat), 11mg chol., 136mg sod., 2g carb. (0 sugars, 0 fiber), 2g pro.

SPINACH & CRAB DIP

We love this recipe! I've lightened it up considerably without losing any of the original's richness, and no one can tell the difference. I also serve it as a topping on baked potatoes.
—Sandie Heindel, Liberty, MO

Takes: 25 min. • **Makes:** 4 cups

- 1 pkg. (10 oz.) frozen chopped spinach, thawed and squeezed dry
- 1 pkg. (8 oz.) reduced-fat cream cheese, cubed
- 1 cup plain yogurt
- ½ cup grated Parmesan cheese
- ½ cup Miracle Whip Light
- 2 garlic cloves, minced
- 1 tsp. crushed red pepper flakes
- ¼ tsp. salt
- ¼ tsp. pepper
- 1 can (6 oz.) lump crabmeat, drained
  Assorted crackers or baked tortilla chip scoops

1. In a large saucepan over low heat, combine first 9 ingredients. Cook and stir until cream cheese is melted. Stir in crab; heat through.
2. Transfer to a serving bowl; serve with crackers. Refrigerate leftovers.
¼ cup: 89 cal., 6g fat (3g sat. fat), 26mg chol., 256mg sod., 3g carb. (2g sugars, 1g fiber), 6g pro.

★ ★ ★ ★ ★ **READER REVIEW**

"Great ... everyone loved it. It had a bit too much kick from pepper flakes for me, but everyone else said it was perfect. A double recipe fits in a Hawaiian bread bowl."

TONIPNC TASTEOFHOME.COM

CURRIED BEEF BITES

These appetizers are so fast and easy to prepare. They are always the first to disappear at any party!
—Karen Kuebler, Dallas, TX

Prep: 15 min. • **Bake:** 15 min.
Makes: 3 dozen

- 12 slices white bread, crusts removed
- 3 Tbsp. butter, melted
- ½ lb. ground beef
- 5 celery ribs, chopped
- ½ cup seasoned bread crumbs
- 2 tsp. curry powder
- ½ tsp. garlic salt
  Optional: Cucumber raita and chopped fresh cilantro

1. Preheat oven to 400°. Flatten bread slices with a rolling pin; brush tops with butter. Set aside.
2. In a large skillet, cook beef and celery over medium heat until beef is no longer pink and celery is tender, 8-10 minutes, breaking beef into crumbles; drain. Stir in bread crumbs, curry powder and garlic salt.
3. Spoon beef mixture evenly among bread slices. Roll up bread slices; secure with toothpicks. Place on a greased baking sheet. Bake until golden brown, 12-15 minutes. When cool enough to handle, discard toothpicks and cut each roll-up crosswise into 3 pieces. If desired, serve warm with cucumber raita and chopped fresh cilantro.
1 roll-up: 52 cal., 2g fat (1g sat. fat), 6mg chol., 114mg sod., 6g carb. (1g sugars, 0 fiber), 2g pro.

CHAMPAGNE SIPPER

This is a terrific cocktail for a holiday celebration. And because you make it by the pitcher, you can mingle with your guests instead of tending bar.
—Moffat Frazier, New York, NY

Takes: 10 min. • Makes: 12 servings

- 1½ cups sugar
- 1 cup lemon juice
- 3 cups cold water
- 1½ cups sweet white wine, chilled
- 1 bottle (750 milliliters) champagne, chilled
  Sliced fresh strawberries, optional

In a 3-qt. pitcher, dissolve sugar in the lemon juice. Add cold water and wine. Stir in the champagne. If desired, serve with strawberries.
¾ cup: 168 cal., 0 fat (0 sat. fat), 0 chol., 2mg sod., 28g carb. (26g sugars, 0 fiber), 0 pro.

MAKE AHEAD
BAKED EGG ROLLS

These egg rolls are low in fat, but the crispiness from baking will fool you into thinking they were fried!
—Barbara Lierman, Lyons, NE

Prep: 30 min. • Bake: 10 min.
Makes: 16 servings

- 2 cups grated carrots
- 1 can (14 oz.) bean sprouts, drained
- ½ cup chopped water chestnuts
- ¼ cup chopped green pepper
- ¼ cup chopped green onions
- 1 garlic clove, minced
- 2 cups finely diced cooked chicken
- 4 tsp. cornstarch
- 1 Tbsp. water
- 1 Tbsp. light soy sauce
- 1 tsp. canola oil
- 1 tsp. brown sugar
  Pinch cayenne pepper
- 16 egg roll wrappers
  Cooking spray

1. Coat a large skillet with cooking spray; heat pan over medium heat. Add the first 6 ingredients; cook and stir until vegetables are crisp-tender, about 3 minutes. Add chicken; heat through.
2. In a small bowl, combine the cornstarch, water, soy sauce, oil, brown sugar and cayenne until smooth; stir into chicken mixture. Bring to a boil. Cook and stir for 2 minutes or until thickened; remove from the heat.
3. Spoon ¼ cup chicken mixture on the bottom third of 1 egg roll wrapper; fold sides toward center and roll tightly. (Keep remaining wrappers covered with a damp paper towel until ready to use.) Place seam side down on a baking sheet coated with cooking spray. Repeat.
4. Spritz tops of egg rolls with cooking spray. Bake at 425° for 10-15 minutes or until lightly browned.
Freeze option: Freeze cooled egg rolls in a freezer container, separating layers with waxed paper. To use, reheat rolls on a baking sheet in a preheated 350° oven until crisp and heated through.
1 egg roll: 146 cal., 2g fat (0 sat. fat), 18mg chol., 250mg sod., 22g carb. (1g sugars, 1g fiber), 9g pro. **Diabetic exchanges:** 1½ starch, 1 lean meat, ½ fat.

CHEESY BBQ BEEF DIP

Barbecued beef dip is a holiday staple in our house. My husband can't get enough!
—Selena Swafford, Dalton, GA

Takes: 30 min. • **Makes:** 8 servings

- 1 pkg. (8 oz.) cream cheese, softened
- 1 pkg. (15 oz.) refrigerated fully cooked barbecued shredded beef
- 1 cup shredded cheddar cheese
- ½ cup chopped red onion
- ¾ cup french-fried onions
  Optional toppings: chopped tomatoes, chopped red onion and minced fresh cilantro
  Tortilla chips

Preheat oven to 350°. Spread cream cheese onto bottom of a greased 9-in. pie plate. Spread evenly with beef. Sprinkle with cheddar cheese and red onion. Bake until heated through, 15-20 minutes. Sprinkle with french-fried onions; bake 5 minutes longer. If desired, top with tomatoes, onion and cilantro. Serve with tortilla chips.
¼ cup: 279 cal., 19g fat (10g sat. fat), 57mg chol., 578mg sod., 16g carb. (10g sugars, 0 fiber), 12g pro.

★ ★ ★ ★ ★ **READER REVIEW**

"I improvised a little and it was still very good. I used my own leftover shredded beef BBQ and a mixture of jalapeno jack and cheddar cheeses. If I were to do this over, I'd use Fritos instead of the french-fried onions. Very tasty!"
SCOTTSGRACETASTEOFHOME.COM

CHEDDAR HAM CUPS

When a college classmate and I threw a party for our professor, a friend contributed these savory appetizers. Everyone in the class requested the recipe before the party was done. Try the cups with chicken instead of ham if you'd like.
—Brandi Ladner, Gulfport, MS

Takes: 30 min. • **Makes:** 2½ dozen

- 2 cups (8 oz.) finely shredded cheddar cheese
- 2 pkg. (2½ oz. each) thinly sliced deli ham, chopped
- ¾ cup mayonnaise
- ⅓ cup bacon bits
- 2 to 3 tsp. Dijon mustard
- 2 tubes (10.20 oz. each) large refrigerated flaky biscuits

1. In a large bowl, combine the cheese, ham, mayonnaise, bacon and mustard. Split biscuits into thirds. Press onto the bottom and up the sides of ungreased miniature muffin cups. Fill each with about 1 Tbsp. of cheese mixture.
2. Bake at 450° until cups are golden brown and cheese is melted, 9-11 minutes. Let stand for 2 minutes before removing from the pans. Serve warm.
1 ham cup: 99 cal., 5g fat (2g sat. fat), 11mg chol., 298mg sod., 9g carb. (1g sugars, 0 fiber), 4g pro.

ITALIAN CHEESE LOAF

Here's a deliciously different sandwich. It's yummy warm from the oven or off the grill at a cookout. Cheese in the filling with garden-fresh ingredients goes great inside crusty bread. I usually serve it with a salad and onion rings.
—Mary Ann Marino, West Pittsburgh, PA

Prep: 15 min. • **Bake:** 25 min.
Makes: 12 servings

- 1   loaf (1 lb.) French bread
- 2   cups diced fresh tomatoes
- 1   cup shredded part-skim mozzarella cheese
- 1   cup shredded cheddar cheese
- 1   medium onion, finely chopped
- ¼   cup grated Romano cheese
- ¼   cup chopped ripe olives
- ¼   cup Italian salad dressing
- 1   tsp. minced fresh basil or ¼ tsp. dried basil
- 1   tsp. minced fresh oregano or ¼ tsp. dried oregano

1. Preheat oven to 350°. Cut top half off loaf of bread. Carefully hollow out both halves of loaf, leaving a ½-in. shell (discard removed bread or save for another use).
2. Combine remaining ingredients. Spoon into bottom half of bread, mounding as necessary; replace top. Wrap in foil. Bake until cheese is melted, about 25 minutes. Slice and serve warm.
1 piece: 204 cal., 8g fat (4g sat. fat), 18mg chol., 478mg sod., 23g carb. (3g sugars, 2g fiber), 9g pro.

EASY DEVILED EGGS

This recipe comes from the Durbin Inn, a well-known restaurant in Rushville, Indiana, from the 1920s until it closed in the late '70s. The eggs are delicious, and it's easy to make more of them for larger gatherings.
—Margaret Sanders, Indianapolis, IN

Takes: 15 min. • **Makes:** 1 dozen

- 6   hard-boiled large eggs
- 2   Tbsp. mayonnaise
- 1   tsp. sugar
- 1   tsp. white vinegar
- 1   tsp. prepared mustard
- ½   tsp. salt
     Paprika

Slice eggs in half lengthwise; remove yolks and set whites aside. In a small bowl, mash yolks with a fork. Add the mayonnaise, sugar, vinegar, mustard and salt; mix well. Stuff or pipe into egg whites. Sprinkle with paprika. Refrigerate until serving.
1 egg half: 55 cal., 4g fat (1g sat. fat), 94mg chol., 146mg sod., 1g carb. (1g sugars, 0 fiber), 3g pro.
Bacon-Cheddar Deviled Eggs: To mashed yolks, add ¼ cup mayonnaise, 2 cooked and crumbled bacon strips. 1 Tbsp. finely shred cheddar cheese, 1½ tsp. honey mustard and ⅛ tsp. pepper. Stuff as directed.
Picnic Stuffed Eggs: To mashed yolks, add ¼ cup mayonnaise, 2 Tbsp. drained sweet pickle relish, 1½ tsp. honey mustard, ½ tsp. garlic salt, ¼ tsp. Worcestershire sauce and ⅛ tsp. pepper. Stuff as directed.

Santa Fe Deviled Eggs: To mashed yolks, add 3 Tbsp. each mayonnaise and canned chopped green chiles, 1½ tsp. chipotle pepper in adobo sauce and ¼ tsp. garlic salt. Stuff as directed. Garnish each with 1 tsp. salsa and a sliver of ripe olive.
Crab-Stuffed Deviled Eggs: Make 12 hard-cooked eggs. To mashed yolks, add 1 can (6 oz.) crabmeat (drained, flaked and cartilage removed), ⅔ cup mayonnaise, ½ cup finely chopped celery, ½ cup slivered almonds, 2 Tbsp. finely chopped green pepper and ½ tsp. salt. Stuff as directed.

BRING IT
No deviled egg plate? No problem! Instead, pack the whites on a covered tray and place the filling in a piping bag. Pipe in the filling at your destination, sprinkle with a little paprika and *voila!*—perfect deviled eggs with no mishaps.

SPINACH & TURKEY PINWHEELS

Need an awesome snack for game day? My kids love these easy 4-ingredient turkey pinwheels. Go ahead and make them the day before; the pinwheels won't get soggy!
—Amy Van Hemert, Ottumwa, IA

Takes: 15 min. • **Makes:** 8 servings

- 1 carton (8 oz.) spreadable garden vegetable cream cheese
- 8 flour tortillas (8 in.)
- 4 cups fresh baby spinach
- 1 lb. sliced deli turkey

Spread cream cheese over tortillas. Layer with spinach and turkey. Roll up tightly; if not serving immediately, cover and refrigerate. To serve, cut rolls crosswise into 1-in. slices.

1 piece: 51 cal., 2g fat (1g sat. fat), 9mg chol., 144mg sod., 5g carb. (0 sugars, 0 fiber), 3g pro.

THE BEST HUMMUS

Hummus is my go-to appetizer when I need something quick, easy and impressive. Over the years I've picked up a number of tricks that make this the best hummus you'll ever have.
—James Schend, Pleasant Prairie, WI

- -

Prep: 25 min. • **Cook:** 20 min. + chilling
Makes: 1½ cups

- 1   can (15 oz.) garbanzo beans or chickpeas, rinsed and drained
- ½   tsp. baking soda
- ¼   cup fresh lemon juice
- 1   Tbsp. minced garlic
- ½   tsp. kosher salt
- ½   tsp. ground cumin
- ½   cup tahini
- 2   Tbsp. extra virgin olive oil
- ¼   cup cold water
     Optional: Olive oil, roasted garbanzo beans, toasted sesame seeds, ground sumac

1. Place garbanzo beans in a large saucepan; add water to cover by 1 in. Gently rub beans together to loosen outer skin. Pour off water and any skins that are floating. Repeat 2-3 times until no skins float to the surface; drain. Return to saucepan; add baking soda and enough water to cover by 1 in. Bring to a boil; reduce heat. Simmer, uncovered, until beans are very tender and just starting to fall apart, 20-25 minutes.
2. Meanwhile, in a blender, process lemon juice, garlic and salt until almost a paste. Let stand 10 minutes; strain, discarding solids. Stir in cumin. In a small bowl, stir together tahini and olive oil.
3. Add beans to blender; add cold water. Loosely cover and process until completely smooth. Add lemon mixture and process. With blender running, slowly add tahini mixture, scraping sides as needed. Adjust seasoning with additional salt and cumin if desired.
4. Transfer mixture to a serving bowl; cover and refrigerate at least 30 minutes. If desired, top with additional olive oil and assorted toppings.
¼ cup: 250 cal., 19g fat (3g sat. fat), 0 chol., 361mg sod., 15g carb. (2g sugars, 5g fiber), 7g pro.

MAKE AHEAD
MINI CHEESE BALLS

These mini cheese balls are the perfect quick appetizer for any party. Roll them in toasted sesame seeds, fresh rosemary and/or paprika to add even more flavor.
—Judy Spivey, Ennice, NC

- -

Prep: 30 min. + chilling
Makes: 36 cheese balls

- 1   pkg. (8 oz.) cream cheese, softened
- 2   cups shredded sharp cheddar cheese
     Optional toppings: Toasted sesame seeds, minced fresh rosemary and paprika
     Optional garnishes: Halved rye crisps and rolled tortilla chips

In a large bowl, combine cheeses. Shape into 36 balls; roll balls in the toppings as desired. Cover and refrigerate for 8 hours or overnight. To serve, if desired, press a rye crisp or rolled corn chip into the top of each cheese ball.
1 cheese ball: 47 cal., 4g fat (2g sat. fat), 13mg chol., 61mg sod., 1g carb. (0 sugars, 0 fiber), 2g pro.

Sunrise Sausage
Enchiladas
page 60

Breakfast for a Bunch

The most important meal of the day is also the most celebratory when these eye-opening dishes are on the menu. Cheesy sausage-hash brown lasagna for breakfast? Sign us up!

BAKED BLUEBERRY GINGER PANCAKE

My kids love pancakes, so I came up with this baked version that saves a lot of time in the morning. My kids always gobble these breakfast squares right up!
—Erin Wright, Wallace, KS

Takes: 30 min. • **Makes:** 9 servings

2	large eggs, room temperature
1½	cups 2% milk
¼	cup butter, melted
2	cups all-purpose flour
2	Tbsp. sugar
3	tsp. baking powder
1½	tsp. ground ginger
½	tsp. salt
2	cups fresh or frozen blueberries
	Maple syrup

1. Preheat oven to 350°. Combine the eggs, milk and butter. Whisk the next 5 ingredients; add to egg mixture. Spoon batter into a 9-in. square baking pan coated with cooking spray. Sprinkle blueberries over the top.

2. Bake until a toothpick inserted in center comes out clean, 20-25 minutes. Cut into squares; serve with warm maple syrup.

1 piece: 213 cal., 7g fat (4g sat. fat), 58mg chol., 368mg sod., 31g carb. (8g sugars, 2g fiber), 6g pro. **Diabetic exchanges:** 2 starch, 1½ fat.

HOW TO QUICKLY WARM EGGS
Many recipes benefit from room-temperature eggs, and it's an easy thing to do. Just place eggs in hot water while you prep your recipe. They'll be ready when it's time to get cracking.

GRITS & BACON CASSEROLE

A Mississippi home cook gave me her recipe for grits casserole. It baked like traditional custard. I garnish it with parsley, crumbled bacon and cheese.
—Theresa Liguori, Elkridge, MD

Prep: 20 min. + cooling • **Cook:** 1¼ hours
Makes: 8 servings

- 4½ cups water
- ½ tsp. salt
- ¼ tsp. pepper
- 1 cup quick-cooking grits
- 8 large eggs
- 8 bacon strips, cooked and crumbled
- 1 cup shredded Gouda cheese

1. Preheat oven to 350°. In a large saucepan, bring water, salt and pepper to a boil. Slowly stir in grits. Reduce heat to medium-low; cook, covered, until thickened, about 5 minutes, stirring occasionally. Remove from heat. Pour grits into a greased 2½-qt. souffle dish; cool completely.

2. In a large bowl, whisk eggs; pour over grits. Sprinkle with bacon and cheese.

3. Place casserole in a larger baking pan; add 1 in. of hot water to larger pan. Bake, covered, 45 minutes. Uncover; bake until knife inserted in the center comes out clean, 30-40 minutes. Let stand for 5-10 minutes before serving.

To make ahead: Refrigerate unbaked casserole, covered, several hours or overnight. To use, preheat oven to 350°. Remove casserole from refrigerator while oven heats. Place casserole in a larger baking pan; add 1 in. of hot water to larger pan. Bake as directed, increasing time as necessary for a knife inserted in the center to come out clean. Let stand 5-10 minutes before serving.

1 piece: 227 cal., 12g fat (5g sat. fat), 210mg chol., 480mg sod., 16g carb. (1g sugars, 1g fiber), 14g pro.

MAPLE APPLE BAKED OATMEAL

I've tried a number of different types of fruit for this recipe, but apple seems to be my family's favorite. I mix the dry and wet ingredients in separate bowls the night before and combine them the next morning to save time.
—Megan Brooks, Saint Lazare, QC

Prep: 20 min. • **Bake:** 25 min.
Makes: 8 servings

 3 cups old-fashioned oats
 2 tsp. baking powder
1¼ tsp. ground cinnamon
 ½ tsp. salt
 ¼ tsp. ground nutmeg
 2 large eggs
 2 cups fat-free milk
 ½ cup maple syrup
 ¼ cup canola oil
 1 tsp. vanilla extract
 1 large apple, chopped
 ¼ cup sunflower kernels or pepitas

1. Preheat oven to 350°. In a large bowl, mix the first 5 ingredients. In a small bowl, whisk eggs, milk, syrup, oil and vanilla until blended; stir into dry ingredients. Let stand 5 minutes. Stir in apple.
2. Transfer to an 11x7-in. baking dish coated with cooking spray. Sprinkle with sunflower kernels. Bake, uncovered, until set and edges are lightly browned, 25-30 minutes.
1 serving: 305 cal., 13g fat (2g sat. fat), 48mg chol., 325mg sod., 41g carb. (20g sugars, 4g fiber), 8g pro. **Diabetic exchanges:** 3 starch, 1½ fat.

GROUND BEEF SNACK QUICHES

A hearty appetizer like these meaty mini quiches is a perfect way to start any meal. They taste super made with ground beef, but I sometimes substitute bacon, ham, ground pork or sausage.
—Stacy Atkinson, Rugby, ND

Prep: 15 min. • **Bake:** 20 min.
Makes: 1½ dozen

 ¼ lb. ground beef
 ⅛ to ¼ tsp. garlic powder
 ⅛ tsp. pepper
 1 cup biscuit/baking mix
 ¼ cup cornmeal
 ¼ cup cold butter, cubed
 2 to 3 Tbsp. boiling water
 1 large egg
 ½ cup half-and-half cream
 1 Tbsp. chopped green onion
 1 Tbsp. chopped sweet red pepper
 ⅛ to ¼ tsp. salt
 ⅛ to ¼ tsp. cayenne pepper
 ½ cup finely shredded cheddar cheese

1. Preheat oven to 375°. In a large saucepan over medium heat, cook the beef, garlic powder and pepper until meat is no longer pink; crumble beef; drain and set aside.
2. Meanwhile, in a small bowl, combine biscuit mix and cornmeal; cut in butter until crumbly. Add enough water to form a soft dough.
3. Press onto the bottoms and up the sides of greased miniature muffin cups. Place a tsp. of the beef mixture into each shell.
4. In a small bowl, combine the egg, cream, onion, red pepper, salt and cayenne; pour over beef mixture. Sprinkle with cheese.
5. Bake for 20 minutes or until a knife inserted in the center comes out clean.
1 snack quiche: 93 cal., 6g fat (3g sat. fat), 27mg chol., 137mg sod., 7g carb. (0 sugars, 0 fiber), 3g pro.

SPIRAL OMELET SUPREME

You can substitute 2 cups of any combination of your favorite omelet fillings for the vegetables in this recipe. A serrated knife works well for slicing it.
—Debbie Morris, Hamilton, OH

Prep: 20 min. • **Bake:** 20 min.
Makes: 8 servings

4	oz. cream cheese, softened
¾	cup 2% milk
¼	cup plus 2 Tbsp. grated Parmesan cheese, divided
2	Tbsp. all-purpose flour
12	large eggs
2	tsp. canola oil
1	large green pepper, chopped
1	cup sliced fresh mushrooms
1	small onion, chopped
1¼	tsp. Italian seasoning, divided
1½	cups shredded part-skim mozzarella cheese
1	plum tomato, seeded and chopped

1. Preheat oven to 375°. Line bottom and sides of a greased 15x10x1-in. pan with parchment; grease paper.

2. Beat cream cheese until soft; gradually beat in milk. Beat in ¼ cup Parmesan cheese and flour. In a large bowl, beat eggs until blended. Add cream cheese mixture; mix well. Pour into prepared pan. Bake until set, 20-25 minutes.

3. Meanwhile, in a large skillet, heat oil over medium-high heat; saute the pepper, mushrooms and onion until crisp-tender, 3-4 minutes. Stir in 1 tsp. Italian seasoning. Keep warm.

4. Remove omelet from the oven; top immediately with mozzarella, tomato and pepper mixture. Starting with a short side, roll up omelet jelly-roll style, lifting with the parchment and removing it as you roll. Transfer to a platter. Sprinkle with the remaining 2 Tbsp. Parmesan cheese and ¼ tsp. Italian seasoning.

1 piece: 275 cal., 19g fat (9g sat. fat), 312mg chol., 372mg sod., 8g carb. (4g sugars, 1g fiber), 18g pro.

QUICK & EASY SAUSAGE GRAVY

Breakfast doesn't get any heartier or more satisfying than this home-style classic. No one will leave hungry!
—John Wilhelm, Richmond, VA

Takes: 25 min. • **Makes:** 8 servings

- 2 **lbs. bulk pork sausage**
- ⅓ **cup all-purpose flour**
- 3 **tsp. pepper**
- 2 **tsp. sugar**
- ½ **tsp. salt**
- 2 **cups 2% milk**
- 2 **cans (5 oz. each) evaporated milk**
  Cooked biscuits

1. In a Dutch oven, cook sausage over medium heat until no longer pink, breaking into crumbles (do not drain), 8-10 minutes. Add flour, pepper, sugar and salt; cook and stir until blended, about 2 minutes.
2. Stir in milks; bring to a boil. Reduce heat; simmer, uncovered, until thickened, 3-5 minutes, stirring occasionally. Serve with biscuits.
¾ cup: 446 cal., 34g fat (12g sat. fat), 93mg chol., 1075mg sod., 14g carb. (7g sugars, 0 fiber), 20g pro.

RUBY BREAKFAST SAUCE

Brighten any breakfast with this delicious cherry sauce on French toast, pancakes or waffles. With a hint of cranberry flavor, the mixture also is nice served over ham, pork or chicken.
—Edie DeSpain, Logan, UT

Takes: 10 min. • **Makes:** about 4 cups

- 1 **can (21 oz.) cherry pie filling**
- 1 **can (8 oz.) jellied cranberry sauce**
- ¼ **cup maple syrup**
- ¼ **cup orange juice**
- 3 **Tbsp. butter**
  Pancakes or French toast

1. In a microwave-safe bowl, combine pie filling, cranberry sauce, syrup, orange juice and butter.
2. Microwave on high for 2 minutes; stir. Microwave 1-2 minutes longer or until butter is melted and mixture is heated through; stir. Serve over pancakes or French toast.
¼ cup: 97 cal., 2g fat (1g sat. fat), 6mg chol., 32mg sod., 19g carb. (16g sugars, 0 fiber), 0 pro.

CREAMY STRAWBERRY FRENCH TOAST BAKE

On Sunday mornings I like to take it easy, but I also want my family to have a nice breakfast. This recipe allows me to sleep in but still feel as if I'm a fabulous mom. Win!
—Alynn Hansen, Mona, UT

Prep: 30 min. + chilling • **Bake:** 40 min.
Makes: 8 servings

- 3 cups sliced fresh strawberries, divided
- 2 Tbsp. sugar
- 1 pkg. (8 oz.) cream cheese, softened
- ½ cup confectioners' sugar
- 1 Tbsp. grated orange zest
- 1 Tbsp. orange juice
- 1 tsp. vanilla extract
- 1 loaf (1 lb.) cinnamon bread, cut into 1-in. pieces
- 5 large eggs
- 1 cup half-and-half cream
  Sweetened whipped cream

1. Toss 2 cups strawberries with sugar. In another bowl, beat the next 5 ingredients until smooth. Place half the bread in a greased 13x9-in. baking dish. Spoon cream cheese mixture over bread. Layer with strawberry mixture and remaining bread. Whisk eggs and cream until blended; pour over top. Refrigerate, covered, overnight.
2. Preheat oven to 350°. Remove casserole from refrigerator while oven heats. Bake, uncovered, until a knife inserted in the center comes out clean, 40-45 minutes. Let stand 5 minutes before serving. Top with the whipped cream and remaining 1 cup strawberries.
1 piece: 431 cal., 21g fat (10g sat. fat), 160mg chol., 382mg sod., 47g carb. (24g sugars, 5g fiber), 13g pro.

HAM & CHEDDAR BRUNCH RING

It's surprisingly easy to transform ordinary breakfast standbys into next-level brunch centerpieces. This looks and smells so good, you might have to fend off guests en route from oven to table. Dig in!
—James Schend, Pleasant Prairie, WI

Prep: 25 min. • **Bake:** 20 min.
Makes: 8 servings

- 1 tube (8 oz.) refrigerated crescent rolls
- 10 pieces thinly sliced deli ham
- 1 cup shredded cheddar cheese, divided
- 11 large eggs, divided use
- ¾ cup roasted sweet red peppers, drained and chopped
- 4 green onions, thinly sliced
- 1 Tbsp. olive oil
- 1 tsp. minced garlic
- 2 tsp. sesame seeds, optional
  Chopped fresh parsley, optional

1. Preheat oven to 375°. Unroll crescent dough and separate into triangles. On an ungreased 12-in. pizza pan, arrange triangles in a ring with points toward the outside and wide ends overlapping to create a 3-in.-diameter hole in the center. Press overlapping dough to seal. Fold ham slices lengthwise and place on top of the wide end of each triangle. Sprinkle with half the cheese.
2. In a large bowl, beat 10 eggs; add chopped peppers. In a large skillet, cook green onions in oil over medium heat until tender, 2-3 minutes. Add garlic; cook for 30 seconds. Pour in egg mixture; cook and stir until eggs are thickened and no liquid egg remains. Spoon mixture over cheese on the wide end of the triangles; sprinkle with remaining cheese. Fold pointed ends of triangles over filling, tucking points under to form a ring with a small hole in the center (filling will be visible). Beat remaining egg; brush over pastry. If desired, sprinkle with sesame seeds.
3. Bake until golden brown and heated through, 20-25 minutes. If desired, top with parsley to serve.
1 serving: 313 cal., 19g fat (5g sat. fat), 282mg chol., 735mg sod., 15g carb. (5g sugars, 0 fiber), 19g pro.

Using a pizza cutter, cut into 2-in.-wide strips. Roll up 1 strip and place in the center of a greased 9-in. deep-dish pie plate; wrap remaining strips around the center to form 1 giant roll. Cover with greased foil; let rise until doubled, about 1 hour. Meanwhile, preheat oven to 350°.

4. Bake until golden brown, 30-40 minutes. If dough starts browning too quickly, cover lightly with foil. Cool on a wire rack.

5. To prepare topping, combine the sugar and water in a small saucepan; cook over medium heat until it turns light amber. Add butter, stirring vigorously. Remove from heat; add cream while continuing to stir vigorously. Cool slightly. Pour ¾ cup sauce over warm roll; sprinkle with salt. Serve with remaining sauce.

1 piece: 416 cal., 21g fat (13g sat. fat), 76mg chol., 354mg sod., 55g carb. (30g sugars, 1g fiber), 5g pro.

COFFEE MILK

Coffee Milk is the official state drink of Rhode Island, and once you taste it, you will understand why it has so many fans!
—Karen Barros, Bristol, RI

- -

Takes: 5 min.
Makes: 8 servings (about 1 cup each)

  2 qt. cold 2% or whole milk
  1 cup Eclipse coffee syrup

In a large pitcher, mix milk and coffee syrup until blended.

1 cup: 135 cal., 5g fat (3g sat. fat), 18mg chol., 122mg sod., 15g carb. (12g sugars, 0 fiber), 8g pro.

To make your own coffee milk syrup: Brew ½ cup finely ground coffee with 2 cups cold water in a coffeemaker. Combine brewed coffee and 1 cup sugar in a saucepan; simmer until reduced by half, about 30 minutes. Refrigerate until cold or up to 2 weeks. Makes 1 cup.

GIANT CINNAMON ROLL

This must-try cinnamon roll is all about the pillowy texture, the sweet spices and the homemade caramel drizzle.
—Leah Rekau, Milwaukee, WI

- -

Prep: 30 min. + rising • **Bake:** 30 min.
Makes: 12 servings

  1 pkg. (¼ oz.) active dry yeast
  ½ cup warm water (110° to 115°)
  ½ cup heavy whipping cream, warmed (110° to 115°)
  ½ cup sugar
  ½ tsp. sea salt
  3 to 4 cups all-purpose flour
  1 large egg, room temperature, beaten
  3 Tbsp. butter, melted

FILLING
  ¼ cup butter, softened
  ¼ cup sugar
  1 Tbsp. ground cinnamon

TOPPING
  1 cup sugar
  2 Tbsp. water
  6 Tbsp. butter
  ½ cup heavy whipping cream
  1 tsp. sea salt

1. Dissolve yeast in warm water and whipping cream until foamy. In another bowl, combine sugar and salt; add 3 cups flour, yeast mixture, egg and melted butter. Stir until moistened. Add enough remaining flour to form a soft dough.

2. Turn onto a lightly floured surface; knead until smooth and elastic, 3-4 minutes. Place in a greased bowl, turning once to grease the top. Cover; let rise in a warm place until doubled, about 30 minutes.

3. Punch down dough. Turn out onto a lightly floured surface; roll into a 15x12-in. rectangle. Spread softened butter over dough. Sprinkle with sugar and cinnamon.

THE BEST QUICHE LORRAINE

Nestled in a buttery, rustic crust, this quiche is filled with sweet onions, bacon bits and cheese. It's the perfect addition to brunch.
—Shannon Norris, Cudahy, WI

- -

Prep: 1 hour • **Bake:** 1¼ hours + cooling
Makes: 8 servings

 Dough for single-crust deep-dish pie
1 pkg. (12 oz.) thick-sliced bacon strips, coarsely chopped
3 large sweet onions, chopped
1 Tbsp. minced fresh thyme
½ tsp. coarsely ground pepper
⅛ tsp. ground nutmeg
1½ cups shredded Gruyere cheese
½ cup grated Parmesan cheese
8 large eggs, room temperature
2 cups whole milk
1 cup heavy whipping cream

1. On a lightly floured surface, roll dough to a 14-in. circle. Transfer to a 9-in. springform pan; press firmly against bottom and sides. Refrigerate while preparing filling.

2. In a large skillet, cook bacon over medium heat until crisp, stirring bacon occasionally. Remove with a slotted spoon; drain on paper towels. Discard drippings, reserving 1 Tbsp. in pan. Add onions to drippings; cook and stir over medium heat until caramelized, 20-25 minutes.

3. Stir in the thyme, pepper and nutmeg; remove from heat. Cool slightly. Stir in cheeses and reserved bacon; spoon into crust. Preheat oven to 350°. In a large bowl, whisk eggs, milk and cream until blended; pour over top. Place springform pan on a rimmed baking sheet.

4. Bake on a lower oven rack until a knife inserted near the center comes out clean, 75-85 minutes. Cool on a wire rack for 15 minutes. Loosen side from pan with a knife. Remove rim from pan.

1 piece: 671 cal., 49g fat (27g sat. fat), 308mg chol., 841mg sod., 33g carb. (10g sugars, 2g fiber), 25g pro.

Dough for single-crust deep-dish pie: Combine 1½ cups all-purpose flour and ¼ tsp. salt; cut in ⅔ cup cold butter until crumbly. Gradually add 3-6 Tbsp. ice water, tossing with a fork until dough holds together when pressed. Shape into a disk; wrap and refrigerate 1 hour.

PEACHY DUTCH PANCAKE

After my daughter attended a slumber party, she raved about a Dutch pancake they had for breakfast. She asked her friend's mom for the recipe so we could make it at home. This is my version.
—Carol Rogers, Tipton, IA

Takes: 30 min. • **Makes:** 8 servings

- ¼ cup butter, cubed
- 2 cups fresh or frozen thinly sliced peaches, thawed and drained
- 4 large eggs
- 1¼ cups fat-free milk
- ½ tsp. almond extract
- 1¼ cups all-purpose flour
- ½ cup sugar
- ¾ tsp. salt
  Warm peach preserves and maple syrup

1. Preheat oven to 425°. Place butter in a 13x9-in. baking dish. Place in the oven for 3-4 minutes or until the «butter is melted; carefully swirl to coat bottom and sides of dish. Carefully add peaches; return to oven for 3-4 minutes or until bubbly.
2. Meanwhile, in a large bowl, whisk eggs until frothy. Add milk and extract. Whisk in flour, sugar and salt. Pour into hot baking dish. Bake 10-12 minutes or until puffed and sides are golden brown.
3. Remove from oven; serve immediately with preserves and syrup.
To make ahead: Prepare pancake batter as directed. Refrigerate, covered, several hours or overnight. Remove from the refrigerator 30 minutes before baking. Preheat oven to 425°. Prepare baking dish as directed. Whisk batter until blended; pour into hot baking dish. Bake, as directed, until puffed and sides are golden brown.
1 piece: 235 cal., 8g fat (4g sat. fat), 109mg chol., 319mg sod., 33g carb. (18g sugars, 1g fiber), 7g pro.

SPICY BREAKFAST LASAGNA

It's fun to cook up something new for family and friends—especially when it gets rave reviews. When I took this dish to our breakfast club at work, people said it really woke up their taste buds!
—Guthrie Torp Jr., Highland Ranch, CO

Prep: 20 min. + chilling • **Bake:** 35 min.
Makes: 16 servings

- 3 cups 4% cottage cheese
- ½ cup minced chives
- ¼ cup sliced green onions
- 18 large eggs
- ⅓ cup 2% milk
- ½ tsp. salt
- ¼ tsp. pepper
- 1 Tbsp. butter
- 8 lasagna noodles, cooked and drained
- 4 cups frozen shredded hash browns, thawed
- 1 lb. bulk pork sausage, cooked and crumbled
- 8 oz. sliced Monterey Jack cheese with jalapeno peppers
- 8 oz. sliced Muenster cheese

1. In a bowl, combine cottage cheese, chives and onions. In another bowl, whisk eggs, milk, salt and pepper until blended. In a large skillet, heat butter over medium heat. Pour in egg mixture; cook and stir until eggs are thickened and no liquid egg remains. Remove from heat.
2. Place 4 lasagna noodles in a greased 13x9-in. baking dish. Layer with 2 cups hash browns, scrambled eggs, sausage and half the cottage cheese mixture. Cover with Monterey Jack cheese. Top with the remaining 4 lasagna noodles, hash browns and remaining cottage cheese mixture. Cover with Muenster cheese. Refrigerate, covered, 8 hours or overnight.
3. Remove dish from the refrigerator 30 minutes before baking. Preheat oven to 350°. Bake, uncovered, until a knife inserted in center comes out clean, 35-40 minutes. Let stand 5 minutes before cutting.
1 piece: 366 cal., 23g fat (11g sat. fat), 256mg chol., 640mg sod., 16g carb. (3g sugars, 1g fiber), 23g pro.

HONEY-NUT COCONUT GRANOLA

I received this lovely recipe from a New Zealand pen pal. My family loves the naturally sweet flavor of the honey, and I like it because it's not loaded with preservatives.
—Ann Belczak, North Tonawanda, NY

- -

Prep: 15 min. • **Bake:** 40 min. + cooling
Makes: 11 cups

- 6 **cups old-fashioned oats**
- 1½ **cups toasted wheat germ**
- 1½ **cups all-bran cereal**
- ½ **cup sweetened shredded coconut**
- 1½ **cups honey**
- ½ **cup chopped walnuts**
- ⅓ **cup chopped dried apricots**

1. Preheat oven to 275°. In a large bowl, combine oats, wheat germ, cereal and coconut. Pour into 2 greased 13x9-in. baking pans.
2. Bake 20 minutes, stirring once. Heat honey in a saucepan until thin, about 5 minutes. Pour half into each pan; stir to coat evenly.
3. Return to the oven for 20-30 minutes or until golden, stirring every 10 minutes. Stir in walnuts and apricots. Cool, stirring occasionally. Store in an airtight container.
¾ cup: 347 cal., 7g fat (2g sat. fat), 0 chol., 31mg sod., 67g carb. (32g sugars, 7g fiber), 11g pro.

BRING IT
Build-your-own granola bowls is a healthy, fun option for brunch. Serve the granola with milk, homemade yogurt (page 53), and fresh fruits such as blueberries and sliced peeled peaches.

MAKE AHEAD

MAKE-AHEAD EGGS BENEDICT TOAST CUPS

When I was growing up, we had a family tradition of having eggs Benedict with champagne and orange juice for our Christmas breakfast. But now that I'm cooking, a fussy breakfast isn't my style. I wanted to come up with a dish I could make ahead that would mimic the flavors of traditional eggs Benedict and would also freeze well. Friends, this is it!
—Lyndsay Wells, Ladysmith, BC

- -

Prep: 30 min. • **Bake:** 10 min.
Makes: 1 dozen

6	English muffins, split
1	envelope hollandaise sauce mix
12	slices Canadian bacon, quartered
1	tsp. pepper
1	Tbsp. olive oil
6	large eggs
1	Tbsp. butter

1. Preheat oven to 375°. Flatten muffin halves with a rolling pin; press into greased muffin cups. Bake until lightly browned, about 10 minutes.

2. Meanwhile, prepare hollandaise sauce according to the package directions; cool slightly. Sprinkle bacon with pepper. In a large skillet, cook bacon in oil over medium heat until partially cooked but not crisp. Remove to paper towels to drain. Divide bacon among muffin cups. Wipe the skillet clean.

3. Whisk eggs and ½ cup of the cooled hollandaise sauce until blended. In the same skillet, heat butter over medium heat. Pour in egg mixture; cook and stir until eggs are thickened and no liquid egg remains. Divide egg mixture among muffin cups; top with remaining hollandaise sauce.

4. Bake until heated through, 8-10 minutes. Serve warm.

Overnight option: Refrigerate unbaked cups, covered, overnight. Bake until golden brown, 10-12 minutes.

Freeze option: Cover and freeze unbaked cups in muffin cups until firm. Transfer to an airtight container; return to freezer. To use, bake the cups in muffin tin as directed, increasing time to 25-30 minutes. Cover loosely with foil if needed in order to prevent overbrowning.

1 toast cup: 199 cal., 11g fat (5g sat. fat), 114mg chol., 495mg sod., 15g carb. (2g sugars, 1g fiber), 9g pro.

MOCHA CINNAMON ROLLS

I came up with this recipe because I love cinnamon rolls and coffee-flavored anything! It's a perfect combination that works as a dessert or snack.
—Victoria Mitchel, Gettysburg, PA

- -

Prep: 45 min. + rising • **Bake:** 25 min.
Makes: 1 dozen

- 1 pkg. (¼ oz.) active dry yeast
- 1 cup warm 2% milk (110° to 115°)
- ¼ cup sugar
- ¼ cup butter, melted
- 2 Tbsp. instant coffee granules
- 1 large egg yolk, room temperature
- 1½ tsp. vanilla extract
- ¾ tsp. salt
- ½ tsp. ground nutmeg
- 2½ to 3 cups all-purpose flour

FILLING

- ¾ cup chopped pecans
- ⅔ cup semisweet chocolate chips
- ¼ cup sugar
- 2 Tbsp. instant coffee granules
- ½ tsp. ground cinnamon
- ¼ cup butter, softened
- ¼ cup butter, melted

FROSTING

- 1 oz. cream cheese, softened
- 1 cup confectioners' sugar
- 3 Tbsp. heavy whipping cream
- ¾ tsp. instant coffee granules
- ⅛ tsp. vanilla extract

1. In a large bowl, dissolve yeast in warm milk. Add sugar, butter, coffee granules, egg yolk, vanilla, salt, nutmeg and 2 cups flour. Beat on medium speed until smooth. Stir in enough remaining flour to form a soft dough (dough will be sticky).

2. Turn onto a floured surface; knead until smooth and elastic, 6-8 minutes. Place in a greased bowl, turning once to grease the top. Cover and let rise in a warm place until doubled, about 1 hour. Place the pecans, chocolate chips, sugar, coffee granules and cinnamon in a food processor; process until finely chopped. Punch dough down; turn onto a floured surface. Roll into an 18x12-in. rectangle; spread with the softened butter. Sprinkle pecan mixture over the dough to within ½ in. of edges.

3. Roll up jelly-roll style, starting with a long side; pinch seam to seal. Cut into 12 slices. Place rolls, cut side down, in a greased 13x9-in. baking pan. Cover and let rise until doubled, about 1 hour.

4. Preheat oven to 350°. Drizzle rolls with melted butter. Bake until golden brown, 22-28 minutes. Place pan on a wire rack. In a small bowl, beat frosting ingredients until smooth. Spread over rolls. Serve warm.

1 roll: 406 cal., 23g fat (11g sat. fat), 55mg chol., 259mg sod., 48g carb. (25g sugars, 2g fiber), 5g pro.

HOMEMADE YOGURT

You'll be surprised how easy it is to make homemade yogurt. Top with granola and your favorite berries.
—*Taste of Home* Test Kitchen

- -

Prep: 5 min. + chilling
Cook: 20 min. + standing
Makes: about 2 qt.

- 2   qt. pasteurized whole milk
- 2   Tbsp. plain yogurt with live active cultures

1. In a Dutch oven, heat milk over medium heat until a thermometer reads 200°, stirring occasionally to prevent scorching. Remove from the heat; let stand until a thermometer reads 112°-115°, stirring occasionally. (If desired, place pan in an ice-water bath for faster cooling.)
2. Whisk 1 cup warm milk into yogurt until smooth; return all to pan, stirring gently. Transfer mixture to warm, clean jars, such as 1-qt. canning jars.
3. Cover jars; place in oven. Turn on oven light to keep mixture warm, about 110°. Let stand, undisturbed, until yogurt is set, 6-24 hours, tilting jars gently to check. (Yogurt will become thicker and more tangy as it stands.)
4. Refrigerate, covered, until cold. Store in refrigerator up to 2 weeks.

1 cup: 151 cal., 8g fat (5g sat. fat), 25mg chol., 107mg sod., 12g carb. (12g sugars, 0 fiber), 8g pro. **Diabetic exchanges:** 1 whole milk.

LEEK TART

This tart has a flaky pastry crust and tasty filling of leeks, bacon, eggs and cream. Satisfying and delicious, it makes a nice brunch dish, but you can serve it for any meal.
—Anneliese Deising, Plymouth, MI

- -

Prep: 30 min. + chilling • **Bake:** 30 min.
Makes: 12 servings

- 2   cups all-purpose flour
- ¼   tsp. salt
- ¼   tsp. sugar
- ½   cup cold butter
- 9   to 11 Tbsp. cold water

FILLING
- 1   lb. thick-sliced bacon, diced
- 3½   lbs. leeks (white portion only), sliced
- 2   Tbsp. all-purpose flour
- 4   large eggs
- 1   cup half-and-half cream
- ½   tsp. salt
- ¼   tsp. pepper
- ⅛   tsp. ground nutmeg

1. In a bowl, combine the flour, salt and sugar; cut in butter until crumbly. Gradually add water, tossing with a fork until a ball forms. Cover and refrigerate dough for 30 minutes.
2. In a large skillet, cook bacon over medium heat until crisp. Using a slotted spoon, remove to paper towels. Drain, reserving 2 Tbsp. drippings. Saute leeks in drippings until tender; stir in the bacon. Stir in flour until blended.
3. On a floured surface, roll dough to ⅛-in. thickness. Transfer to an ungreased 10-in. springform pan. Spoon leek mixture into crust. Trim pastry to ¼ in. above filling; press pastry against side of pan. Bake at 400° for 10 minutes.
4. Meanwhile, in a bowl, beat the eggs, cream, salt, pepper and nutmeg. Pour over leek mixture. Bake until a knife inserted in the center comes out clean, 20-25 minutes longer. Serve warm.

1 piece: 352 cal., 18g fat (9g sat. fat), 112mg chol., 482mg sod., 37g carb. (7g sugars, 3g fiber), 11g pro.

TEST KITCHEN TIP
Use kitchen scissors to cut the bacon into small pieces directly into the pan before cooking it.

SALMON & ARTICHOKE QUICHE SQUARES

Salmon, goat cheese and artichoke hearts make this quiche feel a little fancy and taste extra delicious. Baked in an 11x7-inch dish, it comes together in a snap and makes enough to serve a hungry brunch crowd.
—Jeanne Holt, St. Paul, MN

Prep: 15 min. • **Bake:** 40 min. + cooling
Makes: 15 servings

- 1   tube (8 oz.) refrigerated crescent rolls
- ⅔   cup shredded Parmesan cheese, divided
- ½   cup crumbled goat cheese
- 1   cup thinly sliced smoked salmon fillets
- 1   cup water-packed artichoke hearts, drained
- ¼   cup chopped green onions (green portion only)
- 2   Tbsp. finely chopped fresh dill
- ¼   tsp. pepper
- 5   large eggs
- 1   cup heavy whipping cream

1. Preheat oven to 350°. Unroll crescent roll dough into a long rectangle; place in an ungreased 11x7-in. baking dish. Press dough over bottom and up sides of dish, pressing perforations to seal.

2. Sprinkle with ⅓ cup Parmesan cheese. Top with goat cheese, salmon and artichoke hearts. Sprinkle with onions, chopped dill and pepper. Whisk eggs and cream; pour over salmon mixture. Sprinkle with remaining ⅓ cup Parmesan cheese.

3. Bake until a knife inserted in center comes out clean, 40-45 minutes (loosely cover with foil if edges are getting too dark). Cool 20 minutes. Cut into squares.

1 square: 179 cal., 13g fat (7g sat. fat), 89mg chol., 330mg sod., 8g carb. (2g sugars, 0 fiber), 8g pro.

MAKE AHEAD
BREAKFAST BURRITO CASSEROLE

A friend gave me this burrito casserole recipe and I modified it to fit our family. It's perfect for a brunch, because you can prep it the night before and bake it the next morning.
—Krista Yoder, Abbeville, SC

Prep: 25 min. • **Bake:** 30 min.
Makes: 8 servings

- 8   large eggs
- ⅓   cup 2% milk
- ½   tsp. salt
- ½   tsp. pepper
- 1   lb. bulk pork sausage
- 1   cup sour cream
- 1   can (10¾ oz.) condensed cream of chicken soup, undiluted
- 4   flour tortillas (10 in.), cut into 1-in. pieces
- 1⅓ cups salsa, divided
- ⅔   cup shredded cheddar cheese
- ⅔   cup shredded part-skim mozzarella cheese
-     Optional: Enchilada sauce and thinly sliced green onions,

1. Preheat oven to 350°. Whisk together eggs, milk, salt and pepper. In a large skillet coated with cooking spray, cook and stir egg mixture over medium heat until thickened and no liquid egg remains; remove and set aside.

2. In the same skillet, cook and crumble sausage over medium heat until no longer pink, 5-7 minutes; drain. Stir together sour cream and soup. Spread half the sour cream mixture in an ungreased 13x9-in. baking dish. Layer with half the tortilla pieces, half the salsa, the scrambled eggs, the sausage, and then the remaining tortillas and sour cream mixture. Top with remaining salsa; sprinkle with cheeses.

3. Bake, uncovered, until heated through, 30-35 minutes. If desired, serve with enchilada sauce and sliced green onions.

To make ahead: Refrigerate unbaked casserole, covered, several hours or overnight. To use, preheat oven to 350°. Remove casserole from refrigerator while oven heats. Bake as directed, increasing the time by 5 minutes.

1 cup: 506 cal., 34g fat (14g sat. fat), 243mg chol., 1419mg sod., 27g carb. (5g sugars, 2g fiber), 22g pro.

COFFEE CAKE MUFFINS

These cakelike muffins with heaps of streusel topping are to die for! They're wonderful any time you want a treat.
—Shannon Saltsman, Olmsted Falls, OH

Prep: 25 min. • **Bake:** 20 min.
Makes: 15 muffins

STREUSEL
- ½ cup butter, softened
- 1 cup packed brown sugar
- 1 cup all-purpose flour
- 1 tsp. ground cinnamon
- ½ cup chopped pecans

BATTER
- 1 cup butter, softened
- ¾ cup packed brown sugar
- ½ cup sugar
- 2 large eggs, room temperature
- ⅓ cup half-and-half cream
- 1½ tsp. vanilla extract
- 2 cups all-purpose flour
- 2 tsp. baking powder
- ½ tsp. salt
  Confectioners' sugar, optional

1. Preheat oven to 350°. For streusel, in a small bowl, combine butter, brown sugar, flour and cinnamon until crumbly. Stir in the pecans.
2. In a large bowl, cream butter and sugars until light and fluffy, 5-7 minutes. Add eggs, 1 at a time, beating well after each addition. Beat in cream and vanilla. Combine the flour, baking powder and salt; add to creamed mixture just until moistened.
3. Fill greased or paper-lined muffin cups one-fourth full. Drop 1 Tbsp. streusel into center of each muffin cup; cover with batter. Sprinkle tops with the remaining streusel. Bake until a toothpick inserted in muffin comes out clean, 20-22 minutes. Cool in pan 5 minutes. Remove from pans to a wire rack to cool completely. Dust with confectioners' sugar if desired. Serve warm.
1 muffin: 420 cal., 22g fat (12g sat. fat), 79mg chol., 284mg sod., 52g carb. (32g sugars, 1g fiber), 4g pro.

ZUCCHINI QUICHE

I make this recipe for so many different occasions. It's popular with company and at potluck dinners, and I've passed it around to many friends. My husband and I are growing lots of squash this summer...all for this quiche!
—Dorothy Collins, Winnsboro, TX

Prep: 20 min. • **Bake:** 45 min.
Makes: 8 servings

- 1 lb. zucchini, thinly sliced
- 2 Tbsp. butter
- 1 pie shell (9 in.), baked
- 1½ cups shredded mozzarella cheese
- 1 cup ricotta cheese
- ½ cup half-and-half cream
- 3 large eggs, lightly beaten
- ¾ tsp. salt
- ½ tsp. dried oregano
- ½ tsp. dried basil
- ¼ tsp. garlic powder
  Dash pepper
  Paprika

1. Preheat oven to 350°. In a small skillet, saute zucchini in butter until tender; drain. Place half the zucchini in the crust. Sprinkle with mozzarella cheese.
2. In a large bowl, combine the ricotta cheese, cream, eggs, salt, oregano, basil, garlic powder and pepper. Pour into crust. Arrange remaining zucchini slices over the top. Sprinkle with paprika.
3. Bake for 45 minutes or until a knife inserted in the center comes out clean.
1 piece: 306 cal., 21g fat (11g sat. fat), 129mg chol., 499mg sod., 18g carb. (4g sugars, 1g fiber), 12g pro.

HOME FRIES

When I was little, my dad and I would get up early on Sundays and make these for the family. The rest of the gang would be awakened by the tempting aroma.
—Teresa Koide, Manchester, CT

- -

Prep: 25 min. • **Cook:** 15 min./batch.
Makes: 8 servings

- 1   lb. bacon, chopped
- 8   medium potatoes (about 3 lbs.), peeled and cut into ½-in. pieces
- 1   large onion, chopped
- 1   tsp. salt
- ½ tsp. pepper

1. In a large skillet, cook chopped bacon over medium-low heat until crisp. Remove bacon from pan with a slotted spoon and drain on paper towels. Remove bacon drippings from pan and reserve.
2. Working in batches, add ¼ cup bacon drippings, potatoes, onion, salt and pepper to pan; toss to coat. Cook and stir over medium-low heat until potatoes are golden brown and tender, 15-20 minutes, adding more drippings as needed. Stir in cooked bacon; serve immediately.

1 cup: 349 cal., 21g fat (8g sat. fat), 33mg chol., 681mg sod., 31g carb. (3g sugars, 2g fiber), 10g pro.

★ ★ ★ ★ ★ **READER REVIEW**

"I made this recipe on our beach vacation. I used leftover kielbasa instead of bacon and it turned out great."

—**DANIELLEYLEE** TASTEOFHOME.COM

ORANGE-GLAZED BACON

Just when you thought bacon couldn't get any tastier, we whipped up this tasty recipe starring the breakfast favorite drizzled with a sweet orange glaze.
—*Taste of Home* Test Kitchen

- -

Prep: 20 min. • **Bake:** 25 min.
Makes: 8 servings

- ¾ cup orange juice
- ¼ cup honey
- 1   Tbsp. Dijon mustard
- ¼ tsp. ground ginger
- ⅛ tsp. pepper
- 1   lb. bacon strips

1. Preheat oven to 350°. In a small saucepan, combine the first 5 ingredients. Bring to a boil; cook until liquid is reduced to ⅓ cup.
2. Place bacon on a rack in an ungreased 15x10x1-in. baking pan. Bake for 10 minutes, then drain.
3. Drizzle half of glaze over bacon. Bake for 10 minutes. Turn bacon and drizzle with remaining glaze. Bake until golden brown, 5-10 minutes longer. Place bacon on waxed paper until set. Serve warm.

3 glazed bacon strips: 146 cal., 8g fat (3g sat. fat), 21mg chol., 407mg sod., 12g carb. (11g sugars, 0 fiber), 7g pro.

MAKE AHEAD

MAPLE BACON FRENCH TOAST BAKE

Our family loves Sunday brunch. Each season I try to bring a little different flavor to the table. This French toast bake reminds us of fall.
—Peggie Brott, Milford, KS

Prep: 35 min. + chilling • **Bake:** 50 min.
Makes: 12 servings

- 8 cups cubed bread
- 8 large eggs
- 2 cups 2% milk
- ½ cup packed brown sugar
- ⅓ cup maple syrup
- ½ tsp. ground cinnamon
- 1 lb. bacon strips, cooked and crumbled

1. Place bread in a greased 13x9-in. baking dish. In a large bowl, whisk eggs, milk, brown sugar, syrup and cinnamon. Pour over bread. Sprinkle with the bacon. Refrigerate, covered, 4 hours or overnight.
2. Remove casserole from the refrigerator 30 minutes before baking. Preheat oven to 350°. Bake, uncovered, until a knife inserted in center comes out clean, 50-60 minutes. Let stand 5-10 minutes before serving.
1 piece: 256 cal., 10g fat (3g sat. fat), 141mg chol., 426mg sod., 29g carb. (18g sugars, 1g fiber), 12g pro.

★ ★ ★ ★ ★ **READER REVIEW**

"Very tasty and easy dish. We add more maple syrup when it is on our plates. Have made it three times and will continue, as it's always a crowd-pleaser."
CELESTE415 TASTEOFHOME.COM

MAKE AHEAD

SUNRISE SAUSAGE ENCHILADAS

These delicious enchiladas are equally good made with cubed ham instead of cooked sausage. Prepare ahead, refrigerate, and bake when ready for a convenient breakfast.
—Deb LeBlanc, Phillipsburg, KS

Prep: 30 min. + chilling • **Bake:** 40 min.
Makes: 10 servings

- 1 lb. bulk pork sausage
- 2 Tbsp. canola oil
- 7 cups frozen shredded hash brown potatoes, thawed (20 oz.)
- ½ tsp. salt
- ½ tsp. chili powder
- ¼ tsp. cayenne pepper
- ¼ tsp. pepper
- 1 can (4 oz.) chopped green chiles
- 2 cups shredded cheddar cheese, divided
- 10 flour tortillas (6 in.)
- 2 cans (10 oz. each) green enchilada sauce

Optional toppings: Chopped red onion, chopped sweet red pepper and chopped fresh cilantro

1. In a large skillet, cook and crumble the sausage over medium heat until no longer pink, 5-7 minutes. Remove from pan with a slotted spoon; discard drippings.
2. In same pan, heat oil over medium-high heat; saute potatoes until they are lightly browned, 8-10 minutes. Remove from the heat; stir in seasonings, chiles, sausage and ½ cup cheese.
3. Place ½ cup filling on each tortilla; roll up and place in a greased 13x9-in. baking dish, seam side down. Top with sauce, then cover and refrigerate several hours or overnight.
4. Preheat oven to 375°. Remove enchiladas from the refrigerator while oven heats. Bake, covered, 30 minutes. Sprinkle with the remaining 1 ½ cups cheese. Bake, uncovered, until lightly browned and heated through, an additional 10-15 minutes. If desired, serve with toppings.
1 enchilada: 398 cal., 25g fat (9g sat. fat), 48mg chol., 1116mg sod., 30g carb. (2g sugars, 2g fiber), 14g pro.

VEGETARIAN EGG STRATA

I used to make this with turkey or chicken sausage, but I adapted it for a vegetarian friend, and it was a huge hit. I serve it for brunch with fresh breads or bagels and a big mixed salad featuring arugula, apples and walnuts.
—Danna Rogers, Westport, CT

- -

Prep: 25 min. + chilling
Bake: 45 min. + standing
Makes: 12 servings

- 1 medium zucchini, finely chopped
- 1 medium sweet red pepper, finely chopped
- 1 cup sliced baby portobello mushrooms
- 1 medium red onion, finely chopped
- 2 tsp. olive oil
- 3 garlic cloves, minced
- 2 tsp. minced fresh thyme or ½ tsp. dried thyme
- ½ tsp. salt
- ¼ tsp. pepper
- 1 loaf (1 lb.) day-old French bread, cubed
- 2 pkg. (5.3 oz. each) fresh goat cheese, crumbled
- 1¾ cups grated Parmesan cheese
- 6 large eggs, lightly beaten
- 2 cups fat-free milk
- ¼ tsp. ground nutmeg

1. In a large skillet, saute zucchini, red pepper, mushrooms and onion in oil until tender. Add garlic, thyme, salt and pepper; saute 1 minute longer.
2. In a 13x9-in. baking dish coated with cooking spray, layer half the bread cubes, zucchini mixture, goat cheese and Parmesan cheese. Repeat layers.
3. Whisk eggs, milk and nutmeg. Pour over the top. Cover and refrigerate overnight.
4. Remove from refrigerator 30 minutes before baking. Preheat oven to 350°. Bake, uncovered, until a knife inserted in the center comes out clean, 45-50 minutes. Let stand 10 minutes before cutting.
1 piece: 281 cal., 12g fat (6g sat. fat), 140mg chol., 667mg sod., 27g carb. (4g sugars, 2g fiber), 17g pro.

BACON & EGGS CASSEROLE

Because it requires so little time to prepare and is such a great hit with family and friends alike, this is a favorite of mine to make for brunches.
—Deanna Durward-Orr, Windsor, ON

- -

Prep: 20 min. • **Bake:** 40 min.
Makes: 10 servings

- 4 bacon strips
- 18 large eggs
- 1 cup whole milk
- 1 cup shredded cheddar cheese
- 1 cup sour cream
- ¼ cup sliced green onions
- 1 to 1½ tsp. salt
- ½ tsp. pepper

1. In a large skillet, cook the bacon over medium heat until crisp. Remove to paper towel to drain.
2. In a large bowl, beat the eggs. Add the milk, cheese, sour cream, onions, salt and pepper.
3. Pour into a greased 13x9-in. baking dish. Crumble bacon and sprinkle on top. Bake, uncovered, at 325° until knife inserted in center comes out clean, 40-45 minutes. Let stand for 5 minutes.
1 serving: 289 cal., 22g fat (10g sat. fat), 420mg chol., 508mg sod., 4g carb. (3g sugars, 0 fiber), 16g pro.

SHIITAKE & MANCHEGO SCRAMBLE

This savory breakfast dish takes everyday scrambled eggs up a few notches. The rich flavor is so satisfying in the morning, and it's even better served with buttery toasted Italian bread.
—Thomas Faglon, Somerset, NJ

- -

Takes: 25 min. • **Makes:** 8 servings

- 2 **Tbsp. extra virgin olive oil, divided**
- ½ **cup diced onion**
- ½ **cup diced sweet red pepper**
- 2 **cups thinly sliced fresh shiitake mushrooms (about 4 oz.)**
- 1 **tsp. prepared horseradish**
- 8 **large eggs, beaten**
- 1 **cup heavy whipping cream**
- 1 **cup shredded Manchego cheese**
- 1 **tsp. kosher salt**
- 1 **tsp. coarsely ground pepper**

1. In a large nonstick skillet, heat 1 Tbsp. olive oil over medium heat. Add onion and red pepper; cook and stir until crisp-tender, 2-3 minutes. Add mushrooms; cook and stir until tender, 3-4 minutes. Add horseradish; cook 2 minutes more.

2. In a small bowl, whisk together remaining ingredients and remaining 1 Tbsp. olive oil. Pour into skillet; cook and stir until eggs are thickened and no liquid egg remains.

1 serving: 274 cal., 24g fat (12g sat. fat), 234mg chol., 405mg sod., 4g carb. (2g sugars, 1g fiber), 11g pro.

GET-UP-AND-GO GRANOLA

My family loves to have this soul-warming granola before hiking, biking or even when camping. It smells delicious while baking up, and you can easily make it in large batches for special occasions or to send in care packages to family and friends.
—Sabrina Olson, Otsego, MN

- -

Prep: 15 min. • **Bake:** 30 min. + cooling
Makes: 7½ cups

- 6 **cups old-fashioned oats**
- ½ **cup unblanched almonds, coarsely chopped**
- ¼ **cup packed brown sugar**
- ¼ **cup flaxseed**
- ¼ **cup canola oil**
- ¼ **cup honey**
- 1 **Tbsp. maple syrup**
- 1 **tsp. apple pie spice**
- ½ **tsp. salt**
- ½ **tsp. vanilla extract**
- ½ **cup dried cranberries**
- ½ **cup raisins**

1. Preheat oven to 300°. In a large bowl, combine oats, almonds, brown sugar and flax. In a microwave-safe dish, whisk oil, honey, maple syrup, pie spice and salt. Microwave on high for 30-45 seconds or until heated through, stirring once. Stir in vanilla. Pour over oat mixture; toss to coat.

2. Spread evenly in a 15x10x1-in. baking pan coated with cooking spray. Bake until golden brown, 30-40 minutes, stirring every 10 minutes. Cool completely on a wire rack. Stir in cranberries and raisins. Store in an airtight container.

½ cup: 255 cal., 10g fat (1g sat. fat), 0 chol., 84mg sod., 40g carb. (15g sugars, 5g fiber), 7g pro.

Sweet Horseradish
Glazed Ribs
page 91

Main Dishes

When you're in charge of the main event, rely on these recipes for proven success! Here are the impressive meats, stacked sandwiches and craveworthy casseroles that people adore.

SPINACH & CHICKEN PHYLLO PIE

For a wonderful brunch showstopper, we make chicken pie with phyllo and spinach. Even our kids go for it. It's so good served with a minty fruit salad.
—Katie Ferrier, Houston, TX

- -

Prep: 35 min. • **Bake:** 35 min.
Makes: 8 servings

- 2 lbs. ground chicken
- 1 large onion, chopped
- 1 tsp. pepper
- 1 tsp. dried oregano
- ¾ tsp. salt
- ½ tsp. ground nutmeg
- ¼ tsp. crushed red pepper flakes
- 3 pkg. (10 oz. each) frozen chopped spinach, thawed and squeezed dry
- 4 large eggs, lightly beaten
- 3 cups crumbled feta cheese
- 20 sheets phyllo dough (14x9-in. size)
      Cooking spray

1. Preheat oven to 375°. In a large skillet, cook chicken and onion over medium-high heat 7-9 minutes or until chicken is no longer pink, breaking up meat into crumbles; drain. Stir in seasonings. Add spinach; cook and stir until liquid is evaporated. Transfer to a large bowl; cool slightly. Stir in beaten eggs and cheese.
2. Layer 10 sheets of phyllo dough in a greased 13x9-in. baking dish, spritzing each with cooking spray. (Keep remaining phyllo covered with a damp towel to prevent it from drying out.) Spread spinach mixture over phyllo. Top with remaining sheets of phyllo, spritzing each with cooking spray. Cut into 8 rectangles.
3. Bake, uncovered, 35-40 minutes or until golden brown. If necessary, recut rectangles before serving.
1 piece: 442 cal., 23g fat (8g sat. fat), 191mg chol., 921mg sod., 25g carb. (3g sugars, 6g fiber), 35g pro.

MAKE AHEAD

PEPPERONI PIZZA LOAF

Because this savory stromboli uses frozen bread dough, it comes together in no time. The golden loaf is stuffed with cheese, pepperoni, mushrooms, peppers and olives. I often add a few thin slices of ham, too. It's tasty served with warm pizza sauce for dipping.

—Jenny Brown, West Lafayette, IN

- -

Prep: 20 min. • **Bake:** 35 min.
Makes: 12 pieces

1 loaf (1 lb.) frozen bread dough, thawed
2 large eggs, separated
1 Tbsp. grated Parmesan cheese
1 Tbsp. olive oil
1 tsp. minced fresh parsley
1 tsp. dried oregano
½ tsp. garlic powder
¼ tsp. pepper
8 oz. sliced pepperoni
2 cups shredded part-skim mozzarella cheese
1 can (4 oz.) mushroom stems and pieces, drained
¼ to ½ cup pickled pepper rings
1 medium green pepper, diced
1 can (2¼ oz.) sliced ripe olives
1 can (15 oz.) pizza sauce

1. Preheat oven to 350°. On a greased baking sheet, roll out dough into a 15x10-in. rectangle. In a small bowl, combine egg yolks, Parmesan cheese, oil, parsley, oregano, garlic powder and pepper. Brush over the dough.

2. Sprinkle with the pepperoni, mozzarella cheese, mushrooms, pepper rings, green pepper and olives. Roll up, jelly-roll style, starting with a long side; pinch seam to seal and tuck ends under.

3. Position loaf with seam side down; brush with egg whites. Do not let rise. Bake until golden brown and the dough is cooked through, 35-40 minutes. Warm the pizza sauce; serve with sliced loaf.

Freeze option: Freeze cooled unsliced pizza loaf in heavy-duty foil. To use, remove from freezer 30 minutes before reheating. Remove from foil and reheat loaf on a greased baking sheet in a preheated 325° oven until heated through. Serve as directed.

1 piece: 296 cal., 17g fat (6g sat. fat), 66mg chol., 827mg sod., 24g carb. (4g sugars, 2g fiber), 13g pro.

MAKE AHEAD

WINNING CRANBERRY GLAZED HAM

A friend shared the recipe for this tender ham with me. I've served it at reunions, weddings, graduations, baptisms and holiday gatherings. It's a delicious way to please a crowd.
—Sue Seymour, Valatie, NY

Prep: 15 min. + marinating • **Bake:** 2½ hours
Makes: 16 servings

- 2 cans (16 oz. each) whole-berry cranberry sauce
- 1 cup orange juice
- ⅓ cup steak sauce
- 2 Tbsp. canola oil
- 2 Tbsp. prepared mustard
- 2 Tbsp. brown sugar
- 1 fully cooked bone-in ham (7 to 9 lbs.)

1. In a large bowl, combine the cranberry sauce, orange juice, steak sauce, oil, mustard and brown sugar. Score the surface of the ham with shallow diagonal cuts, making diamond shapes.

2. Place ham in a 2-gal. resealable bag. Add half of cranberry mixture; seal bag and turn to coat. Cover and refrigerate 8 hours or overnight, turning several times. Cover and refrigerate remaining cranberry mixture.

3. Preheat oven to 325°. Drain the ham, discarding marinade. Place ham on a rack in a foil-lined roasting pan; cover with foil. Bake for 1¾ hours.

4. Place reserved cranberry mixture in a small saucepan; heat through. Uncover ham; brush with cranberry mixture.

5. Bake ham until a thermometer reads 140°, 45-60 minutes longer, brushing with cranberry mixture every 15 minutes. Warm remaining cranberry mixture; serve with the ham.

4 oz ham.: 264 cal., 7g fat (2g sat. fat), 87mg chol., 1164mg sod., 22g carb. (15g sugars, 1g fiber), 29g pro.

CAJUN RICE DISH

A variety of vegetables makes this delicious casserole a hit with everyone. I team up generous servings with garlic bread and a tossed salad.
—Rose Kostynuik, Calgary, AB

Prep: 5 min. • **Bake:** 1 hour
Makes: 8 servings

- 5 cups beef broth
- 2 cups uncooked long grain rice
- 1 lb. ground beef
- 1 medium onion, chopped
- 1 cup sliced carrots
- ½ cup sliced celery
- ½ cup frozen corn
- ½ cup frozen peas
- ½ cup chopped sweet red pepper
- 1 tsp. salt
- 1 tsp. Cajun seasoning

1. In a roasting pan, combine broth and rice. Cover and bake at 350° for 30 minutes.
2. Meanwhile, in a large skillet, cook beef and onion over medium heat until meat is no longer pink; drain. Add to rice. Stir in the vegetables, salt and Cajun seasoning.
3. Cover and bake 30 minutes longer or until rice is tender.

1 serving: 303 cal., 6g fat (3g sat. fat), 28mg chol., 953mg sod., 45g carb. (4g sugars, 2g fiber), 16g pro.

TEST KITCHEN TIP
If you're out of Cajun seasoning, you can make your own. There are many different blends, but a typical mix includes salt, cayenne pepper, garlic powder, paprika, thyme, pepper and onion powder.

ITALIAN SAUSAGE SANDWICHES

When my wife and I have friends over, we love to serve these sandwiches. This is a convenient recipe, since it can be prepared the day before and reheated. It is a very good meal, and I have made it several times.

—Mike Yaeger, Brookings, SD

Prep: 30 min. • **Cook:** 30 min.
Makes: 20 servings

> 20 Italian sausages
> 4 large green peppers, thinly sliced
> ½ cup chopped onion
> 1 can (12 oz.) tomato paste
> 1 can (15 oz.) tomato sauce
> 2 cups water
> 1 Tbsp. sugar
> 4 garlic cloves, minced
> 2 tsp. dried basil
> 1 tsp. dried oregano
> 1 tsp. salt
> 20 sandwich buns
>   Shredded mozzarella cheese, optional

1. In a large Dutch oven, brown sausages a few at a time; discard all but 2 Tbsp. drippings. Saute peppers and onion in drippings until crisp-tender; drain.
2. In the same pan, combine the tomato paste, tomato sauce, water, sugar, garlic, basil, oregano and salt. Add the sausages; bring to a boil. Reduce heat; cover and simmer for 30 minutes or until heated through. Serve on buns. Top with cheese if desired.

1 sandwich: 430 cal., 19g fat (8g sat. fat), 45mg chol., 1107mg sod., 44g carb. (11g sugars, 4g fiber), 20g pro.

FAVORITE HAMBURGER STEW

I got this recipe from a woman at our church when I needed a way to use up our bounty of home-canned tomatoes. My husband loves it, and I like that it's easy to warm up for a carefree dinner in the winter months.

—Marcia Clay, Truman, MN

Prep: 20 min. • **Cook:** 65 min.
Makes: 16 servings (4 qt.)

> 2 lbs. ground beef
> 2 medium onions, chopped
> 4 cans (14½ oz. each) stewed tomatoes, undrained
> 8 medium carrots, thinly sliced
> 4 celery ribs, thinly sliced
> 2 medium potatoes, peeled and cubed
> 2 cups water
> ½ cup uncooked long grain rice
> 3 tsp. salt
> 1 tsp. pepper

1. In a Dutch oven, cook beef and onions over medium heat until meat is no longer pink, breaking it into crumbles; drain. Add the tomatoes, carrots, celery, potatoes, water, rice, salt and pepper; bring to a boil. Reduce heat; cover and simmer 30 minutes or until vegetables and rice are tender.
2. Uncover; simmer 20-30 minutes longer or until thickened to desired consistency.
Freeze option: Freeze cooled stew in freezer containers. To use, partially thaw in refrigerator overnight. Heat through in a saucepan, stirring occasionally; add a little water if necessary.

1 cup: 191 cal., 7g fat (3g sat. fat), 35mg chol., 689mg sod., 21g carb. (8g sugars, 2g fiber), 12g pro.

★ ★ ★ ★ ★ **READER REVIEW**

"Added cabbage and loved it! I did go with less salt to begin with, then seasoned to taste when it was almost finished."

-GOTAKLU TASTEOFHOME.COM

CREAMY CAVATAPPI & CHEESE

Dive fork-first into oodles of noodles coated with a to-die-for sharp cheddar cheese sauce in this grown-up mac and cheese. Hot sauce lends a mild heat that's delectable with the smoky topping.
—Barbara Colucci, Rockledge, FL

Prep: 30 min. • **Bake:** 20 min.
Makes: 10 servings

- 6   cups uncooked cavatappi or spiral pasta
- 3   garlic cloves, minced
- ⅓   cup butter
- ¼   cup all-purpose flour
- 1   Tbsp. hot pepper sauce
- 4   cups 2% milk
- 6   cups shredded sharp cheddar cheese
- 1   cup cubed Velveeta
- 3   green onions, chopped

TOPPINGS

- ½   cup panko bread crumbs
- 3   thick-sliced bacon strips, cooked and coarsely crumbled
- 1   Tbsp. butter, melted
- 1   green onion, chopped
  Coarsely ground pepper, optional

1. Cook cavatappi according to package directions.

2. Meanwhile, saute garlic in butter in a Dutch oven. Stir in flour and pepper sauce until blended; gradually add milk. Bring to a boil; cook and stir until thickened, about 2 minutes.

3. Stir in cheeses until melted; add green onions. Drain cavatappi; stir into the cheese mixture.

4. Transfer to a greased 13x9-in. baking dish. Combine the bread crumbs, bacon and melted butter; sprinkle over top.

5. Bake, uncovered, at 350° until bubbly, 20-25 minutes. Sprinkle with green onion and, if desired, pepper.

1 cup: 706 cal., 38g fat (21g sat. fat), 110mg chol., 782mg sod., 60g carb. (8g sugars, 3g fiber), 32g pro.

MAKE AHEAD

CARAMELIZED HAM & SWISS BUNS

My next-door neighbor shared this recipe with me, and I simply cannot improve it! You can make it ahead and cook it quickly when company arrives. The combo of poppy seeds, ham, cheese, brown sugar and horseradish and makes it so delicious.

—Iris Weihemuller, Baxter, MN

Prep: 25 min. + chilling • **Bake:** 30 min.
Makes: 1 dozen

- 1 **pkg. (12 oz.) Hawaiian sweet rolls**
- ½ **cup horseradish sauce**
- ¾ **lb. sliced deli ham**
- 6 **slices Swiss cheese, halved**
- ½ **cup butter, cubed**
- 2 **Tbsp. finely chopped onion**
- 2 **Tbsp. brown sugar**
- 1 **Tbsp. spicy brown mustard**
- 2 **tsp. poppy seeds**
- 1½ **tsp. Worcestershire sauce**
- ¼ **tsp. garlic powder**

1. Without separating rolls, cut rolls in half horizontally; arrange bottom halves of rolls in a greased 9x9-in. baking pan. Spread cut side of roll bottoms with horseradish sauce. Layer with ham and cheese; replace tops.

2. In a small skillet, heat the butter over medium-high heat. Add onion; cook and stir until tender, 1-2 minutes. Stir in remaining ingredients. Pour over rolls. Refrigerate, covered, several hours or overnight.

3. Preheat oven to 350°. Bake, covered, 25 minutes. Bake, uncovered, until golden brown, 5-10 minutes longer.

1 sandwich: 315 cal., 17g fat (9g sat. fat), 61mg chol., 555mg sod., 29g carb. (13g sugars, 2g fiber), 13g pro.

BRING IT

This yummy, comforting dish is also called funeral sandwiches in some circles. Glum name aside, hot ham and Swiss buns are simple to serve and easy to eat, making them perfect for a large gathering. Transport them in foil pans for fuss-free heating and serving. Add a small spatula to help diners cut the little sandwiches apart.

APPLE-GLAZED HOLIDAY HAM

Each Christmas I'm asked to prepare this entree. I'm happy to oblige because it is easy to assemble, bakes for a few hours unattended and is simply delicious.
—Emory Doty, Jasper, GA

- -

Prep: 10 min. • **Bake:** 2½ hours
Makes: 15 servings

- 1   spiral-sliced fully cooked bone-in ham (7 to 9 lbs.)
- ½   cup packed brown sugar
- ½   cup unsweetened applesauce
- ½   cup unsweetened apple juice
- ¼   cup maple syrup
- ¼   cup molasses
- 1   Tbsp. Dijon mustard
  Dash ground ginger
  Dash ground cinnamon

1. Place ham on a rack in a shallow roasting pan. Bake, uncovered, at 325° for 2 hours.
2. In a small saucepan, combine the remaining ingredients. Cook and stir over medium heat until heated through. Brush ham with some glaze; bake 30-60 minutes longer or until a thermometer reads 140°, brushing occasionally with remaining glaze.
4 oz. ham: 242 cal., 6g fat (2g sat. fat), 93mg chol., 1138mg sod., 17g carb. (15g sugars, 0 fiber), 31g pro.

TEST KITCHEN TIP
Leftover ham can be stored for up to 1 week in the refrigerator. To further extend its storage, freeze ham in covered airtight containers or heavy-duty freezer bags for up to 2 months.

CHICKEN SALAD PARTY SANDWICHES

My famous chicken salad arrives at the party chilled in a plastic container. When it's time to set out the food, I stir in the pecans and assemble the sandwiches. They're a hit at buffet-style potlucks.
—Trisha Kruse, Eagle, ID

Takes: 25 min. • **Makes:** 16 servings

- 4 cups cubed cooked chicken breast
- 1½ cups dried cranberries
- 2 celery ribs, finely chopped
- 2 green onions, thinly sliced
- ¼ cup chopped sweet pickles
- 1 cup fat-free mayonnaise
- ½ tsp. curry powder
- ¼ tsp. coarsely ground pepper
- ½ cup chopped pecans, toasted
- 16 whole wheat dinner rolls
    Leaf lettuce

1. In a large bowl, combine first 5 ingredients. Mix mayonnaise, curry powder and pepper; stir into chicken mixture. Refrigerate until serving.
2. To serve, stir in pecans. Spoon onto lettuce-lined rolls.

Note: To toast nuts, bake in a shallow pan in a 350°; oven for 5-10 minutes or cook in a skillet over low heat until lightly browned, stirring occasionally.

1 sandwich: 235 cal., 6g fat (1g sat. fat), 30mg chol., 361mg sod., 33g carb. (13g sugars, 4g fiber), 14g pro.

MAKE AHEAD
CHILI TOTS

Cook once and eat twice with this hearty Southwestern casserole. With help from a few convenience products, it quickly goes together before you freeze it or pop it into the oven to bake.
—Linda Baldwin, Long Beach, CA

Prep: 15 min. • **Bake:** 35 min.
Makes: 2 casseroles (6 servings each)

- 1 lb. ground beef
- 2 cans (15 oz. each) chili without beans
- 1 can (8 oz.) tomato sauce
- 1 can (2¼ oz.) sliced ripe olives, drained
- 1 can (4 oz.) chopped green chilies
- 2 cups shredded cheddar cheese
- 1 pkg. (32 oz.) frozen Tater Tots

1. In a large skillet, cook the beef over medium heat until no longer pink; drain. Stir in the chili, tomato sauce, olives and green chilies. Transfer to 2 greased 8-in. square baking dishes. Sprinkle with cheese; top with Tater Tots.
2. Cover and bake casseroles at 350° for 35-40 minutes or until heated through.

Freeze option: Before baking, cover casseroles and freeze for up to 3 months. Remove from freezer 30 minutes before baking (do not thaw). Cover and bake at 350° for 1¼-1½ hours or until casserole is heated through.

1 serving: 297 cal., 18g fat (7g sat. fat), 44mg chol., 761mg sod., 24g carb. (1g sugars, 3g fiber), 15g pro.

MAKE AHEAD
BBQ CHICKEN SANDWICHES

These are fantastic sandwiches and are a cinch to make. For a spicier taste, eliminate the ketchup and increase the amount of salsa to 1 cup.
—Leticia Lewis, Kennewick, WA

Prep: 25 min. • **Cook:** 15 min.
Makes: 12 servings

- 1 cup chopped onion
- 1 cup diced celery
- 2 garlic cloves, minced
- 2 Tbsp. butter
- 1 cup salsa
- 1 cup ketchup
- ¼ cup brown sugar
- ¼ cup cider vinegar
- 2 Tbsp. Worcestershire sauce
- 1 tsp. chili powder
- ½ tsp. salt
- ¼ tsp. pepper
- 4 cups shredded cooked chicken
- 12 hamburger buns, split and toasted

1. In a large saucepan, saute the onion, celery and garlic in butter until tender. Stir in the salsa, ketchup, brown sugar, vinegar, Worcestershire sauce, chili powder, salt and pepper.
2. Stir in chicken. Bring to a boil. Reduce heat; cover and simmer for 15 minutes. Serve about ⅓ cup chicken mixture on each bun.
Freeze option: Freeze cooled meat mixture in freezer containers. To use, partially thaw in refrigerator overnight. Heat through in a saucepan, stirring occasionally; add water if necessary. Serve in buns.
1 sandwich: 284 cal., 8g fat (3g sat. fat), 47mg chol., 770mg sod., 35g carb. (12g sugars, 3g fiber), 18g pro. **Diabetic exchanges:** 2 starch, 2 lean meat.

BAKED SPAGHETTI

This cheesy crowd-pleasing dish puts a different spin of spaghetti. Leftovers freeze well for a quick future meal.
—Ruth Koberna, Brecksville, OH

Prep: 30 min. • **Bake:** 30 min.
Makes: 12 servings

- 1 cup chopped onion
- 1 cup chopped green pepper
- 1 Tbsp. butter
- 1 can (28 oz.) diced tomatoes, undrained
- 1 can (4 oz.) mushroom stems and pieces, drained
- 1 can (2¼ oz.) sliced ripe olives, drained
- 2 tsp. dried oregano
- 1 lb. ground beef, browned and drained, optional
- 12 oz. spaghetti, cooked and drained
- 2 cups shredded cheddar cheese
- 1 can (10¾ oz.) condensed cream of mushroom soup, undiluted
- ¼ cup water
- ¼ cup grated Parmesan cheese

1. In a large skillet, saute onion and green pepper in butter until tender. Add the tomatoes, mushrooms, olives, oregano and, if desired, ground beef. Simmer, uncovered, for 10 minutes.
2. Place half of the spaghetti in a greased 13x9-in. baking dish. Layer with half of the vegetable mixture and 1 cup cheddar cheese. Repeat layers.
3. In a small bowl, combine soup and water until smooth; pour over casserole. Sprinkle with Parmesan cheese. Bake, uncovered, at 350° until heated through, 30-35 minutes.
1 cup: 239 cal., 9g fat (5g sat. fat), 25mg chol., 500mg sod., 30g carb. (5g sugars, 3g fiber), 10g pro.

TEST KITCHEN TIP
To prevent pasta from sticking together when cooking, use a large pot and 3 qt. water for each 8 oz. of pasta you plan to cook. Add 1 Tbsp. cooking oil to the water. (This also prevents boiling over.) Bring the water to a full rolling boil before stirring in the pasta. Stir several times to separate the pasta until the water returns to a boil.

HOME-STYLE GLAZED MEAT LOAF

Grated carrots and cheese add a hint of color to this down-home glazed meat loaf. We look forward to meat loaf sandwiches the next day!
—Sandra Etelamaki, Ishpeming, MI

Prep: 15 min. • **Bake:** 1 hour + standing
Makes: 12 servings

2	large eggs, beaten
⅔	cup 2% milk
1½	cups shredded cheddar cheese
1	cup crushed saltines (about 30 crackers)
1	cup finely shredded carrots
½	cup finely chopped onion
½	tsp. salt
¼	tsp. garlic powder
¼	tsp. pepper
2	lbs. lean ground beef
½	cup packed brown sugar
½	cup ketchup
2	Tbsp. Dijon mustard
	Minced fresh parsley, optional

1. Preheat the oven to 350°. In a large bowl, combine eggs, milk, cheese, saltines, carrots, onion, salt, garlic powder and pepper. Crumble beef over mixture and mix lightly but thoroughly. Shape into a loaf. Place in a greased 13x9-in. baking dish. Bake, uncovered, for 50 minutes.

2. For glaze, in a small saucepan, bring the brown sugar, ketchup and mustard to a boil. Reduce heat; simmer, uncovered, for 3-5 minutes or until heated through. Spoon over meat loaf.

3. Bake 10-15 minutes longer or until the meat is no longer pink and a thermometer reads 160°. Drain; let stand for 10 minutes before slicing. If desired, top with minced fresh parsley.

1 piece: 266 cal., 12g fat (6g sat. fat), 100mg chol., 494mg sod., 18g carb. (12g sugars, 1g fiber), 20g pro.

CHEESE ENCHILADAS

You won't bring home leftovers when you bring these easy enchiladas to a potluck. With a homemade tomato sauce and cheesy filling, they always go fast. You can substitute any type of cheese you wish.
—Ashley Schackow, Defiance, OH

- -

Prep: 25 min. • **Bake:** 25 min.
Makes: 8 servings

2	cans (15 oz. each) tomato sauce
1⅓	cups water
2	Tbsp. chili powder
2	garlic cloves, minced
1	tsp. dried oregano
½	tsp. ground cumin
1	cup sour cream
¼	cup minced fresh parsley
½	tsp. salt
½	tsp. pepper
4	cups shredded Monterey Jack cheese
2½	cups shredded cheddar cheese, divided
2	medium onions, finely chopped
16	flour tortillas (8 in.), warmed
	Optional toppings: shredded lettuce, sliced ripe olives, chopped tomatoes and additional sour cream

1. Preheat oven to 350°. In a large saucepan, combine first 6 ingredients; bring to a boil. Reduce heat; simmer, uncovered, until thickened, 4-5 minutes, stirring occasionally.

2. Mix sour cream, parsley, salt and pepper; stir in Monterey Jack cheese, 2 cups cheddar cheese and onions. Spread 2 Tbsp. sauce over each tortilla; top each with about ⅓ cup cheese mixture and roll up. Place in 2 greased 13x9-in. baking dishes, seam side down. Pour remaining sauce over top.

3. Bake, uncovered, 20 minutes. Sprinkle with remaining cheddar cheese. Bake until cheese is melted, 4-5 minutes. If desired, serve with toppings.

Freeze option: Cover and freeze enchiladas before baking. To use, partially thaw in refrigerator overnight. Remove from refrigerator 30 minutes before baking. Preheat oven to 350°. Bake as directed, increasing time as necessary to heat through and for a thermometer inserted in center to read 165°.

2 enchiladas: 778 cal., 42g fat (23g sat. fat), 106mg chol., 1741mg sod., 66g carb. (4g sugars, 6g fiber), 34g pro.

4. Bake, covered, 30 minutes. Uncover and bake until golden brown and bubbly, 30-35 minutes longer. Let stand 10-15 minutes before serving. If desired, sprinkle with red pepper flakes.

1 piece: 350 cal., 17g fat (9g sat. fat), 45mg chol., 481mg sod., 37g carb. (8g sugars, 2g fiber), 13g pro.

MOIST TURKEY BREAST

My family always requests this turkey at family gatherings. The Italian dressing adds zip that you don't find in other recipes. If you'd like, you can make a flavorful gravy from the pan drippings.
—Cindy Carlson, Ingleside, TX

- -

Prep: 10 min. • **Bake:** 2 hours + standing
Makes: 14 servings

  1 **bone-in turkey breast (about 7 lbs.)**
  1 **tsp. garlic powder**
  ½ **tsp. onion powder**
  ½ **tsp. salt**
  ¼ **tsp. pepper**
 1½ **cups Italian dressing**

1. Place turkey breast in a greased 13x9-in. baking dish. Combine the seasonings; sprinkle over turkey. Pour dressing over the top.

2. Cover and bake at 325° until a thermometer reads 170°, 2-2½ hours, basting occasionally with pan drippings. Let stand for 10 minutes before slicing.

6 oz. cooked turkey: 406 cal., 22g fat (5g sat. fat), 122mg chol., 621mg sod., 2g carb. (1g sugars, 0 fiber), 47g pro.

Roasted Turkey: Combine 1¾ tsp. garlic powder, ¾ tsp. each onion powder and salt, and ½ tsp. pepper; sprinkle over a 12- to 14-pound turkey. Place in a roasting pan; top with 2½ cups Italian dressing. Cover and bake at 325° until a thermometer inserted in thigh reads 180°, 3-3½ hours, basting occasionally with pan drippings. Let stand for 20 minutes before carving.

ROASTED PUMPKIN LASAGNA

This is a hearty meatless meal that my family enjoys. If you prefer butternut squash, you can use it instead of pumpkin.
—Wendy Masters, East Garafraxa, ON

- -

Prep: 1 hour. • **Bake:** 1 hour + standing
Makes: 12 servings

  1 **medium pie pumpkin (about 3 lbs.)**
  2 **Tbsp. olive oil**
  1 **tsp. salt, divided**
  ¼ **tsp. ground nutmeg**
 12 **uncooked lasagna noodles**
  ½ **cup butter, cubed**
  1 **cup chopped onion**
  3 **garlic cloves, minced**
  ½ **cup all-purpose flour**
4½ **cups 2% milk**
  ¼ **cup chopped fresh sage**
  ½ **cup grated Parmesan cheese**
  2 **cups shredded mozzarella cheese**
      Crushed red pepper flakes, optional

1. Preheat oven to 400°. Peel pumpkin; cut in half lengthwise; discard seeds or save for toasting. Cut into ¼-in. thick slices. Place in a single layer on 2 greased 15x10x1-in. baking pan. Drizzle with oil; sprinkle with ¼ tsp. salt nutmeg. Roast until tender, 30-35 minutes. Reduce oven temperature to 350°.

2. Meanwhile, cook lasagna noodles according to package directions for al dente. In a large saucepan, melt butter over medium heat. Add onion; cook and stir until tender, 6-7 minutes. Add garlic; cook 1 minute longer. Stir in flour and remaining ¾ tsp. salt until smooth; gradually whisk in milk and sage. Bring to a boil, stirring constantly; cook and stir until thickened, 8-10 minutes. Remove from the heat; stir in Parmesan cheese. Drain noodles.

3. Place 3 noodles in a greased 13x9-in. baking dish. Layer with ⅓ of the pumpkin, 1⅓ cups sauce and ½ cup mozzarella cheese. Repeat layers twice. Top with the remaining noodles, sauce and mozzarella cheese.

LIP-SMACKIN' BBQ CHICKEN

The kids always say prepare to lick your lips when we have friends over for barbecue chicken. I'm proud of this dish, the first recipe I ever created.
—Sue Thomas, Moore, SC

Prep: 1¼ hours • **Grill:** 25 min.
Makes: 12 servings

- 2 cups ketchup
- 1 cup cider vinegar
- 1 cup water
- ¼ cup packed brown sugar
- ¼ cup reduced-sodium soy sauce
- ¼ cup molasses
- ¼ cup honey
- 2 Tbsp. prepared mustard
- 3 tsp. ground cumin
- ¼ tsp. salt
- ¼ tsp. pepper
- 6 lbs. assorted bone-in chicken pieces

1. In a large saucepan, combine the first 11 ingredients; bring to a boil. Reduce heat; simmer, uncovered, 1-1½ hours or until thickened, stirring occasionally. Remove half of the sauce; reserve for brushing chicken. Keep remaining sauce warm for serving.

2. Grill chicken, covered, over medium heat 25-35 minutes or until juices run clear, turning occasionally and brushing with reserved sauce during the last 10 minutes. Serve with remaining sauce.

4 oz. cooked chicken: 402 cal., 17g fat (5g sat. fat), 104mg chol., 871mg sod., 27g carb. (26g sugars, 0 fiber), 34g pro.

ONION LOOSE-MEAT SANDWICHES

With French onion soup, these sandwiches don't have the typical flavor of most sloppy joes. My sisters and I rely on this recipe from Mom on days when there's little time to cook.
—Kathy Petorsky, Belle Vernon, PA

Takes: 25 min. • **Makes:** 8 servings

- 1½ lbs. ground beef
- 2 Tbsp. all-purpose flour
  Salt and pepper to taste
- 1 can (10½ oz.) condensed French onion soup, undiluted
- 6 to 8 hamburger buns, split
  Sliced cheddar cheese and dill pickles, optional

1. In a large skillet, cook beef over medium heat until no longer pink; drain. Stir in flour, salt and pepper until blended. Gradually add soup. Bring to a boil; cook and stir for 2 minutes or until thickened.

2. Spoon onto buns; top with cheese and pickles if desired.

1 serving: 253 cal., 10g fat (4g sat. fat), 43mg chol., 526mg sod., 21g carb. (4g sugars, 1g fiber), 19g pro.

TEST KITCHEN TIP
For even more onion flavor, add ½ cup chopped onion to the filling of these sandwiches.

ACAPULCO DELIGHT

This dish always delights family and friends at potlucks and gatherings I take it to.

—Margene Skaggs, Guinda, CA

Prep: 25 min. • Bake: 25 min.
Makes: 10 servings

- 2 lbs. ground beef
- 1 envelope (1¼ oz.) taco seasoning
- ¾ cup water
- 1 bottle (15 oz.) mild green taco sauce
- 9 flour tortillas (6 in.)
- 2 cups shredded cheddar cheese
- 1 can (16 oz.) refried beans
- 2 cups sour cream
- 4 green onions, chopped
- 1 can (2¼ oz.) sliced ripe olives, drained
   Optional: Chopped tomatoes and chopped avocados

1. Preheat oven to 350°. In a large skillet, cook and crumble beef over medium heat until no longer pink; drain. Stir in taco seasoning and water. Add the taco sauce; simmer until slightly thickened, 5-10 minutes.

2. Cover the bottom of a 13x9-in. baking dish with 3 tortillas, tearing them into pieces as necessary. Layer half the meat mixture over tortillas; sprinkle with half the cheese. Layer with 3 more tortillas; spread with refried beans. Cover with sour cream; sprinkle with green onions and olives. Layer remaining tortillas over top; cover with remaining meat mixture and cheese.

3. Bake until heated through, 25-30 minutes. Let stand a few minutes before serving. If desired, serve with chopped tomatoes and avocados.

1 piece: 468 cal., 27g fat (14g sat. fat), 104mg chol., 1064mg sod., 26g carb. (3g sugars, 3g fiber), 28g pro.

MAKE AHEAD

FLAVORFUL MARINATED PORK LOIN

Beautifully glazed with a mouthwatering marinade, this entree is relatively low in fat but still juicy and tender.
—Paula Young, Tiffin, OH

Prep: 20 min. + marinating
Bake: 1 hour + standing
Makes: 12 servings

- 1 cup orange juice
- ¾ cup apricot preserves
- 2 Tbsp. plus ¼ cup sherry or vegetable broth, divided
- 3 Tbsp. lemon juice
- 2 Tbsp. olive oil
- 1 Tbsp. curry powder
- 1 Tbsp. Worcestershire sauce
- 1 tsp. dried thyme
- ½ tsp. pepper
- 1 boneless pork loin roast (3 lbs.)
- 1 Tbsp. cornstarch

1. In a small bowl, combine the orange juice, preserves, 2 Tbsp. sherry, lemon juice, oil, curry, Worcestershire sauce, thyme and pepper. Pour ¾ cup marinade into a large resealable plastic bag; add the pork. Seal bag and turn to coat; refrigerate overnight, turning occasionally. Set aside 1 cup remaining marinade for sauce; cover and refrigerate. Cover and refrigerate the rest of the marinade for basting.

2. Drain and discard marinade; place pork on a rack in a shallow roasting pan. Bake, uncovered, at 350° for 1-1¼ hours or until a thermometer reads 145°, basting occasionally with reserved marinade. Transfer to a serving platter. Let stand for 10 minutes before slicing.

3. Meanwhile, in a small saucepan, combine cornstarch with the remaining sherry and 1 cup marinade. Bring to a boil; cook and stir for 2 minutes or until thickened. Serve with roast.

3 oz. cooked pork with about 2 Tbsp. gravy: 229 cal., 8g fat (3g sat. fat), 55mg chol., 51mg sod., 15g carb. (8g sugars, 0 fiber), 22g pro. **Diabetic exchanges:** 3 lean meat, 1 starch, ½ fat.

ROAST LEG OF LAMB WITH ROSEMARY

Rubbing rosemary, garlic and onion into this delectable roast lamb takes it to a whole new level of deliciousness!
—Suzy Horvath, Milwaukie, OR

Prep: 10 min. • **Bake:** 2 hours + standing
Makes: 8 servings

- ⅓ cup olive oil
- ¼ cup minced fresh rosemary
- ¼ cup finely chopped onion
- 4 garlic cloves, minced
- ½ tsp. salt
- ¼ tsp. pepper
- 1 bone-in leg of lamb (5 to 6 lbs.), trimmed

1. Preheat oven to 325°. Combine the oil, rosemary, onion, garlic, salt and pepper; rub over lamb. Place fat side up on a rack in a shallow roasting pan.
2. Bake, uncovered, 2-2½ hours or until meat reaches desired doneness (for medium-rare, a thermometer should read 135°; medium, 140°; medium-well, 145°), basting occasionally with pan juices. Let stand 15 minutes before slicing.
5 oz. cooked lamb: 316 cal., 18g fat (5g sat. fat), 128mg chol., 206mg sod., 1g carb. (0 sugars, 0 fiber), 36g pro.

★ ★ ★ ★ ★ **READER REVIEW**

"It was well-received. Rosemary and lamb are such a nice pairing. The second time I made this, I served it with a quick balsamic vinegar reduction. Definitely a dish you will be proud to serve."

-EBRAMKAMP TASTEOFHOME.COM

PIGEON RIVER CHICKEN

For a picnic on the Pigeon River, we made chicken marinated in yogurt with a touch of cayenne. It's delectable warm or cold.
—Lib Jicha, Waynesville, NC

Prep: 25 min. + marinating • **Cook:** 15 min.
Makes: 12 servings

- 2 cups plain yogurt
- 2 Tbsp. hot pepper sauce
- 3 tsp. salt
- 2 broiler/fryer chickens (3 to 4 lbs. each), cut up

COATING

- 2 cups all-purpose flour
- 3 Tbsp. paprika
- 4 tsp. cayenne pepper
- 2 tsp. salt
- 2 tsp. pepper
- 1 tsp. dried thyme
    Oil for deep-fat frying

1. In a large bowl, combine the yogurt, pepper sauce and 3 tsp. salt. Add chicken; turn to coat. Cover and refrigerate 8 hours or overnight.
2. Drain chicken, discarding marinade. In a shallow bowl, mix flour and seasonings. Add chicken, a few pieces at a time, and toss to coat; shake off excess. Transfer to a 15x10x1-in. pan; let stand 20 minutes.
3. In a Dutch oven or deep skillet, heat ½ in. of oil over medium heat to 350°. Fry chicken, uncovered, until coating is dark golden brown and meat is no longer pink, 7-8 minutes per side, turning occasionally. Drain on paper towels.
1 serving: 608 cal., 42g fat (7g sat. fat), 109mg chol., 1031mg sod., 19g carb. (2g sugars, 1g fiber), 37g pro.

CHICKEN & CHILES CASSEROLE

This casserole is easy to prepare and can be made ahead if you have a busy day coming up. It makes good use of leftover meat and is very filling.
—Lois Keel, Alburquerque, NM

Prep: 15 min. • **Bake:** 1¼ hours
Makes: 8 servings

- 1 cup sour cream
- 1 cup half-and-half cream
- 1 cup chopped onion
- 1 can (4 oz.) chopped green chiles
- 1 tsp. salt
- ½ tsp. pepper
- 1 pkg. (2 lbs.) frozen shredded hash brown potatoes
- 2½ cups cubed cooked chicken
- 2½ cups shredded cheddar cheese, divided
  Chopped fresh cilantro, optional

1. Preheat oven to 350°. In a large bowl, combine sour cream, half-and-half cream, onion, chiles, salt and pepper. Stir in the potatoes, chicken and 2 cups cheese.

2. Pour the mixture into a greased 13x9-in. or 3-qt. baking dish. Bake, uncovered, until golden brown, about 1¼ hours. Sprinkle with remaining cheese before serving. If desired, sprinkle with chopped cilantro.

1½ cups: 410 cal., 21g fat (14g sat. fat), 111mg chol., 647mg sod., 25g carb. (4g sugars, 2g fiber), 26g pro.

> **TEST KITCHEN TIP**
> Cooked turkey or ham can be substituted for the chicken.

BURGERS WITH SPICY DILL SALSA

When I make burgers or hot dogs for barbecues or boating, I do a topping that tastes like pickle relish meets tomato salsa. You will love piling it on anything!
—Valonda Seward, Coarsegold, CA

Prep: 20 min. • **Grill:** 10 min./batch
Makes: 12 servings (3 cups salsa)

- 1 jar (10 oz.) dill pickle relish
- 3 plum tomatoes, seeded and finely chopped
- 1 small white onion, finely chopped
- ½ cup finely chopped red onion
- ½ cup minced fresh cilantro
- 1 Tbsp. olive oil
- 1 to 2 serrano peppers, seeded and chopped

BURGERS
- 3 lbs. ground beef
- 2 tsp. salt
- 1 tsp. pepper
- 12 hamburger buns, split

1. In a bowl, mix the first 7 ingredients. In another bowl, combine beef, salt and pepper; mix lightly but thoroughly. Shape into twelve ½-in.-thick patties.

2. In 2 batches, grill burgers, covered, over medium heat or broil 4 in. from heat 4-5 minutes on each side or until a thermometer reads 160°. Serve with salsa.

Note: Wear disposable gloves when cutting hot peppers; the oils can burn skin. Avoid touching your face.

1 burger with ¼ cup salsa: 371 cal., 16g fat (6g sat. fat), 70mg chol., 926mg sod., 31g carb. (4g sugars, 2g fiber), 25g pro.

CREAMY CHICKEN LASAGNA ROLL-UPS

The first time I made this I was at home and needed to make dinner, but I didn't want to go out to the store. I used the ingredients I had to make these roll-ups. You won't believe how creamy and cheesy and delicious they are!
—Cyndy Gerken, Naples, FL

- -

Prep: 35 min. • **Bake:** 45 min.
Makes: 10 servings

- 10 lasagna noodles
- ¾ lb. boneless skinless chicken breasts, cubed
- 1½ tsp. herbes de Provence
- ½ tsp. salt, divided
- ½ tsp. pepper, divided
- 1 Tbsp. olive oil
- 2 cups ricotta cheese
- ½ cup grated Parmesan cheese, divided
- ¼ cup 2% milk
- 2 Tbsp. minced fresh parsley
- 4 cups spaghetti sauce
- 8 oz. fresh mozzarella cheese, thinly sliced
- Additional minced fresh parsley, optional

1. Preheat oven to 375°. Cook lasagna noodles according to package directions.
2. Meanwhile, sprinkle chicken with herbes de Provence, ¼ tsp. salt and ¼ tsp. pepper. In a large skillet, cook chicken in oil over medium heat for 5-7 minutes or until no longer pink; set aside.
3. In a large bowl, combine ricotta, ¼ cup Parmesan cheese, milk, fresh parsley and remaining salt and pepper. Add chicken.
4. Drain noodles. Spread 1 cup spaghetti sauce into a greased 13x9-in. baking dish. Spread ⅓ cup chicken mixture over each noodle; carefully roll up. Place seam side down over sauce. Top with remaining sauce and Parmesan cheese.
5. Cover and bake 30 minutes. Uncover; top with mozzarella cheese. Bake 15-20 minutes longer or until bubbly and cheese is melted. Top with additional parsley if desired.
Note: Look for herbes de Provence in the spice aisle.
1 lasagna roll-up: 378 cal., 17g fat (9g sat. fat), 63mg chol., 789mg sod., 32g carb. (11g sugars, 3g fiber), 24g pro.

TEST KITCHEN TIP
Common olive oil works better for cooking at high heat than virgin or extra-virgin oil. These higher grades have ideal flavor for cold foods, but they smoke at lower temperatures.

CHICKEN ENCHILADAS

This is one of the first recipes I created for my husband after we got married. He was so impressed! Now we fix these regularly for our friends.
—Melissa Rogers, Tuscaloosa, AL

Prep: 30 min. • **Bake:** 30 min.
Makes: 2 casseroles (5 servings each)

- 2 cans (14½ oz. each) diced tomatoes with mild green chiles, undrained
- 2 cans (10½ oz. each) condensed cream of chicken soup, undiluted
- 1 can (10¾ oz.) condensed cheddar cheese soup, undiluted
- ¼ cup 2% milk
- 1 Tbsp. ground cumin
- 1 Tbsp. chili powder
- 2 tsp. garlic powder
- 2 tsp. dried oregano
- 5 cups shredded rotisserie chicken
- 1 pkg. (8 oz.) cream cheese, cubed and softened
- 20 flour tortillas (8 in.), warmed
- 4 cups shredded Mexican cheese blend

1. Preheat oven to 350°. For sauce, mix first 8 ingredients. For filling, combine chicken and cream cheese; stir in 3½ cups sauce.
2. Spread ¼ cup sauce into each of 2 greased 13x9-in. baking dishes. Place ⅓ cup filling down the center of each tortilla; roll up and place seam side down in baking dishes. Pour remaining sauce over tops; sprinkle with cheese.
3. Bake, uncovered, 30-35 minutes or until heated through and cheese is melted.
Freeze option: Cover and freeze unbaked enchiladas up to 3 months. Partially thaw in refrigerator overnight. Remove from refrigerator 30 minutes before baking. Bake enchiladas, covered, at 350° until a thermometer inserted in center reads 165°, about 45 minutes. Uncover; bake until cheese is melted, 5-10 minutes longer.
2 enchiladas: 828 cal., 40g fat (17g sat. fat), 132mg chol., 1738mg sod., 72g carb. (5g sugars, 7g fiber), 42g pro.

THREE-CHEESE MEATBALL MOSTACCIOLI

When my husband travels for work, I make a special dinner for my kids to keep their minds off missing Daddy. This tasty mostaccioli is meatball magic.
—Jennifer Gilbert, Brighton, MI

Prep: 15 min. • **Bake:** 35 min.
Makes: 10 servings

- 1 pkg. (16 oz.) mostaccioli
- 2 large eggs, lightly beaten
- 1 carton (15 oz.) part-skim ricotta cheese
- 1 lb. ground beef
- 1 medium onion, chopped
- 1 Tbsp. brown sugar
- 1 Tbsp. Italian seasoning
- 1 tsp. garlic powder
- ¼ tsp. pepper
- 2 jars (24 oz. each) pasta sauce with meat
- ½ cup grated Romano cheese
- 1 pkg. (12 oz.) frozen fully cooked Italian meatballs, thawed
- ¾ cup shaved Parmesan cheese
  Optional: Torn fresh basil or fresh oregano leaves

1. Preheat oven to 350°. Cook mostaccioli according to package directions for al dente; drain. Meanwhile, in a small bowl, mix eggs and ricotta cheese.
2. In a 6-qt. stockpot, cook beef and onion 6-8 minutes or until beef is no longer pink, breaking up beef into crumbles; drain. Stir in brown sugar and seasonings. Add pasta sauce and mostaccioli; toss to combine.
3. Transfer half the pasta mixture to a greased 13x9-in. baking dish. Layer with ricotta mixture and remaining pasta mixture; sprinkle with Romano cheese. Top with meatballs and Parmesan cheese.
4. Bake, uncovered, 35-40 minutes or until heated through. If desired, top with basil or oregano.
1⅓ cups: 541 cal., 23g fat (11g sat. fat), 105mg chol., 1335mg sod., 55g carb. (13g sugars, 5g fiber), 34g pro.

SWEET HORSERADISH GLAZED RIBS

PICTURED ON PAGE 64

If you like to prep ahead of camping, roast these ribs, wrap them and finish with a sweet, savory sauce at your campfire or grill.
—Ralph Jones, San Diego, CA

Prep: 10 min. + chilling • **Cook:** 2¼ hours
Makes: 8 servings

- 3 racks pork baby back ribs (about 8 lbs.)
- 1½ tsp. salt, divided
- 1½ tsp. coarsely ground pepper, divided
- 2 bottles (12 oz. each) beer or 3 cups unsweetened apple juice
- 1 jar (12 oz.) apricot preserves
- ¼ cup prepared horseradish, drained
- 2 Tbsp. honey or maple syrup
- 1 tsp. liquid smoke, optional

1. Preheat oven to 325°. If necessary, remove thin membrane from ribs and discard. Sprinkle 1 tsp. each salt and pepper over ribs. Transfer to a large shallow roasting pan, bone side down; add beer or juice. Bake, covered, until tender, 2-3 hours.
2. Meanwhile, puree apricot preserves, horseradish, honey, remaining ½ tsp. salt and ½ tsp. pepper and, if desired, liquid smoke in a blender.
3. Drain ribs. Place 1 rib rack on a large piece of aluminum foil. Brush with apricot-horseradish mixture; wrap tightly. Repeat with remaining ribs. Refrigerate up to 2 days.
4. Prepare a campfire or grill for medium heat. Remove the ribs from foil; grill until browned, 10-15 minutes, turning occasionally.

1 serving: 690 cal., 42g fat (15g sat. fat), 163mg chol., 674mg sod., 33g carb. (23g sugars, 0 fiber), 45g pro.

SAVORY RUBBED ROAST CHICKEN

A blend of paprika, onion powder, garlic and cayenne creates a delicious, slightly spicy roast chicken. The aroma of this dish while it's cooking drives my family nuts!
—Margaret Cole, Imperial, MO

Prep: 20 min. • **Bake:** 2 hours + standing
Makes: 12 servings

- 2 tsp. paprika
- 1 tsp. salt
- 1 tsp. onion powder
- 1 tsp. white pepper
- 1 tsp. cayenne pepper
- 1 tsp. dried thyme
- ¾ tsp. garlic powder
- ½ tsp. pepper
- 1 roasting chicken (6 to 7 lbs.)
- 1 large onion, cut into wedges

1. Preheat oven to 350°. In a small bowl, mix the first 8 ingredients.
2. Pat chicken dry and place on a rack in a roasting pan, breast side up. Rub the seasoning mixture over the outside and inside of chicken. Place onion inside cavity. Tuck wings under chicken; tie the drumsticks together.
3. Roast 2-2½ hours or until a thermometer inserted in the thickest part of thigh reads 170°-175°. (Cover loosely with foil if chicken browns too quickly.) Remove chicken from oven; tent with foil. Let stand 15 minutes before carving.

4 oz. cooked chicken: 272 cal., 16g fat (4g sat. fat), 90mg chol., 284mg sod., 2g carb. (1g sugars, 1g fiber), 29g pro.

TEST KITCHEN TIP
If you like this recipe, save time in the future by prepping extra batches of the seasoning rub. Next time you decide to make it, you'll be ready to go fast.

PENNSYLVANIA-STYLE PORK ROAST

Our children wouldn't dream of eating sauerkraut until they tasted it with this tender and juicy pork roast at a family celebration. They devoured it and went back for seconds! Now it's a mainstay in my pork recipe file.
—Ronda Jay Holcimb, Farmington, NM

- -

Prep: 10 min.
Cook: 2¼ hours + standing
Makes: 16 servings

1	tsp. onion powder
1	tsp. garlic powder
1	tsp. celery seed, crushed
1	tsp. Worcestershire sauce
¼	tsp. pepper
1	boneless rolled pork loin roast (4 to 5 lbs.)
2	cans (14 oz. each) sauerkraut, undrained
1	tsp. sugar, optional
8	oz. smoked kielbasa or Polish sausage, sliced

1. Preheat oven to 350°. In a small bowl, combine the first 5 ingredients; rub over roast. Place roast fat side up in a Dutch oven. Combine sauerkraut and sugar, if desired. Spoon sauerkraut and sausage over and around roast.

2. Cover and bake until a thermometer inserted in pork reads 145°, 2¼-2¾ hours. Let pork stand about 15 minutes before slicing.

3 oz. cooked pork: 191 cal., 9g fat (3g sat. fat), 66mg chol., 353mg sod., 2g carb. (1g sugars, 1g fiber), 24g pro.

EASY CHICKEN CASSEROLE

This may be a basic chicken casserole, but I never bring home leftovers whenever I take it to a potluck. The stick-to-your-ribs dish has lots of broad appeal, and I especially like that the crumb topping adds crunch to each serving.
—Faye Hintz, Springfield, MO

Prep: 15 min. • **Bake:** 30 min.
Makes: 10 servings

- 8 cups cubed cooked chicken
- 2 cans (10½ oz. each) condensed cream of chicken soup, undiluted
- 1 cup sour cream
- 1 cup crushed Ritz crackers (about 25 crackers)
- 2 Tbsp. butter, melted
- 1 tsp. celery seed
  Minced fresh parsley, optional

1. Preheat oven to 350°. Combine chicken, soup and sour cream; spread into a greased 13x9-in. baking dish. Combine crumbs, butter and celery seed; sprinkle over chicken mixture.

2. Bake, uncovered, until bubbly, 30-35 minutes. If desired, garnish with parsley.

1 cup: 386 cal., 21g fat (8g sat. fat), 116mg chol., 629mg sod., 12g carb. (2g sugars, 1g fiber), 35g pro.

★ ★ ★ ★ ★ **READER REVIEW**

"One of my favorites! It's great to eat when you're not feeling well or when you have lots of people over for a family dinner. Definitely a good dish!"

-ALISASAURUS TASTEOFHOME.COM

MAKE AHEAD

FAVORITE CREAMY CHICKEN CASSEROLE

I created this noodle casserole when my husband was craving a dish his aunt used to make. It tastes and smells wonderful and is now a staple at our house.
—Mari Warnke, Fremont, WI

Prep: 20 min. • **Bake:** 40 min.
Makes: 2 casseroles (5 servings each)

- 4 cups uncooked egg noodles
- 4 cups cubed cooked chicken
- 1 pkg. (16 oz.) frozen peas and carrots
- 2 cups 2% milk
- 2 cans (10½ oz. each) condensed cream of celery soup, undiluted
- 2 cans (10½ oz. each) condensed cream of chicken soup, undiluted
- 1 cup chopped onion
- 2 Tbsp. butter, melted
- ½ tsp. salt
- ½ tsp. pepper

1. Preheat oven to 350°. Cook noodles according to the package directions. Meanwhile, in a large bowl, combine remaining ingredients. Drain noodles; add to chicken mixture.
2. Transfer to 2 greased 8-in. square baking dishes. Cover and bake for 30 minutes. Uncover; bake until heated through, 10-15 minutes.
Freeze option: Cover and freeze unbaked casseroles up to 3 months. To use, partially thaw in refrigerator overnight. Remove from refrigerator 30 minutes before baking. Cover and microwave on high 10-12 minutes or until heated through and a thermometer inserted in center reads 165°, stirring twice.
1⅓ cups: 344 cal., 15g fat (5g sat. fat), 80mg chol., 996mg sod., 29g carb. (4g sugars, 5g fiber), 23g pro.

BALSAMIC PORK SCALLOPINE

I created this dish based on my veal scallopine. Thinly sliced pork is an economical alternative to veal and tasty!
—Mary Cokenour, Monticello, UT

Prep: 25 min. • **Cook:** 30 min.
Makes: 12 servings

- 3 lbs. pork sirloin cutlets
- 1½ cups all-purpose flour
- ½ cup olive oil
- 2 Tbsp. butter
- 1 medium onion, chopped
- ½ cup chopped roasted sweet red peppers
- 6 garlic cloves, minced
- 1 can (14½ oz.) reduced-sodium chicken broth
- ½ cup minced fresh basil or 2 Tbsp. dried basil
- ½ cup balsamic vinegar
- ½ tsp. pepper

NOODLES
- 1 pkg. (16 oz.) egg noodles
- ½ cup half-and-half cream
- ¼ cup grated Romano cheese
- ¼ cup butter, cubed
- ½ tsp. pepper
- ¼ tsp. garlic powder

1. Dredge pork cutlets in flour. Heat oil and butter in a large skillet over medium-high heat; add pork and brown in batches. Set aside.
2. Add onion and red peppers to the pan; saute until onion is tender. Add garlic; cook 1 minute longer. Add the broth, basil, vinegar and pepper. Return pork to the pan, layering if necessary.
3. Cover and cook over low heat for 15-20 minutes or until meat is tender.
4. Meanwhile, in a Dutch oven, cook noodles according to package directions. Drain; stir in cream, cheese, butter, pepper and garlic powder. Serve with pork.
1 serving: 503 cal., 25g fat (9g sat. fat), 127mg chol., 292mg sod., 35g carb. (4g sugars, 2g fiber), 32g pro.

GRILLED RIBEYES WITH BROWNED GARLIC BUTTER

Use the grill's smoke to flavor the ribeyes, then slather them with garlicky butter for a standout entree your friends and family will always remember.
—Arge Salvatori, Waldwick, NJ

- -

Takes: 25 min. • **Makes:** 8 servings

6	Tbsp. unsalted butter, cubed
2	garlic cloves, minced
4	beef ribeye steaks (about 1 in. thick and 12 oz. each)
1½	tsp. salt
1½	tsp. pepper

1. In a small heavy saucepan, melt butter with garlic over medium heat. Heat 4-6 minutes or until butter is golden brown, stirring constantly. Remove from heat.

2. Season steaks with salt and pepper. Grill, covered, over medium heat or broil 4 in. from heat 5-7 minutes on each side or until meat reaches desired doneness (for medium-rare, a thermometer should read 135°; medium, 140°; medium-well, 145°).

3. Gently warm garlic butter over low heat. Serve with steaks.

4 oz. cooked beef with 2 tsp. garlic butter: 449 cal., 36g fat (16g sat. fat), 123mg chol., 521mg sod., 1g carb. (0 sugars, 0 fiber), 30g pro.

★ ★ ★ ★ ★ **READER REVIEW**

"I love ribeyes, and the browned butter with garlic was a delicious addition. Will be making these steaks often."

K. TASTEOFHOME.COM

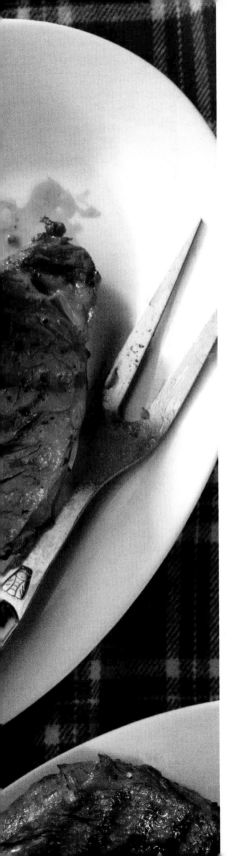

FIRE-ROASTED ZITI WITH SAUSAGE

We punch up our pasta with smoked sausage and fire-roasted tomato sauce. It's an easy recipe to switch up—use whatever noodles and spaghetti sauce are in your pantry.
—Jean Komlos, Plymouth, MI

- -

Takes: 30 min. • **Makes:** 8 servings

8   **oz. uncooked ziti or rigatoni (about 3 cups)**
1   **can (28 oz.) Italian diced tomatoes, drained**
1   **jar (24 oz.) fire-roasted tomato and garlic pasta sauce**
1   **pkg. (16 oz.) smoked sausage, sliced**
2   **cups shredded part-skim mozzarella cheese, divided**
1   **cup 4% cottage cheese**

1. In a Dutch oven, cook ziti according to package directions for al dente. Drain; return to pot.
2. Add tomatoes, pasta sauce and sausage to ziti; heat through over medium heat, stirring occasionally. Stir in 1 cup mozzarella cheese and cottage cheese. Sprinkle with remaining mozzarella cheese. Cook, covered, 2-5 minutes or until cheese is melted.

1¼ cups: 463 cal., 23g fat (11g sat. fat), 66mg chol., 1634mg sod., 41g carb. (15g sugars, 3g fiber), 23g pro.

HOT CHICKEN SALAD PIES

These pies come together in a snap! They're perfect for when you have leftover chicken on hand and need to use it up.
—Shirley Gudenschwager, Orchard, NE

Prep: 20 min. • **Bake:** 30 min.
Makes: 2 pies (6 servings each)

- 1 pkg. (15 oz.) refrigerated pie pastry
- 3 cups diced cooked chicken
- 2 cups cooked long grain rice
- 4 hard-boiled large eggs, chopped
- 1 can (10¾ oz.) condensed cream of mushroom soup, undiluted
- 1 cup mayonnaise
- 1 medium onion, chopped
- ½ cup chopped celery
- ¼ cup lemon juice
- 1 tsp. salt
- 1½ cups crushed cornflakes
- ¼ cup butter, melted

1. Unroll crusts into 9-in. pie plates; flute edges. Refrigerate 30 minutes. Preheat oven to 400°. Line unpricked crusts with a double thickness of foil. Fill with pie weights, dried beans or uncooked rice. Bake on a lower oven rack until edges are light golden brown, 10-15 minutes. Remove foil and weights; bake until crusts are golden brown, 3-6 minutes longer. Cool on a wire rack; reduce heat to 350°.
2. In a large bowl, combine chicken, rice, eggs, soup, mayonnaise, onion, celery, lemon juice and salt. Spoon chicken mixture into crusts. Combine cornflakes and butter; sprinkle over tops. Bake on lowest oven rack until lightly browned, 20-25 minutes.
1 piece: 505 cal., 32g fat (10g sat. fat), 112mg chol., 771mg sod., 38g carb. (3g sugars, 1g fiber), 15g pro.

MAKE AHEAD
GRILLED DIJON PORK ROAST

I came up with this recipe one day after not having much in the house to eat. My husband loved it and it has become the only way I make pork now.
—Cyndi Lacy-Andersen, Woodinville, WA

Prep: 10 min. + marinating
Grill: 1 hour + standing • **Makes:** 12 servings

- ⅓ cup balsamic vinegar
- 3 Tbsp. Dijon mustard
- 1 Tbsp. honey
- 1 tsp. salt
- 1 boneless pork loin roast (3 to 4 lbs.)

1. In a large resealable plastic bag, whisk vinegar, mustard, honey and salt. Add pork; seal bag and turn to coat. Refrigerate at least 8 hours or overnight.
2. Prepare grill for indirect heat, using a drip pan.
3. Drain pork, discarding marinade. Place pork on a greased grill rack over drip pan and cook, covered, over indirect medium heat for 1-1½ hours or until a thermometer reads 145°, turning occasionally. Let stand for 10 minutes before slicing.
3 oz. cooked pork: 149 cal., 5g fat (2g sat. fat), 56mg chol., 213mg sod., 2g carb. (1g sugars, 0 fiber), 22g pro. **Diabetic exchanges:** 3 lean meat.

EASY CHICKEN TETRAZZINI

This easy dish is made with leftover cooked chicken and canned soup. It's the perfect recipe for busy weeknights because it's so easy to assemble. Once you pop the dish in the oven, you'll have time to take care of other things on your to-do list.

—Martha Sue Stroud, Clarksville, TX

Prep: 15 min. • **Bake:** 1 hour
Makes: 8 servings

- 1 pkg. (16 oz.) uncooked spaghetti
- 2 Tbsp. butter
- 1 medium green pepper, chopped
- 1 medium onion, chopped
- 2 cups cubed cooked chicken
- 2 cans (4 oz. each) mushrooms, drained
- 1 jar (2 oz.) diced pimiento, drained
- 1 can (10¾ oz.) condensed cream of mushrooms soup, undiluted
- 2 cups 2% milk
- ½ tsp. garlic powder
- ½ tsp. salt
- 1 to 1½ cups shredded cheddar cheese

1. Preheat oven to 350°. Cook spaghetti according to package directions. Meanwhile, melt butter in a large Dutch oven over medium-high heat; add green pepper and onion. Cook and stir until vegetables are crisp-tender, 4-5 minutes. Stir in chicken, mushrooms, pimientos, soup, milk, garlic powder and salt. Drain spaghetti; add to pan and toss to coat.
2. Pour into a greased 13x9-in. baking dish. Cover and bake until hot and bubbly, 50-60 minutes. Uncover; sprinkle with cheese. Bake, uncovered, until cheese is melted, about 10 minutes.
1¼ cups: 438 cal., 14g fat (6g sat. fat), 59mg chol., 686mg sod., 52g carb. (6g sugars, 3g fiber), 24g pro.

SLOPPY JOE SLIDER BAKE

Ground beef is turned up a notch in these party sliders that are sure to please your crowd. I love how easy they are!
—Rashanda Cobbins, Milwaukee, WI

Prep: 20 min. • **Bake:** 15 min.
Makes: 1 dozen

- 1 pkg. (18 oz.) Hawaiian sweet rolls
- 12 slices cheddar cheese
- 1½ lbs. lean ground beef (90% lean)
- ½ cup chopped onion
- 1 can (15½ oz.) sloppy joe sauce
- 1 Tbsp. packed brown sugar
- 1 Tbsp. soy sauce
- ¾ tsp. pepper

GLAZE
- ¼ cup butter, melted
- 1 Tbsp. packed brown sugar
- 1 Tbsp. Dijon mustard
- 1 tsp. soy sauce
- ½ tsp. garlic powder
- 1 tsp. sesame seeds
- 1 tsp. black sesame seeds
- 1 tsp. dried minced onion
  Dill pickle slices, optional

1. Preheat the oven to 350°. Without separating rolls, cut rolls in half horizontally; arrange bottom halves in a greased 13x9-in. baking pan. Top with half of cheese slices.
2. In a large skillet, cook beef and onion over medium heat until beef is no longer pink and onion is tender, 6-8 minutes, break up beef into crumbles; drain. Stir in sloppy joe sauce, brown sugar, soy sauce and pepper. Cook and stir until combined, 1-2 minutes. Spoon beef mixture evenly over rolls; top with remaining cheese. Replace top halves of rolls.

3. For glaze, stir together butter, brown sugar, mustard, soy sauce and garlic powder. Brush over rolls; sprinkle with sesame seeds and minced onion. Bake, uncovered, until the tops are golden and cheese is melted, 15-20 minutes. If desired, top with pickle slices.
1 slider: 392 cal., 19g fat (10g sat. fat), 91mg chol., 668mg sod., 32g carb. (15g sugars, 2g fiber), 23g pro.

TEST KITCHEN TIP
Everything seasoning works perfectly for sprinkling on top of the rolls instead of sesame seeds and dried onion. If you use it, omit the soy sauce in the glaze to account for salt in the seasoning.

Chestnut Dressing
page 119

Sides & Salads

It's not a potluck without a fresh roundup of stellar side dishes, salads and breads. Each of these mouthwatering mealtime sidekicks is a guaranteed crowd-pleaser. And since they all serve 8 or more, there will be plenty to go around!

RIB SHACK COPYCAT MASHED POTATOES

Idaho is proud to be the nation's potato state—even our license plates say "Famous Potatoes"! This is my delicious version of the scrumptious smashers served at a local barbecue joint. Just about everyone who tries them there begs for the recipe, which is top secret. So I decided to make my own copycat dish. These can be made ahead and kept warm in a slow cooker.
—Trisha Kruse, Eagle, ID

Takes: 30 min. • **Makes:** 12 servings

2½ lbs. potatoes, peeled and cubed
1 cup 2% milk, warmed
½ cup spreadable garlic and herb cream cheese
3 Tbsp. butter, softened
1 lb. bacon strips, cooked and crumbled
1 cup shredded cheddar cheese
½ cup shredded Parmesan cheese
3 green onions, chopped
2 Tbsp. minced fresh parsley or 2 tsp. dried parsley flakes
¼ tsp. salt
¼ tsp. pepper

Place potatoes in a Dutch oven; add water to cover. Bring to a boil. Reduce heat; cook, uncovered, until tender, 15-20 minutes. Drain and return to pan; gently mash the potatoes while gradually adding milk, cream cheese spread and butter to reach desired consistency. Stir in remaining ingredients.
⅔ cup: 238 cal., 15g fat (8g sat. fat), 41mg chol., 477mg sod., 15g carb. (2g sugars, 1g fiber), 10g pro.

SPINACH SALAD WITH GOAT CHEESE & BEETS

Here's a super easy salad perfect for a holiday gathering. Vinaigrette dressing coats the greens nicely. Feel free to use red or golden beets, or a mix of both.
—Nancy Latulippe, Simcoe, ON

Prep: 45 min. + cooling • **Makes:** 10 servings

- 1¼ lbs. fresh beets
- 1 Tbsp. balsamic vinegar
- 1½ tsp. honey
- 1½ tsp. Dijon mustard
- ¼ tsp. salt
- ¼ tsp. pepper
- ¼ cup olive oil
- 5 cups fresh baby spinach
- 2 oz. fresh goat cheese, crumbled
- ½ cup chopped walnuts, toasted

1. Scrub beets and trim tops to 1 in. Place in a Dutch oven and cover with water. Bring to a boil. Reduce heat; cover and simmer until tender, 30-60 minutes. Remove from the water; cool. Peel and cut into 1-in. pieces.

2. In a small bowl, whisk the vinegar, honey, mustard, salt and pepper. Slowly whisk in oil until blended.

3. Place spinach in salad bowl. Drizzle with dressing; toss to coat. Top with beets, goat cheese and walnuts. If desired, sprinkle with additional pepper.

¾ cup: 113 cal., 10g fat (2g sat. fat), 4mg chol., 128mg sod., 5g carb. (3g sugars, 1g fiber), 2g pro.

TEST KITCHEN TIP
Baby spinach is variety of spinach with a small flat leaf that is tender in texture. Sold in bulk or in cellophane bags, these greens can be found in your local grocer's produce section. Consume spinach raw or cooked.

1. Preheat oven to 350°. Cream shortening and sugar until light and fluffy, 5-7 minutes. Add eggs and egg yolks, 1 at a time, beating well after each addition. Beat in ricotta and extract. In another bowl, whisk 5 cups flour, baking powder and salt; add to creamed mixture alternately with milk, beating well after each addition. Stir in final 1 cup flour by hand.

2. Turn onto a lightly floured surface; divide into thirds. Roll each into an 18-in. rope. Place ropes on a parchment-lined baking sheet; braid. Pinch ends to seal; tuck under braid. Bake until a toothpick inserted in center comes out clean, 45-55 minutes (do not overbake). Remove to wire rack to cool.

3. Meanwhile, beat confectioners' sugar, milk and extract until smooth. Brush on bread while still warm; top with sliced almonds or sprinkles.

Note: To toast nuts, bake in a shallow pan in a 350° oven for 5-10 minutes or cook in a skillet over low heat until lightly browned, stirring occasionally.

1 piece: 376 cal., 11g fat (4g sat. fat), 68mg chol., 247mg sod., 60g carb. (28g sugars, 1g fiber), 8g pro.

HOW TO BRAID BREAD
Arrange ropes on a greased baking sheet. Pinch ropes together at 1 end and tuck the ends under for a neat appearance. Then, begin braiding by crossing the right rope over the center rope. Next, cross the left rope over the center. Continue braiding until complete. Pinch ends and tuck under.

ITALIAN RICOTTA EASTER BREAD

I changed our family's traditional Easter bread by adding ricotta and a few other ingredients. The almond flavoring works wonders!
—Tina Mirilovich, Johnstown, PA

- -

Prep: 30 min. • **Bake:** 45 min.
Makes: 18 servings

¾ cup plain or butter-flavored shortening, room temperature
1½ cups sugar
3 large eggs, room temperature
3 large egg yolks, room temperature
1 cup whole-milk ricotta cheese
1 tsp. almond extract (or flavor of choice)
6 cups all-purpose flour
1 Tbsp. baking powder
1 tsp. salt
½ cup 2% milk

GLAZE
1½ cups confectioners' sugar
3 Tbsp. 2% milk
½ tsp. almond extract (or flavor of choice)
Sliced toasted almonds or assorted sprinkles

GRANDMA'S CLASSIC POTATO SALAD

I asked my grandmother how old this potato salad recipe is, and she told me that her own mom used to make it when she was a little girl. I would say it has definitely stood the test of time!

—Kimberly Wallace, Dennison, OH

Prep: 25 min. • **Cook:** 20 min. + chilling
Makes: 10 servings

6	medium potatoes, peeled and cubed
¼	cup all-purpose flour
1	Tbsp. sugar
1½	tsp. salt
1	tsp. ground mustard
1	tsp. pepper
¾	cup water
2	large eggs, beaten
¼	cup white vinegar
4	hard-boiled large eggs, divided use
2	celery ribs, chopped
1	medium onion, chopped
	Sliced green onions, optional

1. Place potatoes in a large saucepan and cover with water. Bring to a boil. Reduce heat; cover and cook until tender, 15-20 minutes. Drain and cool to room temperature.

2. Meanwhile, in a small heavy saucepan, combine flour, sugar, salt, mustard and pepper. Gradually stir in water until smooth. Cook and stir over medium-high heat until thickened and bubbly. Reduce heat; cook and stir 2 minutes longer.

3. Remove from heat. Stir a small amount of hot mixture into beaten eggs; return all to the pan, stirring constantly. Bring to a gentle boil; cook and stir 2 minutes longer. Remove from the heat and cool completely. Gently stir in vinegar.

4. Chop and refrigerate 1 hard-boiled egg; chop the remaining 3 hard-boiled eggs. In a large bowl, combine the potatoes, celery, chopped onion and eggs; add dressing and stir until blended. Refrigerate until chilled. Garnish with reserved chopped egg and, if desired, sliced green onions.

¾ cup: 144 cal., 3g fat (1g sat. fat), 112mg chol., 402mg sod., 23g carb. (3g sugars, 2g fiber), 6g pro. **Diabetic exchanges:** 1½ starch, ½ fat.

TUSCAN-STYLE ROASTED ASPARAGUS

This dish is especially wonderful when locally grown asparagus is in season. It's so easy for celebrations because you can serve it hot or cold.
—Jannine Fisk, Malden, MA

Prep: 20 min. • **Bake:** 15 min.
Makes: 8 servings

- 1½ lbs. fresh asparagus, trimmed
- 1½ cups grape tomatoes, halved
- 3 Tbsp. pine nuts
- 3 Tbsp. olive oil, divided
- 2 garlic cloves, minced
- 1 tsp. kosher salt
- ½ tsp. pepper
- 1 Tbsp. lemon juice
- ⅓ cup grated Parmesan cheese
- 1 tsp. grated lemon zest

1. Preheat the oven to 400°. Place the asparagus, tomatoes and pine nuts on a foil-lined 15x10x1-in. baking pan. Mix 2 Tbsp. oil, garlic, salt and pepper; add to asparagus and toss to coat.

2. Bake for 15-20 minutes or just until the asparagus is tender. Drizzle with remaining oil and the lemon juice; sprinkle with cheese and lemon zest. Toss to combine.

1 serving: 95 cal., 8g fat (2g sat. fat), 3mg chol., 294mg sod., 4g carb. (2g sugars, 1g fiber), 3g pro. **Diabetic exchanges:** 1½ fat, 1 vegetable.

TEST KITCHEN TIP
For the ultimate flavor, use fresh produce when it's in season. In spring, that means asparagus, peas, artichokes and fennel. In summer, eggplant, arugula, summer squash and tomatoes shine. Fall's finest? Butternut squash, Brussels sprouts and carrots, to name a few.

IRISH SODA BREAD MUFFINS

Irish soda bread is traditionally prepared in a loaf shape, but these muffins have the same terrific flavor.
—Lorraine Ballsieper, Deep River, CT

Takes: 30 min. • **Makes:** 1 dozen

- 2¼ cups all-purpose flour
- ½ cup plus 1 Tbsp. sugar, divided
- 2 tsp. baking powder
- ½ tsp. salt
- ¼ tsp. baking soda
- 1 tsp. caraway seeds
- 1 large egg, room temperature
- 1 cup buttermilk
- ¼ cup butter, melted
- ¼ cup canola oil
- ¾ cup dried currants or raisins

1. In a large bowl, combine the flour, ½ cup sugar, baking powder, salt, baking soda and caraway seeds. In another bowl, beat the egg, buttermilk, butter and oil. Stir into the dry ingredients just until moistened. Fold in the currants.

2. Fill greased muffin cups three-fourths full. Sprinkle with remaining sugar. Bake at 400° for 15 minutes or until a toothpick inserted in the center comes out clean. Cool for 5 minutes before removing from pan to wire rack. Serve warm.

Note: To substitute for each cup of buttermilk, use 1 Tbsp. white vinegar or lemon juice plus enough milk to measure 1 cup. Stir, then let stand 5 minutes. Or, use 1 cup plain yogurt or 1¾ tsp. cream of tartar plus 1 cup milk.

1 serving: 235 cal., 9g fat (3g sat. fat), 28mg chol., 247mg sod., 35g carb. (17g sugars, 1g fiber), 4g pro.

GARLIC KNOTS

Here's a handy bread that can be made in no time flat. Refrigerated biscuits make preparation simple. The classic Italian flavors complement a variety of meals.
—Jane Paschke, University Park, FL

Takes: 30 min. • **Makes:** 2½ dozen

- 1 tube (12 oz.) refrigerated buttermilk biscuits
- ¼ cup canola oil
- 3 Tbsp. grated Parmesan cheese
- 1 tsp. garlic powder
- 1 tsp. dried oregano
- 1 tsp. dried parsley flakes

1. Preheat oven to 400°. Cut each biscuit into thirds. Roll each piece into a 4-in. rope and tie into a knot; tuck ends under. Place 2 in. apart on a greased baking sheet. Bake until golden brown, 8-10 minutes.
2. In a large bowl, combine the remaining ingredients; add the warm knots and toss to coat.
1 roll: 46 cal., 2g fat (0 sat. fat), 0 chol., 105mg sod., 6g carb. (0 sugars, 0 fiber), 1g pro.

SWEET ONION SPOON BREAD

This unique recipe has been a family favorite for years. The layers of tangy cheese, sour cream and sweet onions in the moist cornbread taste so amazing together. Add chopped green chiles for extra zip.
—Heather Thomas, Fredericksburg, VA

Prep: 15 min. • **Bake:** 25 min.
Makes: 9 servings

- 1⅓ cups chopped sweet onions
- 1 Tbsp. butter
- 1 can (8¼ oz.) cream-style corn
- 1 pkg. (8½ oz.) cornbread/muffin mix
- 2 large egg whites, lightly beaten
- 2 Tbsp. fat-free milk
- ½ cup reduced-fat sour cream
- ⅓ cup shredded sharp cheddar cheese

1. In a small nonstick skillet, saute onions in butter until tender; set aside.
2. Meanwhile, in a large bowl, combine the corn, muffin mix, egg whites and milk. Pour into a 9-in. square baking dish coated with cooking spray. Combine sour cream and onions; spread over batter. Sprinkle with cheese.
3. Bake cornbread, uncovered, at 350° until a toothpick inserted in the center comes out clean, 25-30 minutes.
1 piece: 191 cal., 6g fat (3g sat. fat), 18mg chol., 361mg sod., 29g carb. (10g sugars, 1g fiber), 6g pro. **Diabetic exchanges:** 2 starch, ½ fat.

ZUCCHINI-GARLIC PASTA

My Italian neighbor gave me the ingredients for this salad, but he didn't have the measurements written down. I experimented and came up with this recipe, which is a nice side dish for many meals. There are many garlic producers here in California, so I think this recipe represents our area well.
—Shelley Smail, Chico, CA

Takes: 25 min. • **Makes:** 8 servings

- 1 pkg. (16 oz.) wagon wheel pasta or other specialty shape pasta
- ½ lb. sliced bacon, diced
- 1 medium onion, chopped
- 4 to 6 garlic cloves, minced
- 2 to 3 medium zucchini (about 1½ lbs.), halved and sliced
- ½ tsp. salt
- 3 Tbsp. lemon juice
- ¼ cup grated Romano or Parmesan cheese

1. Cook the pasta according to package directions. Meanwhile, in a large skillet, cook bacon over medium heat until crisp. Using a slotted spoon, remove to paper towels; drain, reserving 2 Tbsp. drippings. In same skillet, saute onion and garlic in reserved drippings for 3 minutes or until tender. Add the zucchini and salt; cook 6 minutes longer or until tender.
2. Drain pasta and add to the zucchini mixture. Add the lemon juice and bacon; toss. Transfer to a serving bowl or platter; sprinkle with cheese.

1 serving: 293 cal., 7g fat (3g sat. fat), 12mg chol., 354mg sod., 46g carb. (5g sugars, 3g fiber), 13g pro.

MAKE AHEAD
OVERNIGHT LAYERED LETTUCE SALAD

This layered salad is a family favorite from a church cookbook I've had for 40 years. The bacon adds a fabulous crunch.
—Mary Brehm, Cape Coral, FL

Prep: 20 min. + chilling
Makes: 16 servings

- 1 medium head iceberg lettuce, torn
- 1 medium green pepper, chopped
- 1 small sweet red pepper, chopped
- 1 medium onion, sliced and separated into rings
- 2 cups frozen peas (about 10 oz.)
- 1 cup mayonnaise
- 2 Tbsp. sugar
- 1 cup shredded cheddar cheese
- 12 bacon strips, cooked and crumbled
- ¾ cup dried cranberries

1. In a 4-qt. or 13x9-in. glass dish, layer the first 5 ingredients. In a small bowl, mix mayonnaise and sugar; spoon over salad, spreading to cover.
2. Sprinkle the top with cheese, bacon and cranberries. Refrigerate, covered, overnight.

1 cup: 206 cal., 16g fat (4g sat. fat), 19mg chol., 250mg sod., 11g carb. (7g sugars, 2g fiber), 5g pro.

FRESH CORN SALAD

People who prefer food with some tang find this corn salad particularly appealing. It's a pretty dish, too—and economical. If you are like me and enjoy growing your own ingredients, you won't have to pick up much at the store.
—Carol Shaffer, Cape Girardeau, MO

Prep: 20 min. + chilling • **Makes:** 10 servings

- 8 ears fresh corn, husked and cleaned
- ½ cup canola oil
- ¼ cup cider vinegar
- 1½ tsp. lemon juice
- ¼ cup minced fresh parsley
- 2 tsp. sugar
- 1 tsp. salt
- ½ tsp. dried basil
- ⅛ to ¼ tsp. cayenne pepper
- 2 large tomatoes, seeded and coarsely chopped
- ½ cup chopped onion
- ⅓ cup chopped green pepper
- ⅓ cup chopped sweet red pepper

1. In a large saucepan, cook corn in enough boiling water to cover for 5-7 minutes or until tender. Drain, cool and set aside.

2. In a large bowl, mix the oil, vinegar, lemon juice, parsley, sugar, salt if desired, basil and cayenne pepper. Cut cooled corn off the cobs (should measure 4 cups).

3. Add corn, tomatoes, onion and peppers to the oil mixture. Mix well. Cover and chill for several hours or overnight.

½ cup: 102 cal., 2g fat (0 sat. fat), 0 chol., 251mg sod., 21g carb. (0 sugars, 0 fiber), 3g pro. **Diabetic exchanges:** 1 starch, ½ vegetable, ½ fat.

CLASSIC MAKE-AHEAD MASHED POTATOES

This dinnertime staple saves time on holidays. No more frantically whipping the potatoes while hungry family and guests hang around the kitchen!
—Marty Rummel, Trout Lake, WA

Prep: 40 min. + chilling • **Bake:** 55 min.
Makes: 12 servings

- 5 lbs. potatoes, peeled and cut into wedges
- 1 pkg. (8 oz.) reduced-fat cream cheese, cubed
- 2 large egg whites, beaten
- 1 cup reduced-fat sour cream
- 2 tsp. onion powder
- 1 tsp. salt
- ½ tsp. pepper
- 1 Tbsp. butter, melted

1. Place potatoes in a Dutch oven and cover with water. Bring to a boil. Reduce the heat; cover and cook for 15-20 minutes or until tender. Drain.

2. In a large bowl, mash potatoes with cream cheese. Combine the egg whites, sour cream, onion powder, salt and pepper; stir into potatoes until blended. Transfer to a greased 3-qt. baking dish. Drizzle with butter. Cover and refrigerate overnight.

3. Remove from refrigerator 30 minutes before baking. Preheat the oven to 350°. Cover and bake 50 minutes. Uncover; bake 5-10 minutes longer or until a thermometer reads 160°.

¾ cup: 220 cal., 7g fat (4g sat. fat), 22mg chol., 316mg sod., 32g carb. (4g sugars, 3g fiber), 7g pro. **Diabetic exchanges:** 2 starch, 1 fat.

1. Preheat oven to 425°. Process cauliflower in batches in a food processor until finely ground. Microwave cauliflower, covered, in a microwave-safe bowl on high until tender, about 8 minutes. When cauliflower is cool enough to handle, wrap in a clean kitchen towel and squeeze dry. Return to bowl.

2. Meanwhile, in another bowl, mix the cheeses together. Stir half cheese mixture into cauliflower; reserve remaining cheese mixture. Combine next 6 ingredients; stir into cauliflower.

3. On a baking sheet lined with parchment, shape cauliflower mixture into an 11x9-in. rectangle. Bake until the edges are golden brown, 20-25 minutes. Top with reserved cheese; bake until melted and bubbly, 10-12 minutes. Cut into 12 breadsticks. If desired, serve with marinara sauce.

1 breadstick: 66 cal., 4g fat (2g sat. fat), 26mg chol., 340mg sod., 4g carb. (1g sugars, 1g fiber), 5g pro. **Diabetic exchanges:** 1 vegetable, 1 medium-fat meat.

TEST KITCHEN TIP
As long as you line your pan with parchment, these breadsticks can be made in any shape you like. A round pizza pan works nicely as well. Customize to your heart's desire by adding toppings such as pepperoni, mushrooms and olives before baking.

CHEESY CAULIFLOWER BREADSTICKS

These yummy grain-free breadsticks are made with cauliflower instead of flour. Serve with your favorite marinara sauce.

—Nick Iverson, Denver, CO

Prep: 20 min. • **Bake:** 30 min.
Makes: 12 servings

- 1   medium head cauliflower, cut into 1-in. florets (about 6 cups)
- ½   cup shredded part-skim mozzarella cheese
- ½   cup grated Parmesan cheese
- ½   cup shredded cheddar cheese
- 1   large egg
- ¼   cup chopped fresh basil
- ¼   cup chopped fresh parsley
- 1   garlic clove, minced
- 1   tsp. salt
- ½   tsp. pepper
     Marinara sauce, optional

GARLIC-SESAME GREEN BEANS

Sauteed bits of garlic and shallot, plus a sprinkling of toasted sesame seeds, turn ordinary beans into something special. Keep the recipe in mind for your garden crop in summer, too.
—Deirdre Cox, Kansas City, MO

Prep: 25 min. • **Cook:** 10 min.
Makes: 12 servings

- 3 **lbs. fresh green beans, trimmed**
- 1 **Tbsp. sesame oil**
- 1 **Tbsp. canola oil**
- 1 **shallot, finely chopped**
- 6 **garlic cloves, minced**
- 1½ **tsp. salt**
- ½ **tsp. pepper**
- 2 **Tbsp. sesame seeds, toasted**

1. In a Dutch oven, bring 10 cups water to a boil. Add green beans; cook, uncovered, 6-8 minutes or until tender.
2. Meanwhile, in a small skillet, heat oils over medium heat. Add shallot, garlic, salt and pepper; cook and stir 2-3 minutes or until tender.
3. Drain green beans and return to Dutch oven. Add shallot mixture; toss to coat. Sprinkle with sesame seeds.

1 serving: 67 cal., 3g fat (0 sat. fat), 0 chol., 305mg sod., 9g carb. (3g sugars, 4g fiber), 3g pro. **Diabetic exchanges:** 2 vegetable, ½ fat.

MAKE AHEAD
SWEDISH FRUIT SOUP

My mother, who was born in Sweden, made this fruit soup for holidays, and now I do the same for my family. I look forward to all of our Swedish Christmas traditions, but making and enjoying this soup is my favorite.
—Enice Jacobson, Wildrose, ND

Prep: 15 min. + standing • **Cook:** 1 hour
Makes: 10 servings

- 1 **lb. mixed dried fruit (about 4 cups)**
- ¾ **cup small pearl tapioca**
- 6 **cups water, divided**
- 5 **apples, peeled and cubed**
- 1 **cup sugar**
  Ground cinnamon

1. In a large saucepan, combine the fruit, tapioca and 4 cups water. Cover and let stand overnight.
2. Stir in the apples, sugar and remaining water; bring to a boil. Reduce heat; cover and simmer for 1 hour or until the tapioca is transparent. Add additional water if necessary. Serve warm or cold with a dash of cinnamon.

¾ cup: 260 cal., 0 fat (0 sat. fat), 0 chol., 8mg sod., 67g carb. (26g sugars, 5g fiber), 1g pro.

HAM, BROCCOLI & ORZO CASSEROLE

A kid-pleaser and perfect comfort food, this ooey, gooey casserole is a complete meal-in-one. For an extra homey touch, I make mine in my favorite hand-me-down baking dish I inherited from my beloved Grandma Laverne.
—Heather Arndt Anderson, Portland, OR

Prep: 30 min. • **Bake:** 20 min.
Makes: 8 servings

- 4 cups chicken stock
- 2 cups uncooked orzo pasta
- 3 Tbsp. butter
- ¼ cup all-purpose flour
- 2 cups 2% milk
- ½ tsp. salt
- ½ tsp. pepper
- 2 cups shredded sharp cheddar cheese, divided
- 1½ cups cubed fully cooked ham
- 2 cups chopped fresh broccoli
- 2 cups chopped fresh kale
- 1 cup french-fried onions

1. Preheat the oven to 350°. In a large saucepan, bring stock to a boil; stir in orzo. Cook, uncovered, until orzo is al dente and broth is absorbed, 8-10 minutes .
2. Meanwhile, in a large saucepan, heat the butter over medium heat. Stir in flour until blended; cook and stir until lightly browned, 4-5 minutes. Gradually whisk in the milk, salt and pepper. Bring to a boil, stirring constantly; cook and stir until thickened, 1-2 minutes. Stir in 1½ cups cheese; cook until cheese is melted.
3. Add the orzo, ham, broccoli and kale. Transfer to a greased 13x9-in. baking dish; sprinkle with onions and remaining cheese. Bake, uncovered, until bubbly, 20-25 minutes.
1 cup: 637 cal., 27g fat (14g sat. fat), 80mg chol., 1386mg sod., 66g carb. (8g sugars, 3g fiber), 32g pro.

BOHEMIAN COLLARDS

I added unconventional ingredients to give traditional collards a flavorful twist. You'll agree these greens are a unique and exquisite addition to any meal.
—Ally Phillips, Murrells Inlet, SC

Prep: 20 min. • **Cook:** 35 min.
Makes: 8 servings

- 1 large bunch collard greens (about 2 lbs.)
- 6 bacon strips, chopped
- 1 Tbsp. olive oil
- ½ cup chicken broth
- 1½ cups fresh or frozen corn (about 7½ oz.)
- 1 cup chopped sweet red pepper
- ½ tsp. salt
- ¼ tsp. crushed red pepper flakes
- ¼ tsp. pepper

1. Trim thick stems from collard greens; coarsely chop leaves. In a Dutch oven, cook bacon over medium heat until crisp, stirring occasionally. Remove with a slotted spoon; drain on paper towels. Cook and stir collard greens in bacon drippings and oil just until coated. Add broth; bring to a boil. Reduce heat; simmer, covered, until greens are very tender, 25-30 minutes.
2. Add the corn, red pepper, salt, pepper flakes and pepper. Cook and stir until heated through. Sprinkle with bacon.
½ cup: 168 cal., 11g fat (3g sat. fat), 14mg chol., 369mg sod., 13g carb. (2g sugars, 5g fiber), 7g pro. **Diabetic exchanges:** 2 fat, 1 starch.

TEST KITCHEN TIP
If you want to take your collard greens to the next level, try adding chopped prosciutto in addition to the crumbled bacon. Add both cured meats just before serving. Don't discard the pot liquor—the liquid leftover from cooking the greens. It's rich with flavor and nutrients. Dunking a big slice of warm cornbread in it is a marvelous way to sop up all that tasty goodness.

THAI NOODLE WATERMELON SALAD

Our county is famous for its fabulous Green River melons. While you won't find this unique and refreshing salad at the county fair, it's definitely a favorite way to enjoy watermelon all summer long!
—Carmell Childs, Orangeville, UT

- -

Prep: 25 min. • **Cook:** 25 min.
Makes: 10 servings

4½ cups cubed watermelon, divided
½ cup sweet chili sauce
3 Tbsp. fish sauce or soy sauce
2 Tbsp. lime juice
½ tsp. minced fresh gingerroot
7 oz. uncooked stir-fry rice noodles
1½ cups julienned carrots
1 small red onion, halved and thinly sliced
½ cup fresh cilantro leaves, chopped
3 Tbsp. minced fresh mint
1¼ cups salted peanuts, chopped
Lime wedges

1. Place 2 cups watermelon in a blender; cover and puree until smooth. Press through a fine-mesh strainer into a bowl; discard pulp. Pour 1 cup juice into a small saucepan (save any remaining juice for another use). Add chili sauce, fish sauce, lime juice and ginger to saucepan. Bring to a boil; cook until liquid is slightly thickened, 20-25 minutes. Remove mixture from heat. Refrigerate until cooled.
2. Meanwhile, prepare noodles according to package directions; rinse with cold water and drain well. Place the noodles in a large bowl. Add the carrots, red onion, cilantro, mint and remaining 2½ cups watermelon. Drizzle with dressing; toss to coat. Serve with peanuts and lime wedges.
¾ cup: 240 cal., 10g fat (2g sat. fat), 0 chol., 721mg sod., 34g carb. (14g sugars, 3g fiber), 7g pro.

CHESTNUT DRESSING
PICTURED ON PAGE 102

I enjoyed this stuffing when I spent my first Thanksgiving with my husband, Mike. It's a family recipe his mother has been making for years. Italian seasoning and chestnuts add flavor and texture.
—Sharon Brunner, Mohnton, PA

- -

Prep: 25 min. • **Bake:** 20 min.
Makes: 18 servings

4 celery ribs, chopped
1 large onion, chopped
1½ cups butter, cubed
3 cups chestnuts, shelled and coarsely chopped
3 Tbsp. Italian seasoning
10 slices Italian bread (¾ in. thick), cubed

1. Preheat oven to 350°. In a large skillet, saute the celery and onion in butter over medium-high heat until tender, 2-3 minutes. Add chestnuts and Italian seasoning. Bring to a boil. Reduce heat; simmer, uncovered, for 10 minutes. Add bread cubes and stir to coat.
2. Transfer to an ungreased 13x9-in. baking dish. Bake, uncovered, until golden brown, 20-25 minutes.
½ cup: 223 cal., 16g fat (10g sat. fat), 40mg chol., 213mg sod., 18g carb. (3g sugars, 2g fiber), 2g pro.

BRING IT
If you tote hot or cold dishes to potlucks frequently, consider investing in an insulated food carrier. These vessels make easy work of transporting food, especially if you are taking a few items to the party.

BEET SALAD WITH ORANGE-WALNUT DRESSING

Light and refreshing, this salad goes nicely with the heavier dishes served at big meals. Your family and friends will also love the tasty homemade dressing.
—Marian Platt, Sequim, WA

Prep: 20 min. • **Bake:** 40 min. + cooling
Makes: 12 servings (about 1 cup dressing)

1 lb. fresh beets
6 cups torn Bibb or Boston lettuce
3 medium navel oranges, peeled and sectioned
2 cups torn curly endive
2 cups watercress
⅔ cup chopped walnuts, toasted

DRESSING

½ cup canola oil
⅓ cup orange juice
3 Tbsp. white wine vinegar
1 green onion, finely chopped
1 Tbsp. lemon juice
1 Tbsp. Dijon mustard
½ tsp. salt
⅛ tsp. white pepper

1. Place beets in a 13x9-in. baking dish; add 1 in. water. Cover and bake at 400° for 40-45 minutes or until tender. Cool; peel and julienne.

2. In a serving bowl, combine the lettuce, oranges, endive and watercress. Add beets and walnuts.

3. In a small bowl, whisk the oil, orange juice, vinegar, onion, lemon juice, mustard, salt and pepper. Drizzle over salad; toss gently to coat.

1½ cups: 255 cal., 14g fat (1g sat. fat), 0 chol., 274mg sod., 28g carb. (8g sugars, 18g fiber), 9g pro.

CREAMY PINEAPPLE FLUFF SALAD

Guests of all ages will gravitate to this traditional fluff salad. It's chock-full of pineapple, marshmallows and cherry bits, making it perfect for a potluck.
—Janice Hensley, Owingsville, KY

Takes: 25 min. • **Makes:** 16 servings

1 pkg. (8 oz.) cream cheese, softened
1 can (14 oz.) sweetened condensed milk
¼ cup lemon juice
2 cans (20 oz.) pineapple tidbits, drained
1½ cups multicolored miniature marshmallows, divided
1 carton (8 oz.) frozen whipped topping, thawed
½ cup chopped nuts
⅓ cup maraschino cherries, chopped

In a large bowl, beat the cream cheese, milk and lemon juice until smooth. Add pineapple and 1 cup marshmallows; fold in whipped topping. Sprinkle with nuts, cherries and remaining marshmallows. Refrigerate leftovers.

½ cup: 161 cal., 10g fat (6g sat. fat), 16mg chol., 50mg sod., 17g carb. (12g sugars, 1g fiber), 2g pro.

BAKED PARMESAN BROCCOLI

I began making this creamy side dish years ago as a way to get my kids to eat broccoli. They've since grown up but still request this satisfying casserole. It's truly a family favorite.
—Barbara Uhl, Wesley Chapel, FL

- -

Prep: 30 min. • **Bake:** 15 min.
Makes: 12 servings

- 4 bunches broccoli, cut into florets
- 6 Tbsp. butter, divided
- 1 small onion, finely chopped
- 1 garlic clove, minced
- ¼ cup all-purpose flour
- 2 cups 2% milk
- 1 large egg yolk, beaten
- 1 cup grated Parmesan cheese
- ½ tsp. salt
- ⅛ tsp. pepper
- ½ cup seasoned bread crumbs

1. Preheat oven to 400°. Place half broccoli in a steamer basket; place basket in a large saucepan over 1 in. water. Bring to a boil; cover and steam for 3-4 minutes or until crisp-tender. Place in a greased 13x9-in. baking dish; repeat with remaining broccoli.
2. Meanwhile, in a small saucepan over medium heat, melt 4 Tbsp. butter. Add the onion; cook and stir until tender. Add garlic; cook 1 minute longer.
3. Stir in flour until blended; gradually add milk. Bring to a boil; cook and stir 2 minutes or until thickened. Stir a small amount of hot mixture into egg yolk; return all to the pan, stirring constantly. Cook and stir for 1 minute longer. Remove from heat; stir in cheese, salt and pepper. Pour over broccoli.
4. In a small skillet, cook bread crumbs in the remaining butter until golden brown; sprinkle over the top.
5. Bake, uncovered, 15-18 minutes or until heated through.
¾ cup: 191 cal., 10g fat (5g sat. fat), 41mg chol., 388mg sod., 19g carb. (7g sugars, 6g fiber), 11g pro.

FOUR-CHEESE MACARONI

I adapted this recipe from one a friend gave to me. It has a distinctive blue cheese taste and is a filling side dish.
—Darlene Marturano, West Suffield, CT

- -

Takes: 20 min. • **Makes:** 8 servings

- 1 pkg. (16 oz.) elbow macaroni
- ¼ cup butter, cubed
- ¼ cup all-purpose flour
- ½ tsp. salt
- ⅛ tsp. pepper
- 3 cups 2% milk
- 2 cups shredded cheddar cheese
- 1½ cups shredded Swiss cheese
- ½ cup crumbled blue cheese
- ½ cup grated Parmesan cheese

1. Cook macaroni according to package directions. Meanwhile, in a Dutch oven, melt butter over medium heat. Stir in flour, salt and pepper until smooth; gradually whisk in the milk. Bring to a boil, stirring constantly; cook and stir until thickened, about 2 minutes.
2. Reduce heat to low; stir in cheeses until melted. Drain macaroni; add to cheese sauce and stir until coated.
1 cup: 508 cal., 23g fat (13g sat. fat), 65mg chol., 603mg sod., 51g carb. (6g sugars, 2g fiber), 26g pro.

STOLLEN BUTTER ROLLS

My family members enjoy my stollen so much and say it's just too good to be served only on holidays. I created this buttery, less-sweet dinner roll version.
—Mindy White, Nashville, TN

Prep: 45 min. + rising • **Bake:** 15 min.
Makes: 2 dozen

- 1 pkg. (¼ oz.) active dry yeast
- ¼ cup warm water (110° to 115°)
- 1 cup warm 2% milk
- 2 large eggs, room temperature
- ½ cup butter, softened
- 1 Tbsp. sugar
- 1 tsp. salt
- 4¼ to 4¾ cups all-purpose flour
- ¾ cup chopped mixed candied fruit
- ¾ cup dried currants
- ½ cup cold butter, cut into 24 pieces (1 tsp. each)

1. In a small bowl, dissolve yeast in warm water. In a large bowl, combine warm milk, eggs, butter, sugar, salt, yeast mixture and 3 cups flour; beat on medium speed until smooth. Stir in enough remaining flour to form a soft dough (dough will be sticky).

2. Turn dough onto a floured surface; knead until smooth and elastic, 6-8 minutes. Place in a greased bowl, turning once to grease the top. Cover and let rise in a warm place until doubled, about 1 hour.

3. Punch dough down; turn onto a floured surface. Knead candied fruit and currants into the dough (knead in more flour if necessary). Divide and shape into 24 balls; flatten slightly. Place 1 tsp. cold butter in center of each circle. Fold circles in half over butter; press edges to seal. Place in a greased 15x10x1-in. baking pan. Cover and let rise in a warm place until doubled, about 45 minutes.

4. Preheat oven to 375°. Bake rolls until golden brown, 15-20 minutes. Cool in pan 5 minutes; serve warm.

1 roll: 198 cal., 9g fat (5g sat. fat), 37mg chol., 178mg sod., 28g carb. (9g sugars, 1g fiber), 4g pro.

MAKE AHEAD
MOJITO MARINATED FRUIT

All the flavors of the popular mojito cocktail are featured in this fantastic salad. After you eat the fruit, you'll want to sip the luscious syrup!
—Marcy Griffith, Excelsior, MN

Prep: 20 min. + chilling • **Makes:** 8 servings

- ⅔ cup sugar
- ⅓ cup water
- ½ cup light rum
- 2 Tbsp. lime juice
- 1 tsp. grated lime zest
- 2 cups each cantaloupe, honeydew and seedless watermelon balls or chunks
- 2 cups cubed fresh pineapple
- 3 mint sprigs
  Fresh mint leaves, optional

1. In a small saucepan, combine sugar and water; cook and stir over medium heat until sugar is dissolved. Remove from heat. Stir in rum, lime juice and zest. Cool completely.
2. In a large bowl, combine the melon pieces, pineapple and mint sprigs. Add rum mixture; toss to coat. Refrigerate, covered, overnight.
3. Discard mint sprigs. Spoon fruit with syrup into serving dishes. If desired, top with mint.

1 cup: 128 cal., 0 fat (0 sat. fat), 0 chol., 8mg sod., 26g carb. (24g sugars, 1g fiber), 1g pro.

LATTICE CORN PIE

With tender diced potatoes and a fresh, sweet corn flavor, this side dish is full of old-fashioned goodness. Once you've tasted this delicious pie, you'll never want to serve corn any other way!
—Kathy Spang, Manheim, PA

- -

Prep: 25 min. • **Bake:** 35 min.
Makes: 8 servings

- 1 **cup diced peeled potatoes**
- ⅓ **cup 2% milk**
- 2 **large eggs, room temperature**
- 2 **cups fresh or frozen corn, thawed**
- 1 **tsp. sugar**
- ½ **tsp. salt**
- 2 **sheets refrigerated pie crust**

1. Preheat oven to 375°. Place potatoes in a small saucepan and cover with water. Bring to a boil. Reduce heat; cover and cook until potatoes are tender, 6-8 minutes. Drain and set aside.

2. In a blender, combine the milk, eggs, corn, sugar and salt; cover and process until blended.

3. Unroll 1 sheet crust into a 9-in. pie plate. Trim the crust to ½ in. beyond rim of plate; flute edge. Spoon potatoes into crust; top with corn mixture (crust will be full). Roll out remaining crust; make a lattice top with crust. Seal and flute the edges.

4. Bake until crust is golden brown and filling is bubbly, 35-40 minutes.

1 piece: 308 cal., 16g fat (7g sat. fat), 57mg chol., 373mg sod., 37g carb. (5g sugars, 1g fiber), 5g pro.

FRESH TOMATO FLATBREAD

Looking for an easy appetizer or side? All you need are a can of refrigerated crescent rolls, fresh tomatoes, olive oil, a sprinkling of cheese and seasonings.
—Marlene Mohr, Cincinnati, OH

Takes: 25 min. • **Makes:** 12 servings

- 2 **plum tomatoes**
- 1 **tube (8 oz.) refrigerated crescent rolls**
- 1 **small onion, thinly sliced**
- 2 **Tbsp. olive oil**
- 1 **tsp. Italian seasoning**
- 1 **garlic clove, minced**
- ¼ **tsp. salt**
- ⅛ **tsp. pepper**
- 1 **Tbsp. grated Parmesan cheese**

1. Thinly slice the tomatoes; place on paper towels to drain. Unroll crescent dough; place on an ungreased baking sheet. Roll into a 14x10-in. rectangle; seal seams and perforations.
2. Arrange tomatoes and onion over crust. In a small bowl, combine the oil, Italian seasoning, garlic, salt and pepper; brush over top. Sprinkle with cheese.
3. Bake at 375° for 10-14 minutes or until lightly browned. Cut into squares.

1 piece: 101 cal., 6g fat (1g sat. fat), 0 chol., 205mg sod., 9g carb. (2g sugars, 0 fiber), 2g pro.

MAKE AHEAD
PATRIOTIC GELATIN SALAD

Almost as spectacular as the fireworks, this lovely salad makes quite a bang at patriotic celebrations. It's exciting to serve, and friends and family love the cool fruity and creamy layers.
—Sue Gronholz, Beaver Dam, WI

Prep: 20 min. + chilling • **Makes:** 16 servings

- 2 **pkg. (3 oz. each) berry blue gelatin**
- 2 **pkg. (3 oz. each) strawberry gelatin**
- 4 **cups boiling water, divided**
- 2½ **cups cold water, divided**
- 2 **envelopes unflavored gelatin**
- 2 **cups 2% milk**
- 1 **cup sugar**
- 2 **cups sour cream**
- 2 **tsp. vanilla extract**

1. In 4 separate bowls, dissolve each package of gelatin in 1 cup boiling water. Add ½ cup cold water to each and stir. Pour 1 bowl of blue gelatin into a 10-in. fluted tube pan coated with cooking spray; chill until almost set, about 30 minutes.
2. Set the other 3 bowls of gelatin aside at room temperature. Soften unflavored gelatin in remaining cold water; let stand 5 minutes.
3. Heat milk in a saucepan over medium heat just below boiling. Stir in softened gelatin and sugar until sugar is dissolved. Remove from heat; stir in sour cream and vanilla until smooth. When blue gelatin in pan is almost set, carefully spoon 1½ cups sour cream mixture over it. Chill until almost set, about 30 minutes.
4. Carefully spoon 1 bowl of strawberry gelatin over cream layer. Chill until almost set. Carefully spoon 1½ cups cream mixture over the strawberry layer. Chill until almost set. Repeat, adding layers of blue gelatin, cream mixture and strawberry gelatin, chilling in between each. Chill for several hours or overnight.

Note: This recipe takes time to prepare since each layer must be set before the next layer is added.

1 piece: 206 cal., 7g fat (4g sat. fat), 23mg chol., 75mg sod., 34g carb. (33g sugars, 0 fiber), 5g pro.

HASH BROWN BROCCOLI BAKE

Here's a perfect dish for a potluck or holiday buffet. It goes well with fish, poultry, pork or beef. Cheddar cheese can be substituted for Swiss. It's easy to double the recipe to serve a crowd.
—Jeanette Volker, Walton, NE

- -

Prep: 25 min. • **Bake:** 50 min.
Makes: 14 servings

   4 **Tbsp. butter, divided**
   2 **Tbsp. all-purpose flour**
   1 **tsp. salt**
   ⅛ **tsp. ground nutmeg**
   ⅛ **tsp. pepper**
   2 **cups 2% milk**
   1 **pkg. (8 oz.) cream cheese, cubed**
   2 **cups shredded Swiss cheese**
   6 **cups frozen shredded hash brown potatoes (about 20 oz.), thawed**
   1 **pkg. (16 oz.) frozen chopped broccoli, thawed**
   ½ **cup dry bread crumbs**

1. Preheat the oven to 350°. In a large saucepan, melt 2 Tbsp. butter. Stir in the flour, salt, nutmeg and pepper until smooth; gradually add milk. Bring to a boil; cook and stir until thickened, about 2 minutes. Remove from heat. Add cheeses; stir until melted. Stir in potatoes.

2. Spoon half the potato mixture into a greased 2-qt. baking dish. Top with the broccoli and remaining potato mixture. Bake, covered, 35 minutes.

3. Melt remaining butter; toss with bread crumbs. Sprinkle over the casserole. Bake, covered, until heated through and topping is golden, 15-20 minutes.

¾ cup: 216 cal., 15g fat (9g sat. fat), 42mg chol., 334mg sod., 13g carb. (3g sugars, 2g fiber), 9g pro.

MAKE AHEAD

BLACK-EYED PEA TOMATO SALAD

Spending time in the kitchen with my late aunt was so much fun because she was an amazing cook and teacher. This black-eyed pea salad was one of her specialties. It is easy to make and is a nice alternative to pasta or potato salad. Add cooked cubed chicken breast to make it a meal on its own.
—Patricia Ness, La Mesa, CA

- -

Prep: 20 min. + chilling • **Makes:** 12 servings

   4 **cans (15½ oz. each) black-eyed peas, rinsed and drained**
   3 **large tomatoes, chopped**
   1 **large sweet red pepper, chopped**
   1 **cup diced red onion**
   4 **bacon strips, cooked and crumbled**
   1 **jalapeno pepper, seeded and diced**
   ½ **cup canola oil**
   ¼ **cup sugar**
   ¼ **cup rice vinegar**
   2 **Tbsp. minced fresh parsley**
   1½ **tsp. salt**
   ½ **tsp. pepper**
   ⅛ **tsp. garlic powder**

1. Combine the first 6 ingredients. In another bowl, whisk together remaining ingredients. Add to bean mixture; toss to coat. Refrigerate, covered, at least 6 hours or overnight.

2. Stir just before serving.

Note: Wear disposable gloves when cutting hot peppers; the oils can burn skin. Avoid touching your face.

¾ cup: 242 cal., 11g fat (1g sat. fat), 3mg chol., 602mg sod., 29g carb. (9g sugars, 5g fiber), 9g pro. **Diabetic exchanges:** 2 starch, 2 fat.

MAKE AHEAD

GREEK PASTA SALAD

Chock-full of tomato, red and green bell peppers, and tricolor spirals, this full-flavored Greek pasta salad is as attractive as it is delicious. I add feta cheese and black olives to the medley before coating it with a speedy homemade dressing.
—Dawna Waggoner, Minong, WI

- -

Prep: 15 min. + chilling • **Makes:** 10 servings

- 3 cups uncooked tricolor spiral pasta
- 1 medium tomato, cut into wedges
- 1 small sweet red pepper, julienned
- 1 small green pepper, julienned
- 4 oz. crumbled feta cheese
- ½ cup sliced ripe olives

DRESSING
- ⅔ cup olive oil
- ¼ cup minced fresh basil
- 3 Tbsp. white vinegar
- 2 Tbsp. chopped green onions
- 2 Tbsp. grated Parmesan cheese
- ½ tsp. salt
- ¼ tsp. pepper
- ¼ tsp. dried oregano

1. Cook the pasta according to package directions. Rinse in cold water and drain. Place in a large serving bowl; add tomato, peppers, feta cheese and olives.
2. In a blender, combine the dressing ingredients; cover and process until smooth. Pour over salad; toss to coat. Cover and refrigerate for 2 hours or overnight. Toss before serving.
¾ cup: 268 cal., 18g fat (4g sat. fat), 7mg chol., 298mg sod., 21g carb. (2g sugars, 2g fiber), 6g pro.

TEXAS PECAN RICE

For a special holiday side dish, I dressed up an old recipe to give it a little more Texas character. Everyone loved the savory flavor and crunchy pecans.
—Joan Hallford, North Richland Hills, TX

Prep: 30 min. • **Bake:** 1 hour
Makes: 10 servings

½ cup unsalted butter, cubed
1½ cups sliced fresh mushrooms
3 green onions, sliced
2 cups uncooked long grain brown rice
1 garlic clove, minced
1½ cups chopped pecans, toasted
½ tsp. salt
½ tsp. dried thyme
½ tsp. pepper
¼ tsp. ground cumin
3 cans (10½ oz. each) condensed beef consomme, undiluted
2¼ cups water
5 bacon strips, cooked and crumbled
Toasted pecan halves, optional

1. Preheat oven to 400°. In a Dutch oven, heat butter over medium-high heat. Add mushrooms and green onions; cook and stir until tender, 3-5 minutes. Add rice and garlic; cook and stir 3 minutes. Stir in the pecans, salt, thyme, pepper and cumin. Add consomme and water; bring to a boil.
2. Bake, covered, until liquid is absorbed and rice is tender, 1-1¼ hours. Transfer to a serving bowl. Top with bacon and, if desired, pecan halves.

¾ cup: 372 cal., 24g fat (8g sat. fat), 29mg chol., 783mg sod., 32g carb. (2g sugars, 4g fiber), 10g pro.

Smoked Brisket
page 149

Big Batch Dishes

Serving 20 or more? Make everyone happy with these large-yield recipes: hearty entrees, fun finger foods, sensational sides, dreamy desserts and other classic crowd-sized dishes!

CHICKEN CAKES WITH AVOCADO MANGO SAUCE

Here's a fabulous appetizer for your next party. Or serve these chicken cakes for dinner with a side of hot rice and your favorite vegetable.
—Rachael Nodes, La Barge, WY

Prep: 15 min. • **Cook:** 10 min./batch
Makes: 4 dozen (2 cups sauce)

- 2   lbs. ground chicken
- 1   cup dry whole wheat bread crumbs
- ½   cup unsweetened crushed pineapple
- ½   cup finely chopped sweet red pepper
- ½   cup finely chopped red onion
- 1   garlic clove, minced
- 1   tsp. salt
- ½   tsp. pepper
- 3   Tbsp. canola oil

AVOCADO MANGO SAUCE
- 1   medium ripe avocado, peeled and pitted
- ½   cup chopped peeled mango
- 3   Tbsp. unsweetened crushed pineapple
- 2   Tbsp. chopped red onion
- 1   garlic clove, halved
- ½   tsp. salt
- ¼   tsp. ground cumin
- ¼   tsp. pepper

1. In a bowl, combine first 8 ingredients, mixing lightly but thoroughly. Shape into forty-eight ½-in.-thick patties. Heat oil in a large cast-iron skillet; fry the patties in batches until a thermometer inserted reads 165°, 3-5 minutes on each side.

2. Meanwhile, place sauce ingredients in a blender; cover and process until smooth. Serve with chicken patties.

1 cake with 2 tsp. sauce: 51 cal., 3g fat (1g sat. fat), 13mg chol., 98mg sod., 3g carb. (1g sugars, 1g fiber), 3g pro.

HEARTY RICE DRESSING

This satisfying side dish has always been received well at church socials and family reunions. I cut back on the recipe if I'm serving a smaller group.
—Ruth Hayward, Lake Charles, LA

Prep: 25 min. • **Bake:** 1 hour
Makes: 50 servings

- 3   lbs. ground beef
- 2   lbs. ground pork
- 2   large onions, chopped
- 3   celery ribs, chopped
- 1   large green pepper, chopped
- 1   jar (4 oz.) diced pimientos, drained
- 5   cups water
- 2   cans (10¾ oz. each) condensed cream of chicken soup, undiluted
- 2   cans (10½ oz. each) condensed French onion soup
- 1   can (10¾ oz.) condensed cream of mushroom soup, undiluted
- 2   Tbsp. Creole seasoning
- 1   tsp. salt
- 1   tsp. pepper
- ½   tsp. cayenne pepper
- 4   cups uncooked long grain rice

1. Combine beef, pork and onions. Divide mixture evenly among several large Dutch ovens or stockpots. Cook over medium heat until meat is no longer pink, breaking it into crumbles; drain.

2. In a large bowl, combine celery, green pepper and pimientos. Add water, soups and seasonings. Stir into the meat mixture, dividing vegetable-soup mixture evenly among the meat mixtures. Bring each to a boil; stir in rice.

3. Preheat oven to 350°. Carefully transfer mixtures to 3 greased 13x9-in. baking dishes. Cover each and bake for 30 minutes; stir. Cover and bake 30-40 minutes longer or until rice is tender.

Note: If you don't have Creole seasoning in your cupboard, you can make your own using ¼ tsp. each salt, garlic powder and paprika, and a pinch each of dried thyme, ground cumin and cayenne pepper.
¾ cup: 153 cal., 6g fat (2g sat. fat), 26mg chol., 293mg sod., 14g carb. (1g sugars, 1g fiber), 10g pro.

1. In a large bowl, dissolve yeast in warm milk. Add 2 cups flour; mix well. Let stand in a warm place for 30 minutes. Add the egg yolks, egg, sugar, salt, lemon zest and vanilla; mix well. Beat in the butter and remaining flour. Do not knead. Cover and let rise in a warm place until doubled, about 45 minutes.

2. Punch dough down. On a lightly floured surface, roll out to ½-in. thickness. Cut with a 2½-in. biscuit cutter. Place on lightly greased baking sheets. Cover and let rise until nearly doubled, about 35 minutes.

3. In a deep-fat fryer or electric skillet, heat oil to 375°. Fry doughnuts, a few at a time, for 1½-2 minutes on each side or until browned. Drain on paper towels.

4. Cool for 2-3 minutes; cut a small slit with a sharp knife on 1 side of each doughnut. Cut a small hole in the corner of a pastry bag; insert a very small round tip. Fill bag with jelly. Fill each doughnut with about 1 tsp. jelly. Carefully roll warm doughnuts in sugar. Serve warm.

1 doughnut: 185 cal., 5g fat (1g sat. fat), 36mg chol., 125mg sod., 31g carb. (9g sugars, 1g fiber), 4g pro.

★ ★ ★ ★ ★ **READER REVIEW**

"I halved the recipe for my family size. I filled them with lemon filling and—swoon—they were sooo yummy! They are in my keeper file for sure! Can't wait to try them with other fillings."

ANGELA32 TASTEOFHOME.COM

JOLLY JELLY DOUGHNUTS
Plump and filled with jelly, these sugar-coated doughnuts will disappear as fast as you can churn them out.
—Lee Bremson, Kansas City, MO

Prep: 25 min. + rising • **Cook:** 30 min.
Makes: 2½ dozen

- 2 pkg. (¼ oz. each) active dry yeast
- 2 cups warm 2% milk (110° to 115°)
- 7 cups all-purpose flour
- 4 large egg yolks, room temperature
- 1 large egg, room temperature
- ½ cup sugar
- 1 tsp. salt
- 2 tsp. grated lemon zest
- ½ tsp. vanilla extract
- ½ cup butter, melted
  Oil for deep-fat frying
  Red jelly of your choice
  Additional sugar

PINA COLADA CUPCAKES

These treats are fun and colorful for picnics and potlucks. Serve them as cupcakes, or cut them into cubes and layer them in individual dishes to make mini trifles.
—Jennifer Gilbert, Brighton, MI

Prep: 20 min. • **Bake:** 20 min. + cooling
Makes: 2 dozen

- 3 large eggs, lightly beaten, room temperature
- ½ cup unsweetened pineapple juice
- ½ cup canola oil
- 1 cup canned coconut milk
- 2 tsp. rum extract
- 3 cups all-purpose flour
- 2 cups sugar
- 2 tsp. baking powder
- ½ tsp. baking soda
- ½ tsp. salt

FROSTING

- 1 cup butter, softened
- 3 Tbsp. canned coconut milk
- 1 tsp. rum extract
- 3½ cups confectioners' sugar
  Optional: Toasted sweetened shredded coconut, maraschino cherries, pineapple wedges

1. Preheat oven to 350°. Line 24 muffin cups with foil liners. In a large bowl, whisk eggs, juice, oil, milk and extract until well blended. In another bowl, whisk the flour, sugar, baking powder, baking soda and salt; gradually beat into egg mixture.
2. Fill prepared cups two-thirds full. Bake until a toothpick inserted in center comes out clean, 18-20 minutes. Cool in pans 10 minutes before removing to wire racks to cool completely.
3. In a large bowl, beat butter until creamy. Beat in the coconut milk and rum extract. Gradually beat in confectioners' sugar until smooth. Spread over cupcakes. If desired, garnish with shredded coconut, cherries and pineapple wedges.

1 cupcake: 330 cal., 15g fat (7g sat. fat), 44mg chol., 189mg sod., 47g carb. (35g sugars, 0 fiber), 3g pro.

BRING IT
To create an easy-to-transport dessert, bake the cake batter in a 13x9-in. pan instead of muffin tins. Decorate the top with toasted shredded coconut, chopped dried pineapple, or sunbathing Teddy Grahams on a "sand" beach made of graham cracker crumbs and coarse sugar. Parasols are optional.

PHILLY CHEESESTEAK SLIDERS

Here's a wonderful way to use up leftover roast beef. Sliced roast beef from the deli also works.
—Debra Waggoner, Grand Island, NE

Prep: 20 min. + chilling • **Bake:** 25 min.
Makes: 2 dozen

- 2 large green peppers, sliced
- 1 large sweet onion, sliced
- 1 Tbsp. olive oil
- 2 pkg. (12 oz. each) Hawaiian sweet rolls
- 1½ lbs. sliced deli roast beef
- 12 slices provolone cheese
- ¾ cup butter
- 1½ tsp. dried minced onion
- 1½ tsp. Worcestershire sauce
- 1 tsp. garlic powder

1. In a large skillet, cook green peppers and onion in oil over medium-high heat until tender, 8-10 minutes. Without separating rolls, cut each package in half horizontally; arrange bottom halves in a greased 13x9-in. baking pan. Layer with roast beef, pepper mixture and cheese; replace top halves of rolls.
2. In a small saucepan, melt butter, dried onion, Worcestershire sauce and garlic powder. Drizzle over rolls. Cover and refrigerate for 8 hours or overnight.
3. Preheat oven to 350°. Remove rolls from refrigerator 30 minutes before baking. Bake, uncovered, 15 minutes. Cover with foil; bake until the cheese is melted, 10 minutes longer.
1 slider: 247 cal., 14g fat (8g sat. fat), 56mg chol., 413mg sod., 18g carb. (7g sugars, 1g fiber), 14g pro.

CHERRY ICEBOX COOKIES

Maraschino cherries add colorful flecks to these cookies. As a home economics teacher, I often supplied treats for school functions. These delectable treats were always popular.
—Patty Courtney, Jonesboro, TX

Prep: 20 min. + chilling • **Bake:** 10 min./batch
Makes: 16 dozen

- 1 cup butter, softened
- 1 cup sugar
- ¼ cup packed brown sugar
- 1 large egg, room temperature
- ¼ cup maraschino cherry juice
- 4½ tsp. lemon juice
- 1 tsp. vanilla extract
- 3¼ cups all-purpose flour
- ½ tsp. baking soda
- ½ tsp. ground cinnamon
- ¼ tsp. cream of tartar
- ½ cup chopped walnuts
- ½ cup chopped maraschino cherries

1. In a large bowl, cream butter and sugars until light and fluffy, 5-7 minutes. Beat in the egg, cherry and lemon juices, and vanilla. Combine dry ingredients; gradually add to creamed mixture and mix well. Stir in nuts and cherries.
2. Shape the dough into four 12-in. rolls; securely wrap each roll in waxed paper. Refrigerate for 4 hours or until firm.
3. Unwrap and cut into ¼-in. slices. Place 2 in. apart on ungreased baking sheets. Bake at 375° for 8-10 minutes or until the edges begin to brown. Remove to wire racks to cool.
1 cookie: 66 cal., 3g fat (2g sat. fat), 10mg chol., 37mg sod., 9g carb. (4g sugars, 0 fiber), 1g pro.

TERIYAKI MEATBALLS

I tweaked this one-time appetizer recipe so many times based on my family's suggestions that it eventually became a main dish. The homemade sauce sets these meatballs apart.
—Evette Nowicki, Oak Harbor, WA

- -

Prep: 20 min. • **Bake:** 20 min.
Makes: 3½ dozen

- 2 cans (8 oz. each) pineapple chunks
- 1 medium onion, finely chopped
- ¼ cup finely chopped sweet yellow pepper
- ¼ cup finely chopped sweet red pepper
- ½ cup dry bread crumbs
- ½ tsp. ground ginger
- ¼ tsp. salt
- 1 lb. lean ground beef

SAUCE
- ¼ cup canola oil
- ¼ cup soy sauce
- 3 Tbsp. honey
- 2 Tbsp. vinegar
- ¾ tsp. garlic powder
- ½ tsp. ground ginger
  Green onions, optional

1. Preheat oven to 400°. Drain pineapple, reserving ¼ cup juice; set pineapple aside. In a bowl, combine onion, peppers, bread crumbs, ginger, salt and reserved pineapple juice. Crumble beef over mixture and mix well. Shape into 1-in. balls.

2. Place the 6 sauce ingredients in a blender; cover and process 1 minute. Place 2 Tbsp. sauce in a greased 13x9-in. baking dish. Add meatballs. Pour the remaining sauce over meatballs. Bake, uncovered, until the meat is no longer pink, 18-20 minutes. Place 1 pineapple chunk on each meatball; secure with a toothpick. If desired, garnish with green onions.

1 meatball: 55 cal., 3g fat (1g sat. fat), 9mg chol., 119mg sod., 5g carb. (3g sugars, 0 fiber), 3g pro.

PUNCH DELIGHT

When we celebrated my mother's 75th birthday, we wanted a punch everyone could enjoy. This delightful combination of lemonades, juice and soda was perfect and so easy to make.
—Barbara Koehnke, Fremont, WI

- -

Takes: 10 min.
Makes: 20 servings (5 qt.)

- 1 can (12 oz.) frozen orange juice concentrate, thawed
- 1 can (12 oz.) frozen lemonade concentrate, thawed
- 1 can (12 oz.) frozen pink lemonade concentrate, thawed
- 2 liters Mello Yello soda, chilled
- 2 liters 50/50 or lemon-lime soda, chilled
  Ice cubes

In a large punch bowl, combine the 3 concentrates. Gradually stir in sodas. Add ice. Serve immediately.

1 cup: 172 cal., 0 fat (0 sat. fat), 0 chol., 25mg sod., 44g carb. (42g sugars, 0 fiber), 1g pro.

APPLE RED-HOT SLAB PIE

This dessert is my family's favorite because it brings back so many fond memories. Red Hots give the filling a pretty color that makes this pie an instant hit at parties.
—Linda Morten, Somerville, TX

- -

Prep: 45 min. + chilling • **Bake:** 50 min.
Makes: 24 servings

- 5 cups all-purpose flour
- 2 Tbsp. sugar
- 2 tsp. salt
- 2 cups cold butter, cubed
- 1 to 1¼ cups ice water

FILLING
- ⅔ cup sugar
- ⅔ cup all-purpose flour
- ½ tsp. salt
- 6 cups thinly sliced peeled Granny Smith apples (about 6 medium)
- 6 cups thinly sliced peeled Gala or Jonathan apples (about 6 medium)
- 1 cup Red Hots
- ¼ cup cold butter
  Vanilla ice cream, optional

1. In a large bowl, mix flour, sugar and salt; cut in butter until crumbly. Gradually add ice water, tossing with a fork until dough holds together when pressed. Divide dough into 2 portions so that 1 portion is slightly larger than the other. Shape each into a rectangle; cover and refrigerate 1 hour or overnight.
2. Preheat oven to 375°. For filling, in a large bowl, mix sugar, flour and salt. Add apples and Red Hots; toss to coat.
3. On a lightly floured surface, roll out larger portion of dough into an 18x13-in. rectangle. Transfer to an ungreased 15x10x1-in. baking pan. Press onto the bottom and up the sides of pan. Add the filling; dot with butter.
4. Roll out remaining dough; place over filling. Fold bottom crust over edge of top crust; seal and flute or press with a fork to seal. Prick top with a fork.
5. Bake 50-55 minutes or until golden brown and filling is bubbly. Cool on a wire rack. Serve warm. If desired, top with ice cream.
1 piece: 349 cal., 18g fat (11g sat. fat), 46mg chol., 383mg sod., 45g carb. (19g sugars, 2g fiber), 3g pro.

MINI BARBECUED HAM SANDWICHES

These flavorful sandwiches make a perfect mini snack or appetizer. Your guests won't be able to eat just one!
—Susanne Roupe, East Fairfield, VT

- -

Takes: 20 min. • **Makes:** 2 dozen

- 1 cup chili sauce
- ½ cup water
- 2 Tbsp. sugar
- 2 Tbsp. cider vinegar
- 1 Tbsp. Worcestershire sauce
- 1 tsp. onion powder
- 1 lb. fully cooked ham, very thinly sliced
- 24 dinner rolls, split

In a large saucepan, combine the first 6 ingredients. Bring to a boil. Reduce heat; simmer, uncovered, for 6-8 minutes or until slightly thickened. Stir in ham; heat through. Serve on rolls.
1 sandwich: 143 cal., 3g fat (1g sat. fat), 24mg chol., 513mg sod., 23g carb. (5g sugars, 1g fiber), 7g pro.

PIZZA BEANS

Take this pizza-inspired dish to your next party. It makes an amazing side, or enjoy a larger serving alongside a fresh green salad for a delicious entree. It can even be made the day before and reheated.
—*Taste of Home* Test Kitchen

Prep: 20 min. • **Cook:** 6 hours
Makes: 20 servings

- 1 lb. bulk Italian sausage
- 2 cups chopped celery
- 2 cups chopped onion
- 1 can (14½ oz.) cut green beans, drained
- 1 can (14½ oz.) cut wax beans, drained
- 1 can (16 oz.) kidney beans, rinsed and drained
- 1 can (16 oz.) butter beans, drained
- 1 can (15 oz.) pork and beans
- 3 cans (8 oz. each) pizza sauce
  Optional toppings: Grated Parmesan cheese, minced fresh oregano and crushed red pepper flakes

In a large skillet, brown the sausage over medium heat until no longer pink, breaking it into crumbles. Transfer to a 5-qt. slow cooker with a slotted spoon. Add celery and onion to skillet; cook until softened, about 5 minutes. Drain. Add vegetable mixture and the next 6 ingredients to slow cooker; mix well. Cover and cook on low until bubbly, 6-8 hours. If desired, serve with toppings.

Freeze option: Freeze cooled beans in freezer containers. To use, partially thaw in refrigerator overnight. Heat through in a saucepan, stirring occasionally; add a little water or broth if necessary.

¾ cup: 142 cal., 6g fat (2g sat. fat), 12mg chol., 542mg sod., 17g carb. (4g sugars, 5g fiber), 7g pro.

SOUR CREAM SUGAR COOKIE CAKE

My husband requested a giant sugar cookie for his birthday. I wanted to do something a bit more exciting than birthday cookies, so I came up with this sugar cookie cake. The secret to a dense yet cakelike texture is to make sure you don't overbake the cake.
—Carmell Childs, Orangeville, UT

Prep: 20 min. • **Bake:** 20 min. + cooling
Makes: 20 servings

- ½ cup butter, softened
- 1½ cups sugar
- 2 large eggs, room temperature
- 1 tsp. vanilla extract
- 3 cups all-purpose flour
- ¾ tsp. salt
- ½ tsp. baking powder
- ½ tsp. baking soda
- 1 cup sour cream
- 1 can (16 oz.) vanilla frosting
  Optional: Coarse sugar, sprinkles and additional frosting

1. Preheat oven to 350°. In a large bowl, cream butter and sugar until light and fluffy, 5-7 minutes. Beat in the eggs and vanilla. In another bowl, whisk flour, salt, baking powder and baking soda; add to the creamed mixture alternately with the sour cream, beating after each addition just until combined. Spread into a greased 13x9-in. baking pan.

2. Bake until a toothpick inserted in center comes out clean, 20-25 minutes. Cool completely on a wire rack. Spread frosting over top. Decorate with optional toppings as desired.

1 piece: 295 cal., 11g fat (6g sat. fat), 34mg chol., 228mg sod., 46g carb. (29g sugars, 1g fiber), 3g pro.

FARMHOUSE APPLE PIE

Apple slab pie is a terrific contribution to a covered-dish supper, picnic or potluck. It's baked in a large 15x10 baking pan so it's easy to make and tote, too. But be prepared—people always ask for a copy of the recipe!
—Dolores Skrout, Summerhill, PA

Prep: 30 min. • **Bake:** 50 min.
Makes: 24 servings

EGG YOLK PASTRY

5	cups all-purpose flour
4	tsp. sugar
½	tsp. salt
½	tsp. baking powder
1½	cups shortening
2	large egg yolks, lightly beaten
¾	cup cold water

FILLING

5	lbs. tart apples, peeled and thinly sliced
4	tsp. lemon juice
¾	cup sugar
¾	cup packed brown sugar
1	tsp. ground cinnamon
½	tsp. ground nutmeg
¼	tsp. salt
	2% milk
	Additional sugar

1. In a large bowl, combine the flour, sugar, salt and baking powder; cut in shortening until the mixture resembles coarse crumbs. Combine yolks and cold water. Sprinkle over dry ingredients; toss with fork. If needed, add additional water, 1 Tbsp. at a time, until mixture can be formed into a ball.

2. Divide the dough in half. On a lightly floured surface, roll half the dough to fit a 15x10x1-in. baking pan.

3. Sprinkle apples with lemon juice; arrange half of them over dough. Combine sugars, cinnamon, nutmeg and salt; sprinkle half over apples. Top with remaining apples; sprinkle with remaining sugar mixture.

4. Roll remaining dough to fit pan; place on top of filling and seal edges. Brush with milk and sprinkle with sugar. Cut vents in top crust. Bake at 400° until crust is golden brown and filling is bubbly, 50 minutes.

1 piece: 317 cal., 13g fat (3g sat. fat), 18mg chol., 86mg sod., 48g carb. (26g sugars, 3g fiber), 3g pro.

TEST KITCHEN TIP
Granny Smith apples are ideal for this recipe because they are tart and firm and keep their shape while providing a perfect balance to the sweet ingredients.

★ ★ ★ ★ ★ **READER REVIEW**

"This recipe is definitely a keeper! Tastes absolutely delicious. I have made it for the second time already. It's definitely my go-to recipe for apple pie!"

BAKE1985 TASTEOFHOME.COM

GREAT-GRANDMA'S OATMEAL COOKIES

This yummy cookie—a favorite of my husband's—goes back to my great-grandmother. At Christmastime, we use colored sugar for a festive touch.
—Mary Ann Konechne, Kimball, SD

Prep: 35 min. • **Bake:** 15 min./batch
Makes: 12 dozen

- 1½ cups shortening
- 2 cups sugar
- 4 large eggs, room temperature
- 4 tsp. water
- 4 cups all-purpose flour
- 2 tsp. baking soda
- 2 tsp. ground cinnamon
- ½ tsp. salt
- 4 cups quick-cooking oats
- 2 cups chopped raisins
- 1 cup chopped walnuts
  Additional sugar or colored sugar

1. Preheat oven to 350°. Cream shortening and sugar until light and fluffy, 5-7 minutes. Add eggs, 1 at a time, beating well after each addition. Beat in water. Whisk together flour, baking soda, cinnamon and salt; add to creamed mixture, and mix well. Stir in the oats, raisins and walnuts.
2. On a surface sprinkled with additional sugar, roll the dough to ¼-in. thickness. Cut with a floured 2½-in. cookie cutter in desired shapes. Place 2 in. apart on greased baking sheets. Bake until set, 12-15 minutes. Remove to wire racks to cool.
1 cookie: 63 cal., 3g fat (1g sat. fat), 5mg chol., 28mg sod., 9g carb. (4g sugars, 0 fiber), 1g pro.

> **TEST KITCHEN TIP**
> To add a sweet icing, mix 1 cup confectioners' sugar with a ¼ tsp. cinnamon and 5-6 tsp. of water

MAKE AHEAD
ITALIAN PASTA SAUCE

When my daughter Kris got married, her new husband made something special for their wedding buffet—a big batch of this thick, flavorful pasta sauce. His grandmother brought the recipe from Italy nearly 100 years ago.
—Judy Braun, Juneau, WI

Prep: 25 min. • **Cook:** 2½ hours
Makes: 20 servings

- 4 lbs. ground beef
- 1 lb. bulk Italian sausage
- 1 large onion, finely chopped
- 3 celery ribs, finely chopped
- 4 garlic cloves, minced
- 2 Tbsp. olive oil
- 3 cans (28 oz. each) crushed tomatoes in puree
- 3 cans (6 oz. each) tomato paste
- 3 cups chicken or beef broth
- 1 lb. fresh mushrooms, sliced
- ¾ cup minced fresh parsley
- 1 Tbsp. sugar
- 2 to 3 tsp. salt
- ½ tsp. pepper
- ½ tsp. ground allspice, optional
  Hot cooked pasta

1. In a Dutch oven or soup kettle, cook and crumble the beef in 2 batches over medium heat until no longer pink; drain and set aside. Cook and crumble the sausage over medium heat until no longer pink; drain and set aside. In same pan, saute onion, celery and garlic in oil until vegetables are tender.
2. Return beef and sausage to the pan. Add the next 9 ingredients, including allspice if desired, and bring to a boil. Reduce heat; cover and simmer until sauce reaches desired thickness, stirring occasionally, 2-3 hours. Serve over pasta.
Freeze option: Freeze cooled sauce in freezer containers. To use, partially thaw in refrigerator overnight. Heat through in a saucepan, stirring occasionally. Add a little broth or water if necessary.
1 cup: 284 cal., 15g fat (5g sat. fat), 57mg chol., 821mg sod., 16g carb. (9g sugars, 3g fiber), 23g pro.

SMOKED-ALMOND CHEESE TOASTS

I created the recipe for these appetizer toasts while planning the menu for a friend's bridal luncheon. Smoked almonds add a special touch to the chunky cheese spread.
—Laura Stricklin, Jackson, MS

Takes: 30 min. • **Makes:** 3 dozen

- ¾ cup whipped cream cheese, softened
- 2 Tbsp. 2% milk
- 1 cup shredded sharp cheddar cheese
- 1 cup shredded Swiss cheese
- ¾ cup chopped smoked almonds
- ½ cup soft sun-dried tomato halves (not packed in oil), chopped
- ⅛ tsp. pepper
- 1 French bread baguette (10½ oz.), cut into ¼-in. slices
  Chopped fresh chives, optional

1. Preheat oven to 350°. In a large bowl, beat cream cheese and milk until smooth. Stir in the cheeses, almonds, tomato and pepper; spread over bread slices.

2. Place on ungreased baking sheets. Bake until cheese is melted, 10-12 minutes. If desired, top with chopped fresh chives.

Note: This recipe was tested with sun-dried tomatoes that were ready-to-use without soaking. When using other sun-dried tomatoes that are not oil-packed, cover with boiling water and let stand until soft. Drain before using.

1 appetizer: 81 cal., 5g fat (2g sat. fat), 9mg chol., 103mg sod., 6g carb. (1g sugars, 1g fiber), 3g pro.

TURKEY, GOUDA & APPLE TEA SANDWICHES

These fun mini sandwiches are a tasty addition to any function. The cranberry mayo lends a unique flavor twist, and the apples add a nice crunch. These sammies will be the life of the party!
—*Taste of Home* Test Kitchen

Takes: 25 min. • **Makes:** 4 dozen

- ⅔ cup reduced-fat mayonnaise
- 2 Tbsp. whole-berry cranberry sauce
- 24 very thin slices wheat or white bread, crusts removed
- 12 slices deli turkey
- 2 medium apples, thinly sliced
- 12 thin slices smoked Gouda cheese
- 4 cups fresh baby spinach

1. Place mayonnaise and cranberry sauce in a small food processor. Cover and process until blended. Spread over each bread slice.

2. Layer the turkey, apples, cheese and spinach over each of 12 bread slices; top with remaining bread. Cut each sandwich into quarters.

1 tea sandwich: 258 cal., 12g fat (4g sat. fat), 48mg chol., 456mg sod., 22g carb. (5g sugars, 1g fiber), 16g pro.

TEST KITCHEN TIP

When smoked, Gouda's exterior becomes dark brown, while the interior remains pale. Hickory is typically used in Dutch Gouda, but U.S. producers make many variations of the cheese.

CHEESY SPAGHETTI BAKE

With the classic ingredients of spaghetti and meat sauce, this recipe makes two hearty family-style casseroles. It is marvelous for entertaining or a potluck.
—Sue Braunschweig, Delafield, WI

Prep: 45 min. • **Bake:** 40 min.
Makes: 2 casseroles (12 servings each)

- 1   lb. uncooked spaghetti,
       broken into 3-in. pieces
- 4   lbs. ground beef
- 2   large onions, chopped
- 1   large green pepper, chopped
- 4   cups whole milk
- 4   cans (10¾ oz. each) condensed
       tomato soup, undiluted
- 2   cans (10¾ oz. each) condensed
       cream of mushroom soup, undiluted
- 4   cups shredded sharp cheddar
       cheese, divided

1. Cook spaghetti according to package directions. Drain and place in 2 greased 13x9-in. baking dishes; set aside.
2. In 2 Dutch ovens or stockpots, cook the beef, onions and green pepper over medium heat until meat is no longer pink, breaking it into crumbles; drain. To each pot, add 2 cups of milk, 2 cans of tomato soup, 1 can of mushroom soup and 1 cup of cheese. Bring to a boil.
3. Spoon over spaghetti (spaghetti will absorb liquid during baking). Sprinkle with remaining cheese. Bake, uncovered, at 350° for 40-45 minutes or until bubbly and top is lightly browned.
1 serving: 305 cal., 14g fat (8g sat. fat), 63mg chol., 349mg sod., 21g carb. (5g sugars, 1g fiber), 22g pro.

BAKLAVA TARTLETS

Want a quick treat that's delicious and easy to make? These tartlets will do the trick. You can serve them right away, but they're even better after chilling for about an hour in the refrigerator.
—Ashley Eagon, Kettering, OH

Takes: 25 min. • **Makes:** 45 tartlets

- ¾   cup honey
- ½   cup butter, melted
- 1   tsp. ground cinnamon
- 1   tsp. lemon juice
- ¼   tsp. ground cloves
- 2   cups finely chopped walnuts
- 3   pkg. (1.9 oz. each) frozen miniature
       phyllo tart shells

In a small bowl, mix the first 5 ingredients until blended; stir in walnuts. Spoon 2 tsp. mixture into each tart shell. Refrigerate until serving.
1 tartlet: 76 cal., 5g fat (1g sat. fat), 5mg chol., 24mg sod., 6g carb. (4g sugars, 0 fiber), 2g pro.

SCALLOPED POTATOES & HAM

A friend of mine served this hot and hearty casserole at her wedding. I liked it so much, I asked for the recipe. The potatoes and ham taste wonderful covered in a creamy cheese sauce, and the dish is excellent for a big group.
—Ruth Ann Stelfox, Raymond, AB

Prep: 30 min. • **Bake:** 1 hour 20 min.
Makes: 4 casseroles (10 servings each)

2 cans (10¾ oz. each) condensed cream of mushroom soup, undiluted
2 cans (10¾ oz. each) condensed cream of celery soup, undiluted
1 can (10¾ oz.) condensed cheddar cheese soup, undiluted
1 can (12 oz.) evaporated milk
10 lbs. medium potatoes, peeled and thinly sliced
5 lbs. fully cooked ham, cubed
4 cups shredded cheddar cheese

1. Preheat oven to 325°. In 2 large bowls, combine soups and milk. Add the potatoes and ham; toss to coat. Divide the mixture among 4 greased 13x9-in. baking dishes.
2. Cover and bake 1¼ hours or until the potatoes are tender. Uncover; sprinkle with cheese. Bake 5-10 minutes longer or until cheese is melted.
1 cup: 226 cal., 10g fat (5g sat. fat), 46mg chol., 970mg sod., 20g carb. (2g sugars, 1g fiber), 15g pro.

MAKE AHEAD
SMOKED BRISKET

This brisket is always a crowd favorite—it melts in your mouth!
—Jodi Abel, La Jolla, CA

Prep: 20 min. + marinating
Grill: 8 hours + standing
Makes: 20 servings

2 Tbsp. olive oil
1 fresh beef brisket (7 to 8 lbs.)
RUB
2 Tbsp. garlic powder
2 Tbsp. onion powder
2 Tbsp. chili powder
1 Tbsp. ground mustard
1 Tbsp. ground cumin
1 Tbsp. paprika
1 Tbsp. smoked sea salt
MOP SAUCE
2 cups beef broth
¼ cup olive oil
2 Tbsp. Worcestershire sauce
2 Tbsp. hickory-flavored liquid smoke

1. Brush olive oil over brisket. Combine the rub ingredients; rub over both sides of beef. Place the brisket on a rimmed baking sheet. Cover and refrigerate overnight or up to 2 days. Meanwhile, in a small saucepan, combine mop sauce ingredients. Simmer for 15 minutes, stirring occasionally. Refrigerate until ready to grill.
2. Soak hickory and mesquite chips or pellets; add to smoker according to the manufacturer's directions. Heat to 225°. Uncover brisket. Place in smoker fat side up; smoke 2 hours. Brush generously with mop sauce; turn meat. Smoke 2 more hours; brush generously with sauce again. Wrap brisket securely in heavy-duty foil; smoke until a thermometer inserted in beef reads 190°, 4-5 more hours.
3. Let the beef stand 20-30 minutes before slicing; cut diagonally across the grain into thin slices.
Note: This is a fresh beef brisket; it is not corned beef.
4 oz. cooked beef: 252 cal., 11g fat (3g sat. fat), 68mg chol., 472mg sod., 2g carb. (0 sugars, 1g fiber), 33g pro.

SOUR CREAM FAN ROLLS

I received this recipe from an email pen pal in Canada. The dough is so easy to work with, and it makes the lightest yeast rolls. I haven't used another white bread recipe since I started making this one.
—Carrie Ormsby, West Jordan, UT

- -

Prep: 30 min. + rising • **Bake:** 20 min./batch
Makes: 2½ dozen

- 7   to 8 cups all-purpose flour
- ½   cup sugar
- 2   Tbsp. active dry yeast
- 1½   tsp. salt
- ¼   tsp. baking powder
- 2   cups sour cream
- 1   cup water
- 6   Tbsp. butter, cubed
- 2   large eggs, room temperature, lightly beaten

1. In a large bowl, combine 3½ cups flour, sugar, yeast, salt and baking powder. In a small saucepan, heat the sour cream, water and butter to 120°-130°; add to the dry ingredients. Beat on medium speed for 2 minutes. Add eggs and ½ cup flour; beat 2 minutes longer. Stir in enough remaining flour to form a soft dough.

2. Turn onto a floured surface; knead until smooth and elastic, 6-8 minutes. Place in a greased bowl, turning once to grease top. Cover and let rise in a warm place until doubled, about 1 hour.

3. Punch dough down. Turn onto a lightly floured surface; divide in half. Roll each portion into a 23x9-in. rectangle. Cut into 1½-in. strips. Stack 5 strips together; cut into 1½-in. pieces and place cut side up in a greased muffin cup. Repeat with the remaining strips. Cover and let rise until doubled, about 20 minutes.

4. Bake at 350° for 20-25 minutes or until rolls are golden brown. Remove from pans to wire racks.

1 roll: 182 cal., 6g fat (3g sat. fat), 31mg chol., 158mg sod., 27g carb. (5g sugars, 1g fiber), 4g pro.

POLYNESIAN MEATBALLS

With pretty bits of pineapple, these meatballs are sure to attract attention— and the sweet-tart sauce brings people back for seconds.
—Carol Wakley, North East, PA

- -

Prep: 30 min. • **Cook:** 15 min.
Makes: 6 dozen

- 1   can (5 oz.) evaporated milk
- ⅓   cup chopped onion
- ⅔   cup crushed saltines
- 1   tsp. seasoned salt
- 1½   lbs. lean ground beef
SAUCE
- 1   can (20 oz.) pineapple tidbits
- 2   Tbsp. cornstarch
- ½   cup cider vinegar
- 2   Tbsp. soy sauce
- 2   Tbsp. lemon juice
- ½   cup packed brown sugar

1. In a bowl, combine the milk, onion, saltines and seasoned salt. Crumble beef over mixture and mix lightly but thoroughly. With wet hands, shape into 1-in. balls. In a large skillet over medium heat, brown the meatballs in small batches, turning often. Remove with a slotted spoon and keep warm. Drain skillet.

2. Drain pineapple, reserving juice; set the pineapple aside. Add enough water to the juice to measure 1 cup. In a bowl, combine the cornstarch, pineapple juice mixture, vinegar, soy sauce, lemon juice and brown sugar until smooth. Add to skillet. Bring to a boil; cook and stir until thickened, about 2 minutes. Add meatballs. Reduce the heat; cover and simmer for 15 minutes. Add the pineapple; heat through.

1 meatball: 37 cal., 1g fat (1g sat. fat), 9mg chol., 61mg sod., 4g carb. (3g sugars, 0 fiber), 3g pro.

MINI SWEET POTATO PIES

My son Levi was only 2 years old when he helped me create this delicious recipe, and it was the first time he told me "I love you!" I'll always remember making these with him.

—Emily Butler, South Williamsport, PA

- -

Prep: 45 minutes • **Bake:** 20 min. + cooling
Makes: 2 dozen

2 large sweet potatoes,
   peeled and cut into ¾-in. cubes
2 sheets refrigerated pie crust
¼ cup all-purpose flour
3 Tbsp. cold unsalted butter, cubed
1 cup packed brown sugar, divided

1. Preheat oven to 400°. Place sweet potatoes in a greased 15x10x1-in. baking pan; bake until tender, 35-40 minutes.
2. Meanwhile, on a work surface, unroll 1 crust. Using a 2½-in. round cutter, cut out 12 circles. Press circles onto bottoms and up sides of 12 nonstick mini muffin cups. Repeat with second crust. Chill until filling is ready.
3. In a food processor, pulse flour, butter and ¼ cup brown sugar until crumbly; set aside for topping. Add the baked sweet potatoes and remaining brown sugar to food processor; pulse until almost smooth. Fill crust-lined cups three-fourths full. Sprinkle with topping.
4. Decrease oven setting to 325°. Bake until crusts are golden brown, 20-24 minutes. Cool 5-10 minutes before removing from pan to a wire rack.

1 mini pie: 156 cal., 6g fat (3g sat. fat), 7mg chol., 67mg sod., 25g carb. (12g sugars, 1g fiber), 1g pro.

MAKE AHEAD
ALWAYS-TENDER ROASTED TURKEY

For years I prepared my Thanksgiving turkey only to have it turn out dry. That's when I decided to give this recipe a try. Baking the bird in an oven bag keeps it moist and tender—and there's no basting involved. It's so easy!
—Shirley Bedzis, San Diego, CA

- -

Prep: 30 min. • **Bake:** 3 hours + standing
Makes: 24 servings

¼ cup butter, softened
6 garlic cloves, minced
1 turkey (22 to 24 lbs.)
2 tsp. salt
2 tsp. pepper
1 Tbsp. all-purpose flour
1 turkey-size oven roasting bag
4 celery ribs, coarsely chopped
2 medium onions, sliced

1. In a small bowl, combine the butter and garlic. Pat turkey dry. Carefully loosen skin of turkey; rub the butter mixture under the skin. Sprinkle salt and pepper over the skin of turkey and inside cavity. Skewer turkey openings; tie drumsticks together.
2. Place flour in oven bag and shake to coat. Place oven bag in a roasting pan; add celery and onions. Place turkey, breast side up, over vegetables. Cut six ½-in. slits in top of bag; close bag with tie provided.
3. Bake at 350° for 3-3½ hours or until a thermometer reads 180°. Let stand for 15 minutes before carving. Skim fat and thicken drippings if desired.
To make ahead: Prepare turkey the day before. Pour drippings into a measuring cup; skim fat. Arrange slices in an ungreased shallow roasting pan; pour the drippings over the turkey. Cool completely. Cover and refrigerate overnight. The next day, bake at 350° for 45-65 minutes or until heated through.
8 oz. cooked turkey: 512 cal., 24g fat (8g sat. fat), 230mg chol., 375mg sod., 2g carb. (1g sugars, 0 fiber), 67g pro.

CHIPPED BEEF CHEESE BALL

This delicious appetizer is near and dear to my heart. It is a symbol of our family's Christmas and New Year's celebrations. My mom made it for more than 30 years.
—Molly Sumner, Creve Coeur, MO

- -

Prep: 10 min. + chilling • **Makes:** 2 cups

- 5 pkg. (2 oz. each) thinly sliced dried beef
- 12 oz. cream cheese, softened
- ⅓ cup finely chopped sweet onion
- 4 drops Worcestershire sauce
  Ritz crackers and assorted fresh vegetables

1. Place beef in a food processor; pulse until finely chopped. In a large bowl, beat cream cheese until smooth. Stir in ⅔ cup beef and the onion and Worcestershire sauce. Refrigerate, covered, at least 1 hour.

2. Place remaining beef in a small shallow bowl. Shape cheese mixture into a ball; roll in beef to coat evenly. Wrap; refrigerate for at least 1 hour. Serve with crackers and vegetables.

1 Tbsp.: 47 cal., 4g fat (2g sat. fat), 16mg chol., 136mg sod., 1g carb. (0 sugars, 0 fiber), 2g pro.

★ ★ ★ ★ ★ **READER REVIEW**

"This brings back amazing memories. Mom used to make this cheese ball in the '60s. We enjoyed it while watching football games on Christmas and New Year's. She used green onion and a little extra W-sauce. Dee-licious."

RAY233 TASTEOFHOME.COM

SUPER SAUSAGE DIP

I love spicy food, but I married a man who grew up in Tennessee and did not share my love of Mexican-type food. When we moved to the Southwest, he decided to give it a chance. Now he likes his food hotter than I can handle!
—Kaye Christiansen, Freistatt, MO

- -

Prep: 15 min. • **Cook:** 35 min.
Makes: 5 cups

- 1 lb. bulk pork sausage
- 1 small onion, chopped
- ½ cup chopped green pepper
- 3 medium tomatoes, chopped
- 1 can (4 oz.) chopped green chiles
- 1 pkg. (8 oz.) cream cheese, cubed
- 2 cups sour cream
  Green onions, optional
  Tortilla chips

1. In a large skillet, cook sausage, onion and green pepper over medium heat until meat is no longer pink, 5-7 minutes, breaking the sausage into crumbles; drain.

2. Stir in tomatoes and chiles. Bring to a boil. Reduce the heat; simmer, uncovered, 30 minutes, stirring occasionally.

3. Add cream cheese; stir until melted. Stir in sour cream; heat through. (Do not boil.) Transfer to a fondue pot and keep warm. If desired, garnish with green onions. Serve with chips.

2 Tbsp.: 75 cal., 7g fat (3g sat. fat), 20mg chol., 103mg sod., 2g carb. (1g sugars, 0 fiber), 2g pro.

Philly Cheese
Sandwiches
page 172

Slow Cooker

For hot, meaty sandwiches, cheesy dips, saucy ribs and more serves-a-crowd fare, nothing beats the ease of slow-simmered dishes. They're made to party.

ASIAN PULLED PORK BUNS

My pulled pork is a happy flavor mash-up of Vietnamese pho noodle soup and a banh mi sandwich. It's one seriously delicious slow cooker dish.
—Stacie Anderson, VA Beach, VA

Prep: 15 min. • **Cook:** 7 hours
Makes: 18 servings

- ½ cup hoisin sauce
- ¼ cup seasoned rice vinegar
- ¼ cup reduced-sodium soy sauce
- ¼ cup honey
- 2 Tbsp. tomato paste
- 1 Tbsp. Worcestershire sauce
- 2 garlic cloves, minced
- 4 lbs. boneless pork shoulder roast
- 18 French dinner rolls (about 1¾ oz. each), split and warmed
  Optional toppings: Shredded cabbage, julienned carrot, sliced jalapeno pepper, fresh cilantro or basil, and Sriracha chili sauce

1. In a small bowl, whisk together the first 7 ingredients until blended. Place roast in a 4- or 5-qt. slow cooker. Pour sauce mixture over the top. Cook, covered, on low until pork is tender, 7-9 hours.

2. Remove roast; cool slightly. Skim fat from cooking juices. Coarsely shred pork with 2 forks. Return pork to slow cooker; heat through. Using tongs, serve pork on rolls, adding toppings as desired.

Freeze option: Freeze cooled meat mixture in freezer containers. To use, partially thaw in refrigerator overnight. Heat through in a saucepan, stirring occasionally; add broth if necessary. Serve as directed.

1 sandwich: 350 cal., 12g fat (4g sat. fat), 60mg chol., 703mg sod., 35g carb. (8g sugars, 1g fiber), 23g pro.

CHEESEBURGER DIP

This fun and hearty dip recipe uses ingredients I always have in the refrigerator, so it's easy to throw together on short notice.
—Cindi DeClue, Anchorage, AK

- -

Prep: 25 min. • **Cook:** 1¾ hours
Makes: 16 servings

- 1   lb. lean ground beef (90% lean)
- 1   medium onion, chopped
- 1   pkg. (8 oz.) cream cheese, cubed
- 2   cups shredded cheddar cheese, divided
- 1   Tbsp. Worcestershire sauce
- 2   tsp. prepared mustard
- ¼   tsp. salt
- ⅛   tsp. pepper
- 1   medium tomato, chopped
- ¼   cup chopped dill pickles
      Tortilla chips or crackers

1. In a large skillet, cook beef and onion over medium-high heat until the beef is no longer pink and onion is tender, 6-8 minutes, breaking beef into crumbles; drain. Transfer to a greased 1½- or 3-qt. slow cooker. Stir in the cream cheese, 1½ cups cheddar cheese, Worcestershire, mustard, salt and pepper. Sprinkle with remaining ½ cup cheese.

2. Cook dip, covered, on low until mixture is heated through and cheese is melted, 1¾ to 2¼ hours. Top with the tomato and pickles. Serve with tortilla chips or crackers.

¼ cup: 157 cal., 12g fat (6g sat. fat), 46mg chol., 225mg sod., 2g carb. (1g sugars, 0 fiber), 10g pro.

TEST KITCHEN TIP
Keep an eye on the dip toward the end of cooking. If it goes too long, the edges will get dark.

CHICKEN CORDON BLEU SLIDERS

I'm always searching for sandwich ideas. Sandwiches are my favorite food. I like sloppy joes and wondered if I could make a sloppy joe of sorts even better. This experiment earned my family's approval.
—Carolyn Eskew, Dayton, OH

- -

Prep: 20 min. • **Cook:** 2½ hours + standing
Makes: 2 dozen

- 1½ lbs. boneless skinless chicken breasts
- 1 garlic clove, minced
- ¼ tsp. salt
- ¼ tsp. pepper
- 1 pkg. (8 oz.) cream cheese, cubed
- 2 cups shredded Swiss cheese
- 1¼ cups finely chopped fully cooked ham
- 2 pkg. (12 oz. each) Hawaiian sweet rolls, split
- Chopped green onions

1. Place chicken in a greased 3-qt. slow cooker; sprinkle with garlic, salt and pepper. Top with cream cheese. Cook, covered, on low 2½ to 3 hours or until a thermometer inserted in chicken reads 165°. Remove chicken; shred with 2 forks. Return to the slow cooker.

2. Stir in Swiss cheese and ham. Cover and let stand 15 minutes or until the cheese is melted. Stir before serving on rolls. Sprinkle with green onions.

1 slider: 209 cal., 10g fat (5g sat. fat), 53mg chol., 254mg sod., 17g carb. (6g sugars, 1g fiber), 14g pro.

★ ★ ★ ★ ★ **READER REVIEW**

"My family likes some zing, so the second time I made it, I stirred in a cup of sour cream near the end. This gave it a nice twist."

OLIVECLOVER TASTEOFHOME.COM

CINCINNATI-STYLE CHILI

My husband had this type of chili when visiting in Ohio and was super thrilled when I made it at home. You can have it two-way, with just chili and spaghetti, but our favorite is five-way, when you add all three toppings: beans, cheese and onion.
—Tari Ambler, Shorewood, IL

- -

Prep: 35 min. • **Cook:** 6 hours
Makes: 10 servings

- 2 **lbs. extra-lean ground turkey**
- 2 **medium onions, finely chopped**
- 4 **garlic cloves, minced**
- 2 **cans (8 oz. each) no-salt-added tomato sauce**
- 1 **can (14½ oz.) reduced-sodium beef broth**
- 2 **Tbsp. cider vinegar**
- ½ **oz. unsweetened chocolate, chopped**
- 3 **Tbsp. chili powder**
- 1 **bay leaf**
- 2 **tsp. Worcestershire sauce**
- 1 **tsp. ground cumin**
- ¾ **tsp. salt**
- ¾ **tsp. ground cinnamon**
- ¼ **tsp. ground allspice**
- ⅛ **tsp. ground cloves**
- ⅛ **tsp. cayenne pepper**
- 1 **pkg. (16 oz.) whole wheat spaghetti**

TOPPINGS
- 1 **can (16 oz.) kidney beans, rinsed and drained**
- 1¼ **cups shredded reduced-fat cheddar cheese**
- 1 **medium onion, chopped**

1. In a Dutch oven coated with cooking spray, cook turkey, onions and garlic until turkey is no longer pink. Transfer to a 3-qt. slow cooker.

2. In a large bowl, combine tomato sauce, broth, vinegar, chocolate and seasonings; pour over turkey mixture. Cook, covered, on low 6-8 hours.

3. Cook spaghetti according to package directions; drain. Remove bay leaf from chili. For each serving, place ¾ cup of the spaghetti in a bowl. Top with about ⅔ cup chili, 3 Tbsp. kidney beans, 2 Tbsp. cheese and 1 Tbsp. chopped onion.

1 serving: 388 cal., 6g fat (3g sat. fat), 47mg chol., 523mg sod., 52g carb. (9g sugars, 10g fiber), 37g pro.

SLOW-COOKER ITALIAN BEEF SANDWICHES

I have fond memories of my mother in the kitchen preparing her amazing beef dip sandwiches. They always made our house smell like an Old World Italian restaurant. And as good as the aroma was, somehow the taste was even better! Set out a jar of giardiniera for spooning on top.

—Kira Vosk, Muskego, WI

- -

Prep: 1 hour • **Cook:** 7 hours
Makes: 12 servings

- 4 **Tbsp. olive oil, divided**
- 1 **boneless beef chuck eye or other boneless beef chuck roast (4 to 5 lbs.)**
- 2¼ **tsp. salt, divided**
- 2¼ **tsp. pepper, divided**
- 2 **small onions, coarsely chopped**
- 9 **garlic cloves, chopped**
- ¾ **cup dry red wine**
- 4 **cups beef stock**
- 3 **fresh thyme sprigs**
- 4 **tsp. Italian seasoning**
- 1½ **tsp. crushed red pepper flakes**
- 4 **medium green peppers, cut into ½-in. strips**
- 1 **tsp. garlic powder**
- 12 **crusty submarine buns or hoagie buns, split partway**
- 12 **slices provolone or part-skim mozzarella cheese**
  Giardiniera, optional

1. In a 6-qt. stockpot, heat 3 Tbsp. oil over medium-high heat; brown roast on all sides. Sprinkle with 2 tsp. each salt and pepper. Transfer to a 6-qt. slow cooker.
2. Add onions to stockpot; cook and stir until lightly browned, 2-3 minutes. Add garlic; cook 30 seconds longer. Add wine; cook 3-5 minutes, stirring to loosen the browned bits from pan. Stir in stock, thyme, Italian seasoning and pepper flakes; transfer to slow cooker. Cook, covered, on low until beef is tender, 7-9 hours.

3. About ½ hour before serving, preheat oven to 350°. Place peppers in a 15x10x1-in. baking pan. Drizzle with remaining 1 Tbsp. oil. Sprinkle with garlic powder and the remaining ¼ tsp. salt and pepper; toss to coat. Roast until peppers are softened, 15-20 minutes, stirring halfway.
4. Remove roast; cool slightly. Strain cooking juices into a small saucepan, reserving strained mixture and removing thyme stems. Skim fat from juices; heat through and keep warm. Coarsely shred beef with 2 forks; stir in reserved strained mixture. If desired, moisten beef with some of the cooking juices.
5. To serve, preheat broiler. Arrange buns on baking sheets, cut sides up. Broil 3-4 in. from heat until lightly toasted. Remove from oven; top each bun with ⅔ cup beef mixture and 1 slice cheese. Broil until cheese is melted, about 30 seconds.
6. Top with peppers and, if desired, giardiniera. Serve with cooking juices for dipping.
1 sandwich: 595 cal., 30g fat (11g sat. fat), 113mg chol., 1134mg sod., 38g carb. (6g sugars, 3g fiber), 44g pro.

HOW TO CUT PEPPERS LIKE A PRO
Trim stem from pepper so it sits flat on its top. Cut 1 side off the pepper, being careful to leave the seeds and core intact. Rotate pepper and cut off another side. Continue turning and cutting until only the core remains; trim or discard core. Then cut each pepper fillet into strips.

JALAPENO MAC & CHEESE

Many years ago after I had knee surgery, a friend brought me a big casserole of mac and cheese along with the recipe. I have fiddled with the recipe over the years, most recently adding jalapenos at the request of my son. What an awesome spicy twist!
—Teresa Gustafson, Elkton, MD

Prep: 25 min. • **Cook:** 3 hours
Makes: 15 servings

- 1 pkg. (16 oz.) uncooked elbow macaroni
- 6 Tbsp. butter, divided
- 4 jalapeno peppers, seeded and finely chopped
- 3 cups shredded cheddar cheese
- 2 cups shredded Colby-Monterey Jack cheese
- 2 cups whole milk
- 1 can (10¾ oz.) condensed cream of onion soup, undiluted
- 1 can (10¾ oz.) condensed cheddar cheese soup, undiluted
- ½ cup mayonnaise
- ¼ tsp. pepper
- 1 cup crushed Ritz crackers (about 25 crackers)

1. Cook macaroni according to package directions for al dente; drain. Transfer to a greased 5-qt. slow cooker.
2. Melt 2 Tbsp. butter in a large skillet over medium-high heat. Add jalapenos; cook and stir until crisp-tender, about 5 minutes. Add to slow cooker. Stir in the cheeses, milk, soups, mayonnaise and pepper.
3. Cook, covered, on low until cheese is melted and mixture is heated through, about 3 hours. Melt remaining 4 Tbsp. butter; stir in crackers. Sprinkle over macaroni mixture.

Note: Wear disposable gloves when cutting hot peppers; the oils can burn skin. Avoid touching your face.

¾ cup: 428 cal., 27g fat (13g sat. fat), 53mg chol., 654mg sod., 33g carb. (5g sugars, 2g fiber), 14g pro.

TEST KITCHEN TIP
Be sure to cook the pasta just short of tender. It will continue to cook in the slow cooker.

APPLE CIDER PULLED PORK

For potlucks and tailgates, we slow-cook pork with cider, onions and spices. These tangy sliders make a winning barbecue plate with sweet potato fries.
—Rachel Lewis, Danville, VA

Prep: 15 min. • **Cook:** 6¼ hours
Makes: 12 servings

- 2 tsp. seasoned salt
- ½ tsp. ground mustard
- ½ tsp. paprika
- ¼ tsp. ground coriander
- ¼ tsp. pepper
- 2 medium Granny Smith apples, peeled and coarsely chopped
- 1 medium onion, chopped
- 1 celery rib, chopped
- 1½ cups apple cider or juice
- 1 boneless pork shoulder butt roast (3 lbs.)
- 2 Tbsp. cornstarch
- 2 Tbsp. water
- 24 mini buns, warmed
  Additional apple slices, optional

1. Mix first 5 ingredients. Place apples, onion, celery and cider in a 5-qt. slow cooker; top with roast. Sprinkle roast with seasoning mixture. Cook, covered, on low until tender, 6-8 hours.
2. Remove roast; shred with 2 forks. Skim fat from cooking juices. Mix cornstarch and water; stir into cooking juices. Cook, covered, on high until liquid is thickened, 10-15 minutes; stir in pork. Serve on buns. If desired, top with apple slices.

Freeze option: Freeze cooled meat mixture in freezer containers. To use, partially thaw in refrigerator overnight. Heat through in a saucepan, stirring occasionally; add a little broth or water if necessary.

2 sliders: 375 cal., 15g fat (5g sat. fat), 69mg chol., 563mg sod., 35g carb. (9g sugars, 2g fiber), 25g pro.

SLOW-COOKER ARTICHOKE-SPINACH DIP

Little extras like crumbled feta and red wine vinegar take this creamy dip of artichoke hearts, spinach and Parmesan to the next level. Just throw the whole nine yards into a slow cooker and this dip is good to go on game day.
—Alyssa Janis, Green Bay, WI

Prep: 20 min. • **Cook:** 2 hours
Makes: 24 servings

- 2 cans (14 oz. each) water-packed artichoke hearts, drained and chopped
- 1 pkg. (10 oz.) frozen chopped spinach, thawed and squeezed dry
- 1 cup sour cream
- 1 small onion, chopped
- 2 garlic cloves, minced
- ¾ cup grated Parmesan cheese
- ¾ cup 2% milk
- ½ cup crumbled feta cheese
- ⅓ cup mayonnaise
- 1 Tbsp. red wine vinegar
- ¼ tsp. coarsely ground pepper
- 1 pkg. (8 oz.) cream cheese, cubed
  Sweet red pepper slices and tortilla chip scoops

1. Combine first 11 ingredients until well blended. Add cream cheese.

2. Place artichoke mixture in a greased 3- or 4-qt. slow cooker; cook, covered, on low about 2 hours. Stir; cover and keep warm. Serve with red pepper slices and tortilla chip scoops.

¼ cup: 112 cal., 9g fat (4g sat. fat), 22mg chol., 217mg sod., 4g carb. (1g sugars, 0 fiber), 4g pro.

CHILE BEEF DIP

No last-minute party prep needed! Just put this creamy dip together a couple of hours before your shindig, and let your slow cooker do the work.
—Pat Habiger, Spearville, KS

- -

Prep: 25 min. • **Cook:** 2 hours
Makes: 8 cups

2	lbs. lean ground beef (90% lean)
1	large onion, chopped
1	jalapeno pepper, seeded and chopped
2	pkg. (8 oz. each) cream cheese, cubed
2	cans (8 oz. each) tomato sauce
1	can (4 oz.) chopped green chiles
½	cup grated Parmesan cheese
½	cup ketchup
2	garlic cloves, minced
1½	tsp. chili powder
1	tsp. dried oregano
	Tortilla chips

1. In a large skillet, brown the beef, onion and jalapeno until meat is no longer pink; drain. Transfer to a 3- or 4-qt. slow cooker. Stir in the cream cheese, tomato sauce, chilies, Parmesan cheese, ketchup, garlic, chili powder and oregano.
2. Cover and cook on low for 2-3 hours or until heated through. Stir; serve with chips.
Note: Wear disposable gloves when cutting hot peppers; the oils can burn skin. Avoid touching your face.
¼ cup: 110 cal., 8g fat (4g sat. fat), 34mg chol., 204mg sod., 3g carb. (2g sugars, 0 fiber), 7g pro.

> **TEST KITCHEN TIP**
> To cut the spice level, use only half of a jalapeno pepper or leave it out entirely.

BBQ BRATS

In Wisconsin, brats are a food group! We are always looking for new ways to cook them. This recipe is easy and a hit at any tailgate party or cookout, any time of year.
—Jessica Abnet, DePere, WI

- -

Prep: 20 min. • **Cook:** 3 hours
Makes: 10 servings

10	uncooked bratwurst links
1	bottle (12 oz.) beer or 1½ cups chicken broth
1	cup ketchup
1	cup honey barbecue sauce
10	hot dog buns, split
	Spicy brown mustard

1. Grill bratwursts, covered, on an oiled rack over medium heat or broil 4 in. from heat 10 minutes, turning frequently. Transfer to a 5-qt. slow cooker.
2. In a large bowl, mix the beer, ketchup and barbecue sauce; pour over the bratwursts. Cook, covered, on low until cooked through, 3-4 hours. Place bratwursts on buns. Serve with mustard and, if desired, cooking liquid.
1 serving: 480 cal., 27g fat (9g sat. fat), 64mg chol., 1659mg sod., 41g carb. (20g sugars, 1g fiber), 16g pro.

SLOPPY JOE TATER TOT CASSEROLE

This simple casserole is an easy, fun dinner for both you and the kids. Serve it with carrot and celery sticks for a fuss-free feast. You can also stir in a little spicy brown mustard if the adults want more zing.
—Laura Wilhelm,
West Hollywood, CA

Prep: 20 min. • **Cook:** 4 hours + standing
Makes: 10 servings

- 1 bag (32 oz.) frozen Tater Tots, divided
- 2 lbs. ground beef or turkey
- 1 can (15 oz.) tomato sauce
- 1 bottle (8 oz.) sweet chili sauce
- 2 Tbsp. packed brown sugar
- 1 Tbsp. Worcestershire sauce
- 1 Tbsp. dried minced garlic
- 1 Tbsp. dried minced onion
- ½ tsp. salt
- ½ tsp. pepper
- 1¼ cups shredded Colby-Monterey Jack cheese
- ¼ tsp. paprika

1. Place half the Tater Tots in bottom of 5-qt. slow cooker. In a large skillet, cook beef over medium-high heat until no longer pink, 5-6 minutes, breaking into crumbles. Drain. Stir in the next 8 ingredients; reduce heat and simmer 2-3 minutes. Place beef mixture in slow cooker; top with remaining Tater Tots.

2. Cook, covered, on low 4 hours. Top with cheese. Sprinkle with paprika. Let stand, uncovered, 15 minutes before serving.

1 cup: 466 cal., 24g fat (9g sat. fat), 69mg chol., 1332mg sod., 41g carb. (18g sugars, 4g fiber), 22g pro.

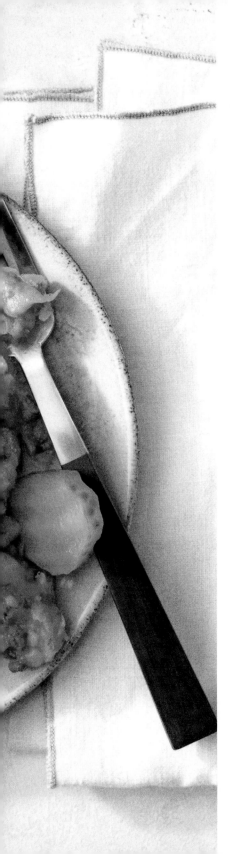

LOW & SLOW HUEVOS RANCHEROS

We love Mexican food, especially for breakfast. My slow cooker version of a favorite, huevos rancheros, is rolled into flour tortillas. It's a perfect way to serve a breakfast crowd.

—Joan Hallford, North Richland Hills, TX

- -

Prep: 25 min. • **Cook:** 3½ hours + standing
Makes: 10 servings

- ½ lb. fresh chorizo
- ½ cup chopped onion
- ½ cup chopped sweet red pepper
- 2 jalapeno peppers, seeded and chopped
- 1 garlic clove, minced
- 3 cups frozen cubed hash brown potatoes, thawed
- 8 large eggs, beaten
- 2 cups shredded Colby-Monterey Jack cheese
- 1 cup salsa
- 4 bacon strips, cooked and crumbled
- 20 flour tortillas (6 in.)
  Fresh chopped cilantro and additional salsa, optional

1. In a large skillet, cook the chorizo, onion, pepper, jalapenos and garlic over medium-high heat until cooked through, 6-8 minutes, breaking into crumbles; drain. Transfer mixture to a 3- or 4-qt. slow cooker. Stir in next 5 ingredients.
2. Cook, covered, until potatoes are tender and eggs are set, 3½-4 hours.
3. Turn off slow cooker; remove insert. Let stand 10 minutes before serving. Serve with tortillas. If desired, top with cilantro and additional salsa.
Note: Wear disposable gloves when cutting hot peppers; the oils can burn skin. Avoid touching your face.
2 tacos: 488 cal., 25g fat (11g sat. fat), 192mg chol., 1028mg sod., 41g carb. (3g sugars, 4g fiber), 21g pro.

TEST KITCHEN TIPS
- This versatile recipe can be served with the toppings of your choice. Try it with avocado, sour cream, Mexican crema or lime wedges.
- For party-sized brunch appetizers, serve the mixture in smaller street taco-sized tortillas or tortilla chip scoops. They're cute and fun!

HEALTHY GREEK BEAN DIP
This crowd-pleasing appetizer is healthy to boot! Folks will love to eat their veggies when they can dip them in this zesty, fresh alternative to hummus.
—Kelly Silvers, Edmond, OK

- -

Prep: 15 min. • **Cook:** 2 hours
Makes: 3 cups

2 cans (15 oz. each) cannellini beans, rinsed and drained
¼ cup water
¼ cup finely chopped roasted sweet red peppers
2 Tbsp. finely chopped red onion
2 Tbsp. olive oil
2 Tbsp. lemon juice
1 Tbsp. snipped fresh dill
2 garlic cloves, minced
¼ tsp. salt
¼ tsp. pepper
1 small cucumber, peeled, seeded and finely chopped
½ cup fat-free plain Greek yogurt
Additional snipped fresh dill
Baked pita chips or assorted fresh vegetables

1. Process beans and water in a food processor until smooth. Transfer to a greased 1½-qt. slow cooker. Add the next 8 ingredients. Cook, covered, on low until heated through, 2-3 hours. Stir in cucumber and yogurt; cool slightly. Sprinkle with additional dill. Serve warm or cold with chips or assorted fresh vegetables.
Freeze option: Omitting cucumber, yogurt and additional dill, freeze cooled dip in freezer containers. To use, thaw in the refrigerator overnight. To serve dip warm, heat through in a saucepan, stirring occasionally. Or serve cold. Stir cucumber and yogurt into finished dip; sprinkle with additional dill. Serve with chips or fresh vegetables.
¼ cup: 86 cal., 3g fat (0 sat. fat), 0 chol., 260mg sod., 11g carb. (1g sugars, 3g fiber), 4g pro. **Diabetic exchanges:** 1 starch, ½ fat.

BOEUF BOURGUIGNON FROM THE SLOW COOKER

I'd wanted to make beef Burgundy ever since I got one of Julia Child's cookbooks, but I wanted to find a way to fix it in a slow cooker. My version of the popular beef stew is still rich, hearty and delicious, but without the need to watch it on the stovetop or in the oven.
—Crystal Jo Bruns, Iliff, CO

- -

Prep: 30 min. + marinating • **Cook:** 8 hours
Makes: 12 servings

3 lbs. beef stew meat
1¾ cups dry red wine
3 Tbsp. olive oil
3 Tbsp. dried minced onion
2 Tbsp. dried parsley flakes
1 bay leaf
1 tsp. dried thyme
¼ tsp. pepper
8 bacon strips, chopped
1 lb. whole fresh mushrooms, quartered
24 pearl onions, peeled (about 2 cups)
2 garlic cloves, minced
⅓ cup all-purpose flour
1 tsp. salt
Hot cooked whole wheat egg noodles, optional

1. Place beef in a large resealable bowl; add wine, oil and seasonings. Turn to coat. Cover and refrigerate overnight.
2. In a large skillet, cook bacon over medium heat until crisp, stirring occasionally. Remove with a slotted spoon; drain on paper towels. Discard drippings, reserving 1 Tbsp. in pan.
3. Add mushrooms and onions to drippings; cook and stir over medium-high heat until tender. Add garlic; cook 1 minute longer.
4. Drain beef, reserving marinade; transfer beef to a 4- or 5-qt. slow cooker. Sprinkle beef with flour and salt; toss to coat. Top with bacon and mushroom mixture. Add reserved marinade.
5. Cook, covered, on low until beef is tender, 8-10 hours. Remove bay leaf. If desired, serve stew with noodles.
⅔ cup beef mixture: 289 cal., 15g fat (5g sat. fat), 77mg chol., 350mg sod., 8g carb. (2g sugars, 1g fiber), 25g pro. **Diabetic exchanges:** 3 lean meat, 1½ fat, 1 vegetable.

CRANBERRY CHILI MEATBALLS

Using packaged meatballs helps save time in the kitchen, and they are just as tasty as homemade. My friends look forward to enjoying these meatballs at our holiday gatherings and there are never any leftovers! The sauce is tangy yet sweet, and the festive color is perfect for any holiday party.
—Amy Scamerhorn, Indianapolis, IN

Prep: 10 min. • **Cook:** 2 hours
Makes: about 5 dozen

- 1 can (14 oz.) jellied cranberry sauce
- 1 bottle (12 oz.) chili sauce
- ¾ cup packed brown sugar
- ½ tsp. chili powder
- ½ tsp. ground cumin
- ¼ tsp. cayenne pepper
- 1 pkg. (32 oz.) frozen fully cooked homestyle meatballs, thawed

1. In a large saucepan over medium heat, combine the first 6 ingredients; stir until sugar is dissolved.
2. Place meatballs in a 4-qt. slow cooker. Add sauce; stir to coat. Cook, covered, on low until heated through, 2-3 hours.
Freeze option: Freeze cooled meatball mixture in freezer containers. To use, partially thaw in refrigerator overnight. Microwave, covered, on high in a microwave-safe dish until heated through, stirring occasionally; add a little water if necessary.
1 meatball: 74 cal., 4g fat (2g sat. fat), 6mg chol., 191mg sod., 8g carb. (5g sugars, 0 fiber), 2g pro.

PHILLY CHEESE SANDWICHES

I'm a big fan of Phillies, so this throw-together recipe is right up my alley. Plus, my slow cooker does all the work. Win-win.
—Christina Addison, Blanchester, OH

Prep: 20 min. • **Cook:** 8 hours
Makes: 8 servings

- 1 boneless beef chuck roast (2½ to 3 lbs.), trimmed and cut into 1-in. cubes
- 2 medium onions, halved and sliced
- ¼ cup Worcestershire sauce
- 2 garlic cloves, minced
- 1 tsp. dried oregano
- ½ tsp. dried basil
- 1 medium sweet red pepper, sliced
- 1 medium green pepper, sliced
- 8 slices American cheese or pepper jack cheese
- 8 hoagie buns, split and toasted

1. In a 3- or 4-qt. slow cooker, combine the first 6 ingredients. Cook, covered, on low for 7 hours. Stir in peppers; cook, covered, until meat and peppers are tender, 1-3 hours.
2. Stir to break up meat. Serve beef mixture and cheese on buns.
1 sandwich: 546 cal., 23g fat (9g sat. fat), 97mg chol., 754mg sod., 42g carb. (9g sugars, 2g fiber), 40g pro.

TEST KITCHEN TIPS

- American cheese is traditional on Philly-style sandwiches, but we won't tell if you top yours with pepper jack and pickled jalapenos. *
- Toast the split hoagie buns under the broiler for 2-3 minutes, but don't turn your back—they go from perfect to burnt in a hurry.

SLOW-COOKED BEEF BURRITOS WITH GREEN CHILES

I created this recipe years ago, and it has become such a favorite that the wonderful aroma as it cooks makes my family instantly happy. It is hearty, flavorful and easy to prepare, and it uses the long, slow cooking method that truly defines comfort food.
—Sally J. Pahler, Palisade, CO

Prep: 20 min. • **Cook:** 7 hours
Makes: 14 servings

- 2 garlic cloves, minced
- 1 tsp. salt
- 2 tsp. ground cumin
- 1 tsp. cayenne pepper
- 1 boneless beef chuck roast (4 lbs.)
- 1 can (28 oz.) diced tomatoes
- 4 cans (7 oz. each) whole green chiles, drained and coarsely chopped
- 1 large onion, diced
- 14 whole wheat tortillas (8 in.), warmed
  Optional toppings: Shredded cheddar cheese, salsa, sour cream, sliced ripe olives

1. Combine garlic, salt, cumin and cayenne; rub over roast. Place in a 5- or 6-qt. slow cooker. Add the tomatoes, chiles and onion. Cook, covered, on low until meat is tender, 7-8 hours.
2. Remove roast from slow cooker; shred with 2 forks. Remove vegetables with a slotted spoon; discard the cooking juices. Return beef and vegetables to slow cooker and heat through. Serve in tortillas, with toppings as desired.

1 burrito: 355 cal., 13g fat (5g sat. fat), 84mg chol., 499mg sod., 28g carb. (4g sugars, 4g fiber), 30g pro. **Diabetic exchanges:** 4 lean meat, 2 starch.

SLOW-COOKER CHORIZO BREAKFAST CASSEROLE

My kids ask for this slow-cooked casserole for breakfast and dinner. I've served it with white country gravy or salsa— it's delightful either way.
—Cindy Pruitt, Grove, OK

- -

Prep: 25 min. • **Cook:** 4 hours + standing
Makes: 8 servings

- 1 lb. fresh chorizo or bulk spicy pork sausage
- 1 medium onion, chopped
- 1 medium sweet red pepper, chopped
- 2 jalapeno peppers, seeded and chopped
- 1 pkg. (30 oz.) frozen shredded hash brown potatoes, thawed
- 1½ cups shredded Mexican cheese blend
- 12 large eggs
- 1 cup 2% milk
- ½ tsp. pepper
- Optional: Chopped avocado and tomato

1. In a large skillet, cook chorizo, onion, red pepper and jalapenos over medium heat until cooked through and vegetables are tender, 7-8 minutes, breaking chorizo into crumbles; drain. Cool slightly.
2. In a greased 5-qt. slow cooker, layer a third of the potatoes, chorizo mixture and cheese. Repeat layers twice. In a large bowl, whisk eggs, milk and pepper until blended; pour over top.
3. Cook, covered, on low until the eggs are set and a thermometer reads 160°, 4-4½ hours. Uncover and let stand for 10 minutes before serving. If desired, top with chopped avocado and tomato.

Note: Wear disposable gloves when cutting hot peppers; the oils can burn skin. Avoid touching your face.

1½ cups: 512 cal., 32g fat (12g sat. fat), 350mg chol., 964mg sod., 25g carb. (4g sugars, 2g fiber), 30g pro.

COUNTRY-STYLE BARBECUE RIBS

These get a good sear under the broiler, then go into the slow cooker to become fall-apart tender. Enjoy them with great sides, or shredded on a bun. Either way, they're the most amazing ribs you'll ever have.

—Shannon Copley, Upper Arlington, OH

Prep: 15 min. • **Cook:** 3 hours
Makes: 10 servings

2 Tbsp. paprika
2 Tbsp. brown sugar
2 tsp. salt
2 tsp. garlic powder
2 tsp. chili powder
1 tsp. onion powder
1 tsp. ground chipotle pepper
1 tsp. pepper
¾ tsp. dried thyme
4 lbs. boneless country-style pork ribs
1 bottle (18 oz.) barbecue sauce
¾ cup amber beer or reduced-sodium chicken broth

1. Preheat broiler. Mix first 9 ingredients. Place pork in a foil-lined 15x10x1-in. pan; rub generously with seasonings. Broil ribs 4-5 in. from heat until browned, 2-3 minutes per side.

2. Transfer to a 5-qt. slow cooker. Whisk together barbecue sauce and beer; pour over ribs. Cook, covered, on low until tender, 3-4 hours.

3. Remove ribs. Reserve 2 cups cooking juices; discard remaining juices. Skim fat from reserved juices. Serve with ribs.

1 serving: 393 cal., 17g fat (6g sat. fat), 105mg chol., 1098mg sod., 26g carb. (20g sugars, 1g fiber), 33g pro..

TEST KITCHEN TIP
Country-style ribs come from the loin end close to the shoulder. They're sold as a bone-in rack and as single ribs, with bones or boneless. Like any other shoulder cut, they're best cooked low and slow.

HAWAIIAN KIELBASA

Savory sausage teams up with juicy, tangy pineapple for a winning combination that you can prep in a flash. The sweet barbecue-style sauce is a tasty way to tie them together.
—Louise Kline, Fort Myers, FL

Prep: 15 min. • **Cook:** 2½ hours
Makes: 12 servings

- 2 lbs. smoked kielbasa or Polish sausage, cut into 1-in. pieces
- 1 can (20 oz.) unsweetened pineapple chunks, undrained
- ½ cup ketchup
- 2 Tbsp. brown sugar
- 2 Tbsp. yellow mustard
- 1 Tbsp. cider vinegar
- ¾ cup lemon-lime soda
- 2 Tbsp. cornstarch
- 2 Tbsp. cold water

1. Place sausage in a 3- or 4-qt. slow cooker. Drain pineapple, reserving ¾ cup juice; set pineapple aside. In a small bowl, whisk the ketchup, brown sugar, mustard and vinegar. Stir in soda and reserved pineapple juice. Pour mixture over sausage; stir to coat. Cover and cook on low until heated through, 2-3 hours.
2. Stir in pineapple. In a small bowl, combine cornstarch and water until smooth. Stir into slow cooker. Cover and cook until sauce is thickened, 30 minutes longer. Serve with toothpicks if desired.

½ cup: 289 cal., 21g fat (7g sat. fat), 51mg chol., 975mg sod., 15g carb. (12g sugars, 0 fiber), 10g pro.

Jalapeno Peach Kielbasa: Use 1 (20-oz.) can unsweetened peach chunks and add 2 thinly sliced fresh jalapenos. Proceed with recipe as directed.

SAUSAGE JALAPENO DIP

This creamy dip cooks up like a dream in the slow cooker. Scoop it up with crunchy tortilla chips or raw veggies.
—Gina Fensler, Cincinnati, OH

Prep: 15 min. • **Cook:** 5½ hours
Makes: 6 cups

- 1 lb. bulk Italian sausage
- 2 large sweet red peppers, finely chopped
- 3 jalapeno peppers, finely chopped
- 1 cup whole milk
- 2 pkg. (8 oz. each) cream cheese, softened
- 1 cup shredded part-skim mozzarella cheese
  Tortilla chips

1. In a large skillet, cook sausage over medium heat until it's no longer pink, 6-8 minutes, breaking it into crumbles as it cooks; drain.
2. Place the red peppers, jalapenos and sausage in a 3-qt. slow cooker; add milk. Cook, covered, on low until peppers are tender, 5-6 hours.
3. Stir in cheeses. Cook, covered, on low until cheese is melted, about 30 minutes longer. Serve with tortilla chips.

Note: Wear disposable gloves when cutting hot peppers; the oils can burn skin. Avoid touching your face.

¼ cup: 137 cal., 12g fat (6g sat. fat), 33mg chol., 211mg sod., 3g carb. (2g sugars, 0 fiber), 5g pro.

SLOW-COOKER TURKEY BREAST WITH GRAVY

This quick-prep recipe lets you feast on turkey at any time of year. We save the rich broth for gravy, noodles and soup making.

—Joyce Hough, Annapolis, MD

Prep: 25 min. • **Cook:** 5 hours + standing
Makes: 12 servings

- 2 tsp. dried parsley flakes
- 1 tsp. salt
- 1 tsp. poultry seasoning
- ½ tsp. paprika
- ½ tsp. pepper
- 2 medium onions, chopped
- 3 medium carrots, cut into ½-in. slices
- 3 celery ribs, coarsely chopped
- 1 bone-in turkey breast (6 to 7 lbs.), skin removed
- ¼ cup all-purpose flour
- ½ cup water

1. Mix the first 5 ingredients in a small bowl. Place vegetables in a 6- or 7-qt. slow cooker; top with turkey. Rub turkey with the seasoning mixture.
2. Cook, covered, on low until a thermometer inserted in turkey reads at least 170°, 5-6 hours. Remove from slow cooker; let stand, covered, for 15 minutes before slicing.
3. Meanwhile, strain cooking juices into a small saucepan. Mix flour and water until smooth; stir into cooking juices. Bring to a boil; cook and stir until thickened, 1-2 minutes. Serve with turkey.
6 oz. cooked turkey with 3 Tbsp. gravy : 200 cal., 1g fat (0 sat. fat), 117mg chol., 270mg sod., 2g carb. (0 sugars, 0 fiber), 43g pro. **Diabetic exchanges:** 6 lean meat.

SPICY SAUSAGE HASH BROWNS

I love to develop my own recipes and have people calling for them often. My family members and friends from our church tend to be my favorite and most honest critics, and they love this meal!

—Angela Sheridan, Opdyke, IL

Prep: 15 min. • **Cook:** 5 hours
Makes: 9 servings

- 1 lb. bulk spicy pork sausage
- 1 pkg. (30 oz.) frozen shredded hash brown potatoes, thawed
- 2 cups sour cream
- 1 jar (16 oz.) double-cheddar cheese sauce
- 2 cans (4 oz. each) chopped green chiles
- ½ tsp. crushed red pepper flakes

In a large skillet, cook sausage over medium heat until no longer pink; drain. Transfer to a 4-qt. slow cooker. Stir in the remaining ingredients. Cover and cook on low for 5-6 hours or until heated through.
1 cup: 368 cal., 25g fat (12g sat. fat), 73mg chol., 723mg sod., 22g carb. (4g sugars, 2g fiber), 10g pro.

CHRISTMAS PUNCH

This holiday, why not indulge in a warm ruby red punch made in the slow cooker? We use cinnamon and Red Hots to give it that cozy spiced flavor and welcome-home aroma.
—Angie Goins, Tazewell, TN

- -

Prep: 5 min. • **Cook:** 3 hours
Makes: 10 servings

- 4 cups unsweetened pineapple juice
- 4 cups cranberry juice
- ⅓ cup Red Hots
- 2 cinnamon sticks (3 in.)
  Fresh cranberries and additional cinnamon sticks

In a 3- or 4-qt. slow cooker, combine the first 4 ingredients. Cook, covered, on low until heated through and te candies are melted, 3-4 hours. Garnish with cranberries and additional cinnamon sticks.
¾ cup: 129 cal., 0 fat (0 sat. fat), 0 chol., 4mg sod., 33g carb. (28g sugars, 0 fiber), 1g pro.

BRING IT
Let the grown-ups customize their punch by providing a bottle of Fireball whiskey or cinnamon schnapps alongside. Cheers!

EASY & ELEGANT HAM

I love to serve my large family this moist, tender ham. It can be readied quickly in the morning, it frees up my oven, it tastes outstanding, and it feeds a crowd. Pineapple, cherries and an orange glaze make it a real showstopper.
—Denise DiPace, Medford, NJ

- -

Prep: 5 min. • **Cook:** 6 hours
Makes: 20 servings

- 2 cans (20 oz. each) sliced pineapple
- 1 fully cooked boneless ham (about 6 lbs.), cut in half
- 1 jar (6 oz.) maraschino cherries, well drained
- 1 jar (12 oz.) orange marmalade

1. Drain pineapple, reserving juice; set juice aside. Place half of the pineapple in an ungreased 6-qt. slow cooker. Top with the ham pieces. Add cherries, remaining pineapple and reserved pineapple juice. Spoon marmalade over ham. Cover and cook on low until heated through, 6-7 hours.

2. Remove to a warm serving platter. Serve pineapple and cherries with sliced ham.
5 oz. ham: 212 cal., 5g fat (2g sat. fat), 69mg chol., 1424mg sod., 18g carb. (18g sugars, 0 fiber), 25g pro.

SPICY TOUCHDOWN CHILI

Football, cool weather and chili just seem to go together. Whether I'm cheering on the local team on a Friday night or enjoying a Saturday afternoon of Oklahoma Sooner football with some friends, I enjoy serving this chili on game day.
—Chris Neal, Quapaw, OK

- -

Prep: 30 min. • **Cook:** 4 hours
Makes: 12 servings (3 qt.)

- 1 **lb. ground beef**
- 1 **lb. bulk pork sausage**
- 2 **cans (16 oz. each) kidney beans, rinsed and drained**
- 2 **cans (15 oz. each) pinto beans, rinsed and drained**
- 2 **cans (14½ oz. each) diced tomatoes with mild green chiles, undrained**
- 1 **can (14½ oz.) diced tomatoes with onions, undrained**
- 1 **can (12 oz.) beer**
- 6 **bacon strips, cooked and crumbled**
- 1 **small onion, chopped**
- ¼ **cup chili powder**
- ¼ **cup chopped pickled jalapeno slices**
- 2 **tsp. ground cumin**
- 2 **garlic cloves, minced**
- 1 **tsp. dried basil**
- ¾ **tsp. cayenne pepper**
  Optional: Shredded cheddar cheese, sour cream and chopped green onions

1. In a large skillet, cook beef over medium heat until no longer pink, 6-8 minutes; crumble beef; drain. Transfer to a 6-qt. slow cooker. Repeat with sausage.

2. Stir in the next 13 ingredients. Cook, covered, on low until heated through, 4-5 hours. If desired, top individual servings with shredded cheddar cheese, sour cream and chopped green onions.

1 cup: 365 cal., 15g fat (5g sat. fat), 48mg chol., 901mg sod., 34g carb. (7g sugars, 9g fiber), 22g pro.

BACON & SWISS BREAKFAST

When we have overnight guests, I like to prepare things ahead of time so we can enjoy our company. It often gets crazy when everyone first wakes up, and I like to have food available whenever people are ready to eat. I devised this slow-cooker breakfast recipe when I was feeding 22 people breakfast at a destination wedding.
—Donna Gribbins, Shelbyville, KY

- -

Prep: 15 min. • **Cook:** 4 hours + standing
Makes: 12 servings

- 1 **pkg. (28 oz.) frozen O'Brien potatoes, thawed**
- 1 **lb. bacon strips, cooked and crumbled**
- 2 **cups shredded Swiss cheese**
- 12 **large eggs**
- 2 **cups 2% milk**
- 1 **tsp. seasoned salt**
- 1 **tsp. pepper**
  Minced chives, optional

In a greased 4- or 5-qt. slow cooker, layer potatoes, bacon and cheese. In a large bowl, whisk the eggs, milk, seasoned salt and pepper; pour over the top. Cook, covered, on low until eggs are set, 4-5 hours. Turn off slow cooker. Remove crock insert to a wire rack; let stand, uncovered, 30 minutes before serving. Garnish with minced chives if desired.

1 serving: 277 cal., 16g fat (7g sat. fat), 220mg chol., 507mg sod., 13g carb. (3g sugars, 2g fiber), 18g pro.

Berry-Patch
Brownie Pizza
page 192

The Sweetest Treats

Save room for dessert! These luscious cakes, crisp cookies, tempting pies and delectable candies will have folks coming back for more.

CLASSIC CHOCOLATE CAKE

This recipe was on a can of Hershey's Cocoa way back in 1943. I tried it, my boys liked it, and I've been making it ever since. I make all my cakes from scratch, and this is one of the best!
—Betty Follas, Morgan Hill, CA

- -

Prep: 15 min. • **Bake:** 35 min.
Makes: 15 servings

⅔ cup butter, softened
1⅔ cups sugar
3 large eggs, room temperature
2 cups all-purpose flour
⅔ cup baking cocoa
1¼ tsp. baking soda
1 tsp. salt
1⅓ cups whole milk
Confectioners' sugar or favorite frosting

1. In a bowl, cream butter and sugar until light and fluffy, 5-7 minutes. Add the eggs, 1 at a time, beating well after each addition.
2. Combine flour, cocoa, baking soda and salt; add to creamed mixture alternately with milk, beating until smooth after each addition. Pour batter into a greased and floured 13x9-in. baking pan.
3. Bake at 350° until a toothpick inserted in center comes out clean, 35-40 minutes. Cool on a wire rack. When cake is cool, dust with confectioners' sugar or top with your favorite frosting.

1 piece: 257 cal., 10g fat (6g sat. fat), 67mg chol., 368mg sod., 38g carb. (23g sugars, 1g fiber), 4g pro.

TEST KITCHEN TIP
To ensure a tender and lump-free cake, take the extra step and sift together your flour, cocoa, baking soda and salt. If you don't have a sifter, shake the ingredients through a mesh strainer.

MAKE AHEAD

NUTTY PIE-CRUST COOKIES

I like Italian cream cake, so I used it as inspiration for this cookie recipe. The splash of orange liqueur in the filling makes it special.

—Sonji McCarty-Onezine, Beaumont, TX

Prep: 15 min. + chilling
Bake: 10 min./batch + cooling
Makes: about 3 dozen

1	cup butter, softened
1¾	cups all-purpose flour
¼	cup confectioners' sugar
⅛	tsp. salt
⅓	cup heavy whipping cream

FILLING

½	cup finely chopped pecans, toasted
½	cup sweetened shredded coconut, toasted
½	cup butter, softened
½	cup cream cheese, softened
⅛	tsp. salt
2	tsp. orange liqueur, optional
¾	cup confectioners' sugar

1. In a large bowl, beat the butter, flour, confectioners' sugar and salt until crumbly. Beat in cream. Divide dough in half. Shape each into a disk; wrap and refrigerate for 30 minutes or until firm enough to roll.

2. Preheat oven to 350°. On a lightly floured surface, roll each portion of dough to ¼-in. thickness. Cut with a floured 1½-in. round cookie cutter. Place circles 1 in. apart on ungreased baking sheets.

3. Bake 10-12 minutes or until edges begin to brown. Cool on pans 2 minutes. Remove to wire racks to cool completely.

4. For filling, place pecans and coconut in a small bowl; toss to combine. Reserve ½ cup coconut mixture. In another bowl, beat the butter, cream cheese, salt and liqueur, optional, until creamy. Gradually beat in confectioners' sugar until smooth. Fold in coconut mixture. Spread over the bottoms of half of the cookies; cover with remaining cookies. Place reserved coconut mixture in a shallow bowl. Roll sides of the cookies in the mixture.

Freeze option: Transfer wrapped disks to a resealable container; freeze. To use, thaw dough in the refrigerator until soft enough to roll. Prepare, bake and fill the cookies as directed.

1 sandwich cookie: 120 cal., 10g fat (6g sat. fat), 24mg chol., 79mg sod., 8g carb. (3g sugars, 0 fiber), 1g pro.

1. Preheat the oven to 350°. Grease a 15x10x1-in. baking pan.
2. In a small bowl, combine the zucchini, buttermilk, lemon zest and lemon juice; toss to combine. In a large bowl, cream butter and sugar until light and fluffy, 5-7 minutes. Beat in eggs, 1 at a time. In another bowl, whisk 3¼ cups flour, baking soda and salt; gradually add to the creamed mixture alternately with zucchini mixture, mixing well after each addition. Toss berries with remaining flour; fold into the batter.
3. Transfer the batter to prepared pan, spreading evenly (pan will be full). Bake 30-35 minutes or until light golden brown and a toothpick inserted in center comes out clean. Cool completely in the pan on a wire rack.
4. In a small bowl, mix glaze ingredients until smooth; spread over top. Let stand until set.

Note: If using frozen blueberries, mix in without thawing to avoid discoloring the batter.

1 piece: 270 cal., 8g fat (5g sat. fat), 36mg chol., 197mg sod., 47g carb. (33g sugars, 1g fiber), 3g pro.

★ ★ ★ ★ ★ **READER REVIEW**

"My husband has diabetes, so I substitute Truvia Cane Sugar Blend and follow the substitution measurements. The recipe still comes out excellent. I don't tell guests and they still ask to take some 'to go.' Family favorite!"

—**LYNNECARR** TASTEOFHOME.COM

BLUEBERRY ZUCCHINI SQUARES

I saw a bar recipe using apple and lemon zest on a muffin mix box. I tried it from scratch with shredded zucchini and fresh blueberries instead of the apple. It's a nifty combo.

—Shelly Bevington, Hermiston, OR

Prep: 30 min. • **Bake:** 30 min. + cooling
Makes: 2 dozen

- 2 cups shredded zucchini (do not pack)
- ½ cup buttermilk
- 1 Tbsp. grated lemon zest
- 3 Tbsp. lemon juice
- 1 cup butter, softened
- 2½ cups sugar
- 2 large eggs, room temperature
- 3¼ cups plus 2 Tbsp. all-purpose flour, divided
- 1 tsp. baking soda
- ½ tsp. salt
- 2 cups fresh or frozen blueberries

GLAZE
- 2 cups confectioners' sugar
- ¼ cup buttermilk
- 1 Tbsp. grated lemon zest
- 2 tsp. lemon juice
- ⅛ tsp. salt

MARSHMALLOW-ALMOND KEY LIME PIE

Summer is peak season for Key limes—a must for this pie's distinctive sweet-tart flavor. Unlike other Key lime pies, mine has a smooth marshmallow layer on top. This makes it stand out as a crowd favorite.
—Judy Castranova, New Bern, NC

- -

Prep: 40 min. • **Bake:** 15 min. + chilling
Makes: 8 servings

- 1 cup all-purpose flour
- 3 Tbsp. brown sugar
- 1 cup slivered almonds, toasted, divided
- ¼ cup butter, melted
- 1 Tbsp. honey
- 1 pkg. (8 oz.) cream cheese, softened, divided
- 1 can (14 oz.) sweetened condensed milk
- 1 Tbsp. grated Key lime peel
- ½ cup Key lime juice
   Dash salt
- 1 large egg yolk
- 1¾ cups miniature marshmallows
- 4½ tsp. butter
- ½ cup heavy whipping cream

1. Preheat oven to 350°. Place the flour, brown sugar and ½ cup almonds in a food processor; process until almonds are finely chopped. Add melted butter and honey; process until crumbly. Press onto bottom and up side of a greased 9-in. pie plate. Bake until lightly browned, 8-10 minutes. Cool on a wire rack.

2. In a large bowl, beat 5 oz. cream cheese, milk, lime peel, lime juice and salt until blended. Add egg yolk; beat on low speed just until combined. Pour into crust. Bake until center is almost set, 15-20 minutes. Cool on a wire rack.

3. Meanwhile, place the marshmallows and butter in a small heavy saucepan; cook and stir over medium-low heat until melted. Transfer to a large bowl; beat in remaining cream cheese until blended. Beat in cream. Refrigerate, covered, until cold.

4. Beat chilled marshmallow mixture until light and fluffy. Spread over pie; sprinkle with remaining almonds. Refrigerate until serving.

Note: To toast nuts, bake in a shallow pan in a 350° oven for 5-10 minutes or cook in a skillet over low heat until lightly browned, stirring occasionally.

1 piece: 587 cal., 35g fat (18g sat. fat), 115mg chol., 235mg sod., 60g carb. (42g sugars, 2g fiber), 12g pro.

PINK LEMONADE STAND CAKE

If you love a moist and creamy cake, this one's for you. The lemon juice and lemonade give the layers a tangy, citrusy touch, and the cream cheese frosting with sprinkles makes it extra pretty.
—Lauren McAnelly, Des Moines, IA

Prep: 50 min. • **Bake:** 20 min. + cooling
Makes: 12 servings

- 1 cup buttermilk
- 2 Tbsp. lemon juice
- 2 Tbsp. seedless strawberry jam, warmed
- 2 Tbsp. thawed pink lemonade concentrate
- 2 Tbsp. grenadine syrup
- 1 cup unsalted butter, softened
- 1¼ cups sugar
- 3 Tbsp. grated lemon zest
- 4 large eggs, room temperature
- ½ tsp. vanilla extract
- 2½ cups all-purpose flour
- 1 tsp. baking powder
- ½ tsp. baking soda
- ½ tsp. salt

FROSTING
- 1 cup unsalted butter, softened
- 1 pkg. (8 oz.) cream cheese, softened
- 1 Tbsp. grated lemon zest
- 4 cups confectioners' sugar
- ⅓ cup plus 3 Tbsp. thawed pink lemonade concentrate, divided
  Pink sprinkles

1. Preheat oven to 350°. Line bottoms of 3 greased 8-in. round baking pans with parchment; grease parchment.
2. In a small bowl, whisk the first 5 ingredients until blended. In a large bowl, cream butter, sugar and lemon zest until light and fluffy, 5-7 minutes. Add the eggs, 1 at a time, beating well after each addition. Beat in vanilla. In another bowl, whisk flour, baking powder, baking soda and salt; add to creamed mixture alternately with buttermilk mixture, beating well after each addition.
3. Transfer batter to prepared pans. Bake until a toothpick inserted in center comes out clean, 20-24 minutes. Cool in pans for 10 minutes before removing to wire racks; remove parchment. Cool completely.
4. For frosting, in a large bowl, beat butter, cream cheese and lemon zest until smooth. Gradually beat in confectioners' sugar and ⅓ cup lemonade concentrate. If necessary, refrigerate until spreadable, up to 1 hour.
5. Place 1 cake layer on a serving plate. Brush 1 Tbsp. lemonade concentrate over cake; spread with ½ cup frosting. Repeat layers. Top with remaining cake layer; brush remaining lemonade concentrate over top. Spread remaining frosting over top and sides of cake.
6. Decorate with sprinkles. Refrigerate cake until serving.
Note: To substitute for each cup of buttermilk, use 1 Tbsp. white vinegar or lemon juice plus enough milk to measure 1 cup. Stir, then let stand 5 min. Or, use 1 cup plain yogurt or 1¾ tsp. cream of tartar plus 1 cup milk.
1 piece: 732 cal., 39g fat (24g sat. fat), 172mg chol., 291mg sod., 91g carb. (68g sugars, 1g fiber), 7g pro.

TEST KITCHEN TIP
If desired, add a few drops of red food coloring to the cake batter and/or frosting to make it a pretty pink masterpiece.

BERRY-PATCH BROWNIE PIZZA

I just love the combination of fruit, almonds and chocolate that makes this brownie so distinctive. The fruit lightens the chocolate a bit and makes it feel as though you're eating something both decadent and healthy.
—Sue Kauffman, Columbia City, IN

Prep: 20 min. + chilling
Bake: 15 min. + cooling
Makes: 12 servings

- 1 pkg. fudge brownie mix (13x9-in. pan size)
- ⅓ cup chopped unblanched almonds
- 1 tsp. almond extract

TOPPING
- 1 pkg. (8 oz.) cream cheese, softened
- 1 Tbsp. sugar
- 1 tsp. vanilla extract
- ½ tsp. grated lemon zest
- 2 cups whipped topping
  Assorted fresh berries
  Optional: Fresh mint leaves and coarse sugar

1. Preheat oven to 375°. Prepare brownie batter according to package directions for fudgelike brownies, adding almonds and almond extract. Spread into a greased 14-in. pizza pan.
2. Bake until a toothpick inserted in center comes out clean, 15-18 minutes. Cool crust completely on a wire rack.
3. Beat first 4 topping ingredients until smooth; fold in whipped topping. Spread mixture over crust to within ½ in. of edge; refrigerate, loosely covered, 2 hours.
4. To serve, cut into 12 pieces; top with berries of choice. If desired, top with mint and sprinkle with coarse sugar.
1 piece: 404 cal., 26g fat (8g sat. fat), 51mg chol., 240mg sod., 39g carb. (26g sugars, 2g fiber), 5g pro.

WATERMELON CUPCAKES

My granddaughter was inspired by all of her mommy's flavored syrups, so we came up with this watermelon cupcake. If you have watermelon flavoring, it can replace some of the lemon-lime soda in the cake batter and frosting. But the gelatin adds a lot of watermelon flavor on its own. If you are not going to pipe the frosting, you can reduce the amount you make by half.
—Elizabeth Bramkamp, Gig Harbor, WA

Prep: 30 min. • **Bake:** 20 min. + cooling
Makes: 2 dozen

- 1 pkg. white cake mix (regular size)
- 1 cup lemon-lime soda
- 3 large egg whites, room temperature
- ¼ cup canola oil
- 1 pkg. (3 oz.) watermelon gelatin
- 2 drops watermelon flavoring, optional

FROSTING
- 2 cups butter, softened
- 6 cups confectioners' sugar
- 1 pkg. (3 oz.) watermelon gelatin
- 5 to 6 Tbsp. lemon-lime soda
- 15 drops red food coloring
- 3 Tbsp. miniature semisweet chocolate chips

1. Preheat oven to 350°. Line 24 muffin cups with paper liners. In a large bowl, combine the cake mix, soda, egg whites, oil, gelatin and, if desired, watermelon flavoring; beat on low speed 30 seconds. Beat on medium speed 2 minutes. Fill prepared cups three-fourths full. . Bake until a toothpick inserted in the center comes out clean, 18-21 minutes. Cool in pans 10 minutes before removing to wire racks to cool completely.
2. For frosting, in a large bowl, combine butter, confectioners' sugar, gelatin, soda and food coloring; beat until smooth. Frost cupcakes. Sprinkle with chocolate chips. Store in the refrigerator.
1 cupcake: 385 cal., 19g fat (11g sat. fat), 41mg chol., 282mg sod., 54g carb. (46g sugars, 1g fiber), 2g pro.

SWEET POTATO DESSERT SQUARES

I prepare sweet potatoes every week for my family, mostly as a side dish. But I've also found that they make desserts even more delightful. These moist, rich squares have a great pecan crunch.
—Betty Janway, Ruston, LA

Prep: 15 min. • **Bake:** 1 hour + cooling
Makes: 16 servings

- 1 pkg. yellow cake mix (regular size), divided
- ½ cup butter, melted
- 1 large egg, room temperature, lightly beaten

FILLING
- 3 cups cold mashed sweet potatoes (without added milk or butter)
- ⅔ cup 2% milk
- ½ cup packed brown sugar
- 2 large eggs, lightly beaten
- 1 Tbsp. pumpkin pie spice

TOPPING
- 6 Tbsp. cold butter
- 1 cup chopped pecans
- ¼ cup sugar
- 1 tsp. ground cinnamon
  Optional: Whipped cream and pecan halves

1. Set aside ¾ cup of the cake mix. Combine the remaining mix with butter and egg until crumbly; spread into a greased 13x9-in. baking pan. Whisk the filling ingredients until smooth; pour over crust.
2. For topping, cut butter into the reserved cake mix until crumbly. Stir in pecans, sugar and cinnamon; sprinkle over the filling.
3. Bake at 350° for 60-65 minutes or until a knife inserted in the center comes out clean. Cool. Garnish with whipped cream and pecan halves if desired.
1 serving: 399 cal., 20g fat (8g sat. fat), 68mg chol., 332mg sod., 52g carb. (32g sugars, 3g fiber), 5g pro.

PEANUT BUTTER FUDGE

This delicious fudge is one of my favorite "never-fail" recipes. You have to love its simplicity.
—Eleanore Peterson, Fort Atkinson, WI

Prep: 10 min. + chilling • **Makes:** 64 pieces

- 1 lb. white candy coating, chopped
- 1 cup creamy peanut butter
- 1 cup coarsely chopped walnuts, optional

Melt the candy coating in a saucepan over medium-low heat, stirring constantly until smooth. Remove from the heat; stir in peanut butter and, if desired, walnuts. Spread into a greased 8-in. square pan. Chill until firm. Cut into 1-in. squares.
1 piece: 62 cal., 4g fat (2g sat. fat), 0 chol., 17mg sod., 6g carb. (5g sugars, 0 fiber), 1g pro.

TEST KITCHEN TIP
You'll generally find candy coating in the cake decorating section of your market. Almond bark also would work.

MINT CHOCOLATE CHEESECAKE

I created this mint chocolate cheesecake for our high school's annual fundraiser. We were told that it brought a hefty price and was one of the first desserts to go! The cookie pieces can be stirred into the batter instead of being added in a layer. Keep the pieces fairly small or they have a tendency to rise to the top.
—Sue Gronholz, Beaver Dam, WI

- -

Prep: 20 min. • **Bake:** 1¼ hours + chilling
Makes: 16 pieces

- 1 **cup Oreo cookie crumbs**
- 3 **Tbsp. sugar**
- 2 **Tbsp. butter, melted**

FILLING
- 4 **pkg. (8 oz. each) cream cheese, softened**
- 1 **cup sugar**
- 1 **cup white baking chips, melted and cooled**
- 6 **Tbsp. creme de menthe**
- ¼ **cup all-purpose flour**
- 2 **Tbsp. creme de cacao**
- ½ **tsp. peppermint extract**
- 4 **large eggs, room temperature, lightly beaten**
- 1 **cup coarsely crushed Oreo cookies (about 10 cookies)**

GANACHE
- ¾ **cup semisweet chocolate chips**
- 6 **Tbsp. heavy whipping cream**

1. Preheat oven to 325°. Place a greased 9-in. springform pan on a double thickness of heavy-duty foil (about 18 in. square). Wrap foil securely around pan. In a small bowl, mix cookie crumbs and sugar; stir in butter. Press onto bottom of prepared pan.
2. In a large bowl, beat cream cheese and sugar until smooth. Beat in cooled chips, creme de menthe, flour, creme de cacao and extract. Add eggs; beat on low speed just until blended. Pour half the batter over crust; sprinkle with the crushed Oreos.

Carefully spoon remaining batter over the top. Place springform pan in a larger baking pan; add 1 in. hot water to the larger pan.
3. Bake until center is just set and the top appears dull, 75-80 minutes. Remove the springform pan from water bath. Cool the cheesecake on a wire rack for 10 minutes. Loosen edge of cake from pan with a knife; remove foil. Cool 1 hour longer. Refrigerate the cheesecake overnight, covering when completely cooled.

4. Remove rim from pan. Place chocolate chips in a small bowl. In a small saucepan, bring cream just to a boil. Pour over the chocolate; stir with a whisk until smooth. Spread over cheesecake.
1 piece: 518 cal., 33g fat (18g sat. fat), 116mg chol., 296mg sod., 46g carb. (38g sugars, 1g fiber), 7g pro.

CITRUS POKE CAKE

This old-fashioned citrus cake tastes even better the day after it is made. It is perfect for picnics or other gatherings because it transports easily and tastes wonderful room temperature or chilled.
—Judi Stowell, West Kelowna, BC

- -

Prep: 25 min. • **Bake:** 20 min.
Makes: 15 servings

1	cup 2% milk
2	Tbsp. white vinegar
½	cup butter, softened
1⅔	cups sugar, divided
1	large egg, room temperature
2	cups all-purpose flour
2	tsp. baking powder
1	tsp. baking soda
⅛	tsp. salt
⅔	cup raisins
⅔	cup sweetened shredded coconut or chopped walnuts
1	Tbsp. grated orange zest
2	tsp. grated lemon zest
½	cup orange juice
3	Tbsp. lemon juice

1. Preheat oven to 350°. Grease and flour a 13x9-in. baking pan. In a small bowl, mix the milk and vinegar; let stand 5 minutes.

2. In a large bowl, cream butter and 1 cup sugar until light and fluffy, 5-7 minutes. Beat in milk mixture and egg. In another bowl, whisk flour, baking powder, baking soda and salt; gradually add to creamed mixture. Stir in raisins, coconut and orange and lemon zests. Pour batter into prepared pan. Bake 20-25 minutes or until a toothpick inserted in center comes out clean.

3. Meanwhile, in a small saucepan, bring juices and remaining sugar to a boil. Reduce heat; cook and stir until sugar is dissolved. Remove cake from oven; place on a wire rack. Poke holes in warm cake with a skewer or chopstick. Pour sugar mixture evenly over cake.

1 piece: 259 cal., 8g fat (6g sat. fat), 30mg chol., 241mg sod., 44g carb. (30g sugars, 1g fiber), 3g pro.

CHOCOLATE MARSHMALLOW PEANUT BUTTER SQUARES

I combined a couple of recipes to create crunchy, chocolaty bars that burst with peanut butter flavor, marshmallows and pretzel pieces. These treats could also pass for fudge!
—Dawn E. Lowenstein, Huntingdon Valley, PA

Prep: 15 min. • **Cook:** 5 min. + chilling
Makes: 5 dozen

- 1 can (14 oz.) sweetened condensed milk
- 1 pkg. (11 oz.) peanut butter and milk chocolate chips
- ½ cup milk chocolate chips
- ½ cup creamy peanut butter
- 1 tsp. vanilla extract
- 1½ cups miniature marshmallows
- 1 cup broken miniature pretzels
- 1 cup Rice Krispies

1. Place first 5 ingredients in a large heavy saucepan; cook and stir over low heat until smooth and blended, about 5 minutes (mixture will be very thick). Remove from heat; stir in remaining ingredients. Spread into a greased 13x9-in. pan.

2. Refrigerate, covered, until firm, about 4 hours. Cut into squares. Store in an airtight container in the refrigerator.

1 square: 85 cal., 4g fat (2g sat. fat), 3mg chol., 50mg sod., 12g carb. (8g sugars, 0 fiber), 1g pro.

TEST KITCHEN TIPS

- For easier cutting, line your pan with greased foil, letting the ends extend up the sides. This makes it simple to pull the candy out and cut even pieces without scratching your pan.
- For a rocky-road-inspired look, sprinkle the top with chopped peanuts.

NECTARINE PLUM COBBLER

I live in northern Manitoba, where fresh, juicy nectarines and plums are usually available only at summer's end. I make the fruit filling and freeze it for use all winter. My family really enjoys this recipe, and it's wonderful topped with vanilla ice cream.
—Darlene Jackson, The Pas, MB

Prep: 30 min. + cooling • **Bake:** 30 min.
Makes: 12 servings

1¼	cups sugar, divided
2	Tbsp. cornstarch
¾	cup unsweetened apple juice
5	cups sliced peeled fresh plums
5	cups sliced peeled nectarines or peaches
2½	cups all-purpose flour
3	tsp. baking powder
½	tsp. baking soda
½	tsp. salt
½	cup cold butter
1½	cups buttermilk
	Vanilla ice cream, optional

1. Preheat oven to 375°. In a large saucepan, combine ¾ cup sugar and the cornstarch. Gradually stir in apple juice until smooth. Stir in the plums and nectarines. Cook and stir until the mixture comes to a boil; cook 1-2 minutes longer or until thickened and bubbly. Reduce heat; simmer, uncovered, for 5 minutes.
2. Remove from heat; cool for 10 minutes. Pour into a greased 13x9-in. baking dish.
3. In a large bowl, whisk the flour, baking powder, baking soda, salt and remaining ½ cup sugar. Cut in butter until crumbly. Make a well in the center; stir in buttermilk just until a soft dough forms. Drop dough by tablespoonfuls over fruit mixture. Bake until golden brown, 30-35 minutes. Serve warm, with ice cream if desired.
1 serving: 333 cal., 9g fat (5g sat. fat), 22mg chol., 361mg sod., 61g carb. (36g sugars, 3g fiber), 5g pro.

RHUBARB UPSIDE-DOWN CAKE

I've baked this cake every spring for many years, and my family loves it! At potlucks it gets eaten up quickly, even by folks who don't normally go for rhubarb. Use your own fresh rhubarb, check out a farmers market or find a neighbor who will trade stalks for the recipe!
—Helen Breman, Mattydale, NY

Prep: 20 min. • **Bake:** 35 min.
Makes: 10 servings

3	cups sliced fresh or frozen rhubarb
1	cup sugar
2	Tbsp. all-purpose flour
¼	tsp. ground nutmeg
¼	cup butter, melted

BATTER

¼	cup butter, melted
¾	cup sugar
1	large egg, room temperature
1½	cups all-purpose flour
2	tsp. baking powder
½	tsp. ground nutmeg
¼	tsp. salt
⅔	cup 2% milk
	Sweetened whipped cream, optional

1. Place the rhubarb in a greased 10-in. cast-iron or other heavy ovenproof skillet. Combine sugar, flour and nutmeg; sprinkle over rhubarb. Drizzle with butter; set aside. For batter, in a large bowl, beat the butter and sugar until blended. Beat in the egg. Combine the flour, baking powder, nutmeg and salt. Gradually add to the egg mixture alternately with milk, beating well after each addition.
2. Spread over rhubarb mixture. Bake at 350° until a toothpick inserted in the center comes out clean, about 35 minutes. Loosen edge immediately and invert onto a serving dish. Serve cake warm. If desired, top with whipped cream.
1 piece: 316 cal., 10g fat (6g sat. fat), 48mg chol., 248mg sod., 53g carb. (36g sugars, 1g fiber), 4g pro.

FRUIT & ALMOND BITES

With big handfuls of dried apricots, cherries, almonds and pistachios, these are some seriously tasty and satisfying no-bake treats. You can take them anywhere.
—Donna Pochoday-Stelmach, Morristown, NJ

- -

Prep: 40 min. + chilling
Makes: about 4 dozen

- 3¾ **cups sliced almonds, divided**
- ¼ **tsp. almond extract**
- ¼ **cup honey**
- 2 **cups finely chopped dried apricots**
- 1 **cup finely chopped dried cherries or cranberries**
- 1 **cup finely chopped pistachios, toasted**

1. Place 1¼ cups almonds in a food processor; pulse until finely chopped. Remove the almonds to a shallow bowl; reserve for coating.
2. Add remaining 2½ cups almonds to food processor; pulse until finely chopped. Add extract. While processing, gradually add the honey. Remove to a large bowl; stir in apricots and cherries. Divide mixture into 6 portions; shape each into a ½-in.-thick roll. Wrap and refrigerate until firm, about 1 hour.
3. Unwrap and cut rolls into 1½-in. pieces. Roll half the pieces in reserved almonds, pressing gently to adhere. Roll remaining half in pistachios. If desired, wrap each piece individually in waxed paper, twisting ends to close. Store in airtight containers, layered between waxed paper if pieces are unwrapped.
Note: To toast nuts, bake in a shallow pan in a 350° oven for 5-10 minutes or cook in a skillet over low heat until lightly browned, stirring occasionally.
1 piece: 86 cal., 5g fat (0 sat. fat), 0 chol., 15mg sod., 10g carb. (7g sugars, 2g fiber), 2g pro. **Diabetic exchanges:** 1 fat, ½ starch.

HONEY-PEANUT BUTTER COOKIES

It's not unusual for my husband to request these cookies by name. You'll love 'em.
—Lucile Proctor, Panguitch, UT

- -

Prep: 15 min. • **Bake:** 10 min./batch
Makes: 5 dozen

- ½ **cup shortening**
- 1 **cup creamy peanut butter**
- 1 **cup honey**
- 2 **large eggs, room temperature, lightly beaten**
- 3 **cups all-purpose flour**
- 1 **cup sugar**
- 1½ **tsp. baking soda**
- 1 **tsp. baking powder**
- ½ **tsp. salt**

1. Preheat oven to 350°. In a bowl, mix the shortening, peanut butter and honey. Add eggs; mix well. Combine flour, sugar, baking soda, baking powder and salt; add to peanut butter mixture and mix well.
2. Roll dough into 1-1½-in. balls and place on ungreased baking sheets. Flatten balls with a fork dipped in flour. Bake until set, 8-10 minutes. Remove to wire racks to cool.
1 cookie: 95 cal., 4g fat (1g sat. fat), 6mg chol., 80mg sod., 14g carb. (8g sugars, 0 fiber), 2g pro.

TOPPING
- ½ cup sugar
- ½ cup all-purpose flour
- ¼ cup butter, melted
- ½ tsp. ground cinnamon
  Optional: Whipped cream and additional raspberries

1. Preheat oven to 350°. In a large bowl, cream butter and sugar until light and fluffy, 5-7 minutes. Add eggs and egg yolk, 1 at a time, beating well after each addition. Beat in vanilla. In another bowl, whisk the flour, baking powder and salt; add to the creamed mixture alternately with buttermilk, beating well after each addition. Transfer mixture to a greased 13x9-in. baking dish.

2. In a bowl, combine 4 cups raspberries and sugar; sprinkle over batter. Drop lemon curd by tablespoonfuls over raspberries. Combine topping ingredients; sprinkle over batter. Bake until the fruit is bubbly and a toothpick inserted into the buckle comes out clean, 45-50 minutes. Let buckle stand 20 minutes before serving. If desired, serve with whipped cream and more raspberries.

Note: To substitute for each cup of buttermilk, use 1 Tbsp. white vinegar or lemon juice plus enough milk to measure 1 cup. Stir, then let stand 5 min. Or, use 1 cup plain yogurt or 1¾ tsp. cream of tartar plus 1 cup milk.

1 piece: 335 cal., 12g fat (7g sat. fat), 76mg chol., 206mg sod., 54g carb. (38g sugars, 3g fiber), 4g pro.

LEMON RASPBERRY BUCKLE

I've given a fresh summery twist to the classic blueberry buckle everyone loves by using raspberries (my favorite) instead of blueberries and adding sweet and tart lemon curd. This berry buckle cake recipe tastes great with vanilla ice cream!

—Jenna Fleming, Lowville, NY

Prep: 30 min. • **Bake:** 45 min. + standing
Makes: 15 servings

- ½ cup butter, softened
- 1 cup sugar
- 2 large eggs plus 1 large egg yolk, room temperature
- 1 tsp. vanilla extract
- 1½ cups all-purpose flour
- 1½ tsp. baking powder
- ¼ tsp. salt
- ⅔ cup buttermilk
- 4 cups fresh raspberries
- ¼ cup sugar
- 1 jar (10 oz.) lemon curd

TEST KITCHEN TIP
Buckle gets its name from the heavy streusel topping that weighs the batter down while the dessert bakes, causing the top of the cake to buckle in spots.

MINI S'MORES

Want to sink your teeth into s'mores all year long? Here's the answer! Just combine marshmallow creme, chocolate and graham crackers for an awesome bite.
—Stephanie Tewell, Elizabeth, IL

- -

Prep: 50 min. + standing • **Cook:** 5 min.
Makes: about 4 dozen

- 2 **cups milk chocolate chips**
- ½ **cup heavy whipping cream**
- 1 **pkg. (14.4 oz.) graham crackers, quartered**
- 1 **cup marshmallow creme**
- 2 **cartons (7 oz. each) milk chocolate for dipping**

1. Place chocolate chips in a small bowl. In a small saucepan, bring cream just to a boil. Pour over chocolate; stir with a whisk until smooth. Cool to room temperature or until mixture reaches a spreading consistency, about 10 minutes.

2. Spread chocolate mixture over half of the graham crackers. Spread the marshmallow creme over remaining graham crackers; place over chocolate-covered crackers, pressing to adhere.

3. Melt the dipping chocolate according to package directions. Dip each s'more halfway into dipping chocolate; allow the excess to drip off. Place on waxed paper-lined baking sheets; let stand until dipping chocolate is set. Store s'mores in an airtight container in the refrigerator.

1 piece: 145 cal., 7g fat (4g sat. fat), 5mg chol., 66mg sod., 19g carb. (13g sugars, 1g fiber), 2g pro.

PEANUT BUTTER PRETZEL BARS

My secret to these rich no-bake bites? Pretzels in the crust. They add a salty crunch to the classic peanut butter and chocolate pairing.
—Jennifer Beckman, Falls Church, VA

Prep: 15 min. + chilling • **Makes:** 4 dozen

- 1 pkg. (16 oz.) miniature pretzels
- 1½ cups butter, melted
- 1½ cups peanut butter
- 3 cups confectioners' sugar
- 2 cups semisweet chocolate chips
- 1 Tbsp. shortening

1. Line a 13x9-in. baking pan with foil; let the ends extend up the sides. Set aside 1½ cups pretzels for topping. In a food processor, pulse remaining pretzels until fine crumbs form. In a large bowl, mix butter, peanut butter, confectioners' sugar and pretzel crumbs.
2. Press into prepared pan. In a microwave, melt chocolate chips and shortening; stir until smooth. Spread over peanut butter layer. Break reserved pretzels and sprinkle over top; press down gently. Refrigerate, covered, until set, about 1 hour. Lifting with foil, remove from pan. Cut into bars.
1 piece: 201 cal., 13g fat (6g sat. fat), 15mg chol., 233mg sod., 22g carb. (12g sugars, 1g fiber), 3g pro.

★ ★ ★ ★ ★ **READER REVIEW**

"I made these the night before a Memorial Day cookout. Before I could get the pan in the fridge to harden, both daughters and my grandson had eaten four large pieces!"

—**KBBRADFORD** TASTEOFHOME.COM

PINEAPPLE PRETZEL FLUFF

I often bring this salad to potlucks, and everyone goes crazy for the sweet and crunchy combination. Be sure to add the pretzel mixture right before serving to keep it crispy.
—Beth Olby, Ashland, WI

Prep: 15 min. + chilling
Bake: 10 min. + cooling
Makes: 12 servings

- 1 cup coarsely crushed pretzels
- ½ cup butter, melted
- 1 cup sugar, divided
- 1 pkg. (8 oz.) cream cheese, softened
- 1 can (20 oz.) unsweetened crushed pineapple, drained
- 1 carton (12 oz.) frozen whipped topping, thawed

1. Preheat oven to 400°. Mix pretzels, melted butter and ½ cup sugar. Press into a 13x9-in. pan. Bake 7 minutes. Cool completely on a wire rack.
2. Meanwhile, in a large bowl, beat cream cheese and remaining sugar until creamy. Fold in pineapple and whipped topping; refrigerate, covered, until serving.
3. To serve, break pretzel mixture into small pieces. Stir into pineapple mixture.
½ cup: 334 cal., 19g fat (13g sat. fat), 39mg chol., 230mg sod., 37g carb. (31g sugars, 1g fiber), 2g pro.

STRAWBERRY LADYFINGER ICEBOX CAKE

This cake is inventive and yet familiar. Be sure to use a springform pan so you can easily remove the cake. If it breaks while you're transferring it to the serving plate, just push the pieces back together, pressing gently.
—Stella Ohanian, Porter Ranch, CA

- -

Prep: 35 min. + chilling • **Makes:** 12 servings

6	cups fresh strawberries, sliced
4	tsp. balsamic vinegar
38	crisp ladyfinger cookies (about 23 oz.)
2	cartons (8 oz. each) mascarpone cheese, softened
2	cups heavy whipping cream
½	cup sugar
2	tsp. vanilla extract
12	fresh strawberries

1. In a large bowl, mix strawberries and vinegar. Let stand 30 minutes. Line bottom of a 9-in. ungreased springform pan with parchment. Trim ½ in. off 1 end of each of 22 ladyfingers. Arrange the ladyfingers, rounded sides up, along sides of prepared pan. Line bottom of pan with 8 ladyfingers, trimming to fit if necessary.

2. In a large bowl, beat mascarpone cheese on low speed until fluffy. Add cream, sugar and vanilla; beat on medium until stiff peaks form. Spread 1½ cups cheese mixture evenly over cookies. With a slotted spoon, spread half of sliced strawberry mixture over top. Repeat the layers. Layer with the remaining ladyfingers, trimming to fit if necessary. Spread remaining cheese over the top.

3. Carefully cover and refrigerate at least 8 hours or overnight. Remove rim from pan; arrange fresh strawberries over top.

1 piece: 456 cal., 33g fat (19g sat. fat), 120mg chol., 72mg sod., 36g carb. (25g sugars, 2g fiber), 7g pro.

ZUCCHINI WALNUT CAKE

What gardener doesn't have extra zucchini? When it's abundant, I shred and freeze plenty so I have it on hand to bake this moist sheet cake all year long. The cream cheese frosting is yummy, and the even a big pan of cake always goes fast at picnic or potluck. I've made this cake for the last 13 years. It's a winner! I have a friend that started growing zucchini just to make this cake!
—Marie Hoyer, Hodgenville, KY

- -

Prep: 20 min. • **Bake:** 35 min. + cooling
Makes: 24 servings

2	cups shredded zucchini
2	cups sugar
1	cup canola oil
4	large eggs, room temperature
2½	cups all-purpose flour
1½	tsp. ground cinnamon
1	tsp. salt
½	tsp. baking powder
½	tsp. baking soda
½	cup chopped toasted walnuts, optional

FROSTING

3	oz. cream cheese, softened
¼	cup butter, softened
1	Tbsp. 2% milk
1	tsp. vanilla extract
2	cups confectioners' sugar
	Chopped toasted walnuts, optional

1. Preheat oven to 350°. Grease a 13x9-in. baking pan; set aside.

2. In a large bowl, beat the zucchini, sugar, oil and eggs until well blended. Combine flour, cinnamon, salt, baking powder and baking soda; gradually beat into zucchini mixture until blended. Fold in walnuts if desired.

3. Pour into prepared pan. Bake until a toothpick inserted in the center comes out clean, 35-40 minutes. Cool completely on a wire rack.

4. For frosting, in a small bowl, beat the cream cheese, butter, milk and vanilla until smooth. Add confectioners' sugar and mix well. Frost cake. Sprinkle with walnuts if desired. Store in the refrigerator.

1 piece: 275 cal., 13g fat (3g sat. fat), 45mg chol., 174mg sod., 37g carb. (26g sugars, 1g fiber), 3g pro.

TART CRANBERRY CAKE

You can't beat this recipe to showcase true fall flavor. The ruby cranberries stay bright and beautiful, and their tartness is irresistible. I've made this cake many times to share.
—Marilyn Paradis, Woodburn, OR

Prep: 15 min. • **Bake:** 45 min.
Makes: 20 servings

- 3 large eggs, room temperature
- 2 cups sugar
- ¾ cup butter, softened
- 1 tsp. almond extract
- 2 cups all-purpose flour
- 2½ cups fresh or frozen cranberries, thawed
- ⅔ cup chopped pecans
  Optional: Whipped cream and cranberries

1. Preheat oven to 350°. In a large bowl, beat eggs and sugar until slightly thickened and lemon-colored, about 5 minutes. Add the butter and extract; beat 2 minutes. Gradually stir in flour just until combined. Stir in cranberries and pecans. Spread in a greased 13x9-in. baking dish.
2. Bake until a toothpick inserted in the center comes out clean, 45-50 minutes. If desired, serve each piece with whipped cream and a cranberry.
1 piece: 227 cal., 10g fat (5g sat. fat), 46mg chol., 66mg sod., 32g carb. (21g sugars, 1g fiber), 3g pro.

CARROT CAKE

This wonderful recipe dates back to my great-grandmother. You will love the texture the cake gets from pineapple, coconut and, of course, carrots! For lighter appetites or to serve more people, cut it into smaller pieces and place them in pretty cupcake liners.
—Debbie Terenzini-Wilkerson, Lusby, MD

Prep: 20 min. • **Bake:** 50 min.
Makes: 12 servings

- 2 cups all-purpose flour
- 2 cups sugar
- 2 tsp. ground cinnamon
- 1 tsp. baking soda
- ½ tsp. salt
- 3 large eggs, room temperature
- 1½ cups canola oil
- 2 cups finely grated carrots
- 1 tsp. vanilla extract
- 1 cup well-drained crushed pineapple
- 1 cup sweetened shredded coconut
- 1 cup chopped nuts

CREAM CHEESE FROSTING

- 6 oz. cream cheese, softened
- 6 Tbsp. butter, softened
- 3 cups confectioners' sugar
- 1 tsp. vanilla extract
  Additional chopped nuts

1. In a large bowl, combine the flour, sugar, cinnamon, baking soda and salt. Add the eggs, oil, carrots and vanilla; beat until combined. Stir in the pineapple, coconut and nuts.
2. Pour into a greased 13x9-in. baking pan. Bake at 350° for 50-60 minutes or until a toothpick inserted in the center comes out clean. Cool on a wire rack.
3. For frosting, beat cream cheese and butter in a small bowl until fluffy. Add the confectioners' sugar and vanilla; beat until smooth. Frost cake. Sprinkle with additional nuts. Store in the refrigerator.
1 piece: 819 cal., 49g fat (12g sat. fat), 76mg chol., 346mg sod., 91g carb. (72g sugars, 3g fiber), 8g pro.

EASY COCONUT CREAM PIE

This pie has been a favorite dessert for decades. I even made several of these pies to serve a threshing crew of 21 men!
—Vera Moffitt, Oskaloosa, KS

Prep: 20 min. + chilling
Cook: 10 min. + cooling
Makes: 8 servings

- 1 sheet refrigerated pie crust
- ¾ cup sugar
- 3 Tbsp. all-purpose flour
- ⅛ tsp. salt
- 3 cups whole milk
- 3 large eggs, beaten
- 1½ cups sweetened shredded coconut, toasted, divided
- 1 Tbsp. butter
- 1½ tsp. vanilla extract

1. Unroll the crust into a 9-in. pie plate; flute edge. Refrigerate 30 minutes. Preheat the oven to 400°.
2. Line the crust with a double thickness of foil. Fill with pie weights, dried beans or uncooked rice. Bake on a lower oven rack or until edge is golden brown, 15-20 minutes. Remove foil and weights; bake until bottom is golden brown, 3-6 minutes longer. Cool on a wire rack.
3. In a medium saucepan, combine the sugar, flour and salt. Stir in milk; cook and stir over medium-high heat until thickened and bubbly. Reduce heat; cook and stir 2 minutes longer.
4. Remove from the heat; gradually stir about 1 cup of hot mixture into beaten eggs. Return all to saucepan; cook and stir over medium heat until nearly boiling. Reduce heat; cook and stir about 2 minutes more (do not boil). Remove from the heat; stir in 1 cup coconut, butter and vanilla.
5. Pour into crust; sprinkle with remaining coconut. Chill several hours before serving.
1 piece: 376 cal., 18g fat (11g sat. fat), 84mg chol., 249mg sod., 47g carb. (32g sugars, 1g fiber), 7g pro.

PEANUT BUTTER CAKE BARS

These cakelike bars are packed with peanut butter and chocolate chips, and are perfect for any occasion. Kids and adults alike will love the tasty gems.
—Charlotte Ennis, Lake Arthur, NM

Prep: 15 min. • **Bake:** 45 min. + cooling
Makes: 2 dozen

- ⅔ cup butter, softened
- ⅔ cup peanut butter
- 1 cup sugar
- 1 cup packed brown sugar
- 4 large eggs, room temperature
- 2 tsp. vanilla extract
- 2 cups all-purpose flour
- 2 tsp. baking powder
- ½ tsp. salt
- 1 pkg. (11½ oz.) milk chocolate chips

1. Preheat the oven to 350°. In a large bowl, cream the butter, peanut butter, sugar and brown sugar. Add eggs, 1 at a time, beating well after each addition. Beat in the vanilla. Combine the flour, baking powder and salt; gradually add to creamed mixture. Stir in chocolate chips.
2. Spread into a greased 13x9-in. baking pan. Bake until a toothpick inserted in the center comes out clean, 45-50 minutes. Cool on a wire rack. Cut into bars.
1 bar: 277 cal., 14g fat (6g sat. fat), 52mg chol., 178mg sod., 35g carb. (25g sugars, 1g fiber), 5g pro.

TEST KITCHEN TIP
For a gourmet touch, sprinkle the tops of these bars with flaky sea salt after removing from the oven.

BUTTERMILK PECAN PIE

Branch out from the usual pecan pie with a creamy-crunchy version that comes out of the oven golden brown. Big pieces are even better with a generous dollop of whipped cream.
—Kathy Harding, Richmond, MO

- -

Prep: 40 min. • **Bake:** 50 min. + cooling
Makes: 8 servings

       Pastry for single-crust pie (9 in.)
½ cup butter, softened
1¾ cups sugar
3 large eggs
3 Tbsp. all-purpose flour
¼ tsp. salt
1 cup buttermilk
2 tsp. vanilla extract
1 cup chopped pecans
       Sweetened whipped cream, optional

1. Preheat oven to 425°. On a lightly floured surface, roll dough to a ⅛-in.-thick circle; transfer to a 9-in. pie plate. Trim pastry to ½ in. beyond rim of plate; flute edge. Line unpricked pastry with a double thickness of foil. Fill with pie weights, dried beans or uncooked rice.

2. Place on a baking sheet; bake until edge is light golden brown, 15 minutes. Remove foil and weights; bake until bottom is golden brown, 5 minutes longer. Cool on a wire rack. Reduce oven setting to 325°.

3. In a large bowl, beat butter and sugar until blended. Add eggs, 1 at a time, beating well after each addition. Beat in flour and salt. Gradually stir in buttermilk and vanilla.

4. Sprinkle pecans into crust; add filling. Bake until center is set, 50-60 minutes. Cover the top loosely with foil during the last 15 minutes to prevent overbrowning if necessary.

5. Cool completely on a wire rack. If desired, top the pie with whipped cream. Serve or refrigerate within 2 hours.

1 piece: 591 cal., 35g fat (16g sat. fat), 132mg chol., 405mg sod., 65g carb. (47g sugars, 2g fiber), 7g pro.

BLUEBERRY LEMON TRIFLE

A refreshing lemon filling and fresh blueberries give this sunny dessert sensation plenty of color. Don't worry about heating up the oven—this trifle doesn't require baking.
—Ellen Peden, Houston, TX

- -

Prep: 15 min. + chilling • **Makes:** 14 servings

3 cups fresh blueberries, divided
2 cans (15¾ oz. each) lemon pie filling
2 cups lemon yogurt
1 prepared angel food cake (8 to 10 oz.), cut into 1-in. cubes
1 carton (8 oz.) frozen whipped topping, thawed

1. Set aside ¼ cup blueberries for garnish. In a large bowl, combine the pie filling and the yogurt.

2. In a 3½-qt. serving or trifle bowl, layer a third of the cake cubes, lemon mixture and blueberries. Repeat layers twice. Top with whipped topping. Cover bowl and refrigerate for at least 2 hours. Garnish with reserved blueberries.

1 serving: 230 cal., 4g fat (3g sat. fat), 2mg chol., 235mg sod., 44g carb. (27g sugars, 1g fiber), 3g pro.

★ ★ ★ ★ ★ **READER REVIEW**

"This was delicious. I made this for a work celebration right around Memorial Day and added strawberries to make it look patriotic. Everyone loved it. Makes a lot."

RUTHIEBURD TASTEOFHOME.COM

BANANA CRUMB PUDDING
*Friends and family ask me to make my
banana pudding for all occasions.*
—Yvonnia Butner, Pinnacle, NC

Prep: 15 min. • **Cook:** 20 min. + chilling
Makes: 15 servings

- 1   **cup sugar**
- ½   **cup cornstarch**
- 6   **cups 2% milk**
- 5   **large egg yolks**
- ¼   **cup butter, cubed**
- 2   **tsp. vanilla extract**
- 1   **tsp. kosher salt**
- 2   **pkg. (11 oz. each) vanilla wafers**
- 7   **medium bananas, sliced**

TOPPING
- 2   **cups heavy whipping cream**
- 6   **Tbsp. sugar**

1. In a large heavy saucepan, mix sugar and cornstarch. Whisk in milk. Cook and stir over medium heat until thickened and bubbly. Reduce heat to low; cook and stir 2 minutes longer. Remove from heat.
2. In a bowl, whisk a small amount of hot mixture into egg yolks; return all to pan, whisking constantly. Bring to a gentle boil; cook and stir 2 minutes. Remove from heat. Stir in the butter, vanilla and salt. Cool for 15 minutes, stirring occasionally.
3. Reserve 1 banana and 1 cup whole wafers for topping. Crush 2 cups wafers and set aside. In a 13x9-in. baking dish, place a single layer of whole wafers, filling gaps with crushed wafers. Layer with a third of the bananas and pudding. Repeat layers twice. Press waxed paper onto surface of pudding. Refrigerate, covered, overnight.
4. In a bowl, beat heavy cream until it begins to thicken. Add sugar; beat until soft peaks form (do not overmix). Just before serving, remove paper and spread whipped cream over pudding; top with reserved banana and wafers.
¾ cup: 535 cal., 27g fat (13g sat. fat), 121mg chol., 370mg sod., 70g carb. (46g sugars, 1g fiber), 7g pro.

CHOCOLATE HAZELNUT PUDDING TORTE

This recipe is a busy mom's twist on a favorite dessert—tiramisu. The dish is simple to assemble and perfect to make the day before you want to serve it. The hardest thing about this tasty recipe is waiting for it to chill so you can eat it!
—Cheryl Snavely, Hagerstown, MD

Prep: 15 min. + chilling • **Makes:** 8 servings

24 soft ladyfingers, divided
½ cup Nutella, divided
1½ cups half-and-half cream
1 pkg. (3.4 oz.) instant French vanilla
    pudding mix

1 carton (12 oz.) frozen whipped
    topping, thawed
    Grated or shaved chocolate

1. Arrange 12 ladyfingers in an 11x7-in. dish. Spread with half of the Nutella.
2. In a large bowl, whisk cream and pudding mix 2 minutes. Stir in whipped topping. Spread half the mixture over the Nutella. Top with remaining ladyfingers; spread with remaining Nutella and then the remaining pudding mixture. Sprinkle with grated or shaved chocolate. Refrigerate, covered, 8 hours or overnight. Refrigerate leftovers.
1 piece: 390 cal., 18g fat (11g sat. fat), 67mg chol., 347mg sod., 46g carb. (37g sugars, 1g fiber), 5g pro.

BRING IT
This dessert should hold up well even on a hot day. To help keep it cold, place the dish in a large foil pan filled with ice. Replenish ice as necessary. For added insurance on a very hot day, pop the pudding torte into the freezer for several hours to get extra cold. Give it time to come up to temperature at the event.

Birthday Cake
Fudge
page 218

Kids' Simple Favorites

Here are the silly sandwiches, fun pizzas, fancy floats and amazing treats that kids love to make, share and eat. These easy dishes let the good times roll!

CANDY PIZZA HEART

I found this recipe in an old cookbook and changed a few ingredients to suit my family's taste. My children really enjoy this candy pizza. Get the kids to help you spread the toppings.
—Becky Thesman, Enid, OK

Prep: 15 min. + chilling • **Makes:** 1¾ lbs.

- 1½ cups milk chocolate chips
- 1 cup butterscotch chips
- ¾ cup miniature marshmallows
- ¾ cup chopped salted peanuts
- ¾ cup crushed potato chips
- 2 Tbsp. sweetened shredded coconut
- 7 maraschino cherries, halved
- ¼ cup milk chocolate M&M's
- 2 Tbsp. vanilla or white chips
- ½ tsp. shortening

1. Using a pencil, draw a 10-in. heart on waxed paper. Place paper, pencil mark down, on a baking sheet; set aside.
2. In a large microwave-safe bowl, melt chocolate and butterscotch chips; stir until smooth. Stir in marshmallows, peanuts and potato chips. Immediately spread on prepared pan into heart shape. Sprinkle with coconut; top with cherries and M&M's.
3. In a microwave, melt vanilla chips and shortening; stir until smooth. Drizzle over top. Refrigerate until firm, about 1½ hours. Remove the waxed paper. Let stand for 10 minutes at room temperature before cutting.
1 piece: 291 cal., 17g fat (9g sat. fat), 5mg chol., 82mg sod., 31g carb. (15g sugars, 1g fiber), 5g pro.

BACON CHEESEBURGER ROLL-UPS

My husband and I both love these roll-ups. I often serve them with broccoli and cheese. They must be good because this recipe won a first-place prize at the Iowa State Fair!

—Jessica Cain, Des Moines, IA

- -

Prep: 25 min. • **Bake:** 20 min.
Makes: 8 servings

- 1   **lb. ground beef**
- 6   **bacon strips, diced**
- ½   **cup chopped onion**
- 1   **pkg. (8 oz.) Velveeta, cubed**
- 1   **tube (16.3 oz.) large refrigerated buttermilk biscuits**
- 1   **large egg, beaten, optional**
     Sesame seeds, optional
- ½   **cup ketchup**
- ¼   **cup yellow mustard**

1. Preheat oven to 400°. In a large skillet, cook beef, bacon and onion over medium heat until meat is no longer pink, breaking beef into crumbles; drain. Add cheese; cook and stir until melted. Remove from heat.

2. Flatten biscuits into 5-in. circles; top each with ⅓ cup beef mixture. Fold sides and ends over filling, and roll up. Place seam side down on a greased baking sheet. If desired, brush with egg and sprinkle with sesame seeds.

3. Bake until golden brown, 18-20 minutes. In a small bowl, combine ketchup and mustard; serve with roll-ups.

1 roll-up: 429 cal., 24g fat (10g sat. fat), 63mg chol., 1372mg sod., 32g carb. (11g sugars, 1g fiber), 21g pro.

BIRTHDAY CAKE FUDGE

This decadent treat is the perfect thing to make your birthday special. Or prepare it ahead and package it as a surprise gift for a friend.
—Rashanda Cobbins, Milwaukee, WI

- -

Prep: 10 min. + chilling • **Makes:** 64 pieces

- 1 **can (14 oz.) sweetened condensed milk**
- 1½ **cups white baking chips**
- 3 **Tbsp. butter**
- ⅛ **tsp. salt**
- 1½ **cups unprepared Funfetti cake mix**
- 3 **Tbsp. sprinkles**

1. Line an 8-in. square pan with foil or parchment; grease foil lightly. In a large heavy saucepan, cook and stir milk, baking chips, butter and salt over low heat until smooth. Remove from heat; stir in cake mix until dissolved. Spread into prepared pan; top with sprinkles. Refrigerate, covered, until firm, about 2 hours.
2. Using foil, lift fudge out of pan. Remove foil; cut fudge into 1-in. squares. Store in an airtight container in the refrigerator.
1 piece: 59 cal., 2g fat (2g sat. fat), 4mg chol., 47mg sod., 9g carb. (7g sugars, 0 fiber), 1g pro.

CHILI CONEY DOGS

From the youngest kids to the oldest adults, everyone in our family loves these hot dogs. They're so easy to throw together in the morning or even the night before.
—Michele Harris, Vicksburg, MI

Prep: 20 min. • **Cook:** 4 hours
Makes: 8 servings

- 1 lb. lean ground beef (90% lean)
- 1 can (15 oz.) tomato sauce
- ½ cup water
- 2 Tbsp. Worcestershire sauce
- 1 Tbsp. dried minced onion
- ½ tsp. garlic powder
- ½ tsp. ground mustard
- ½ tsp. chili powder
- ½ tsp. pepper
  Dash cayenne pepper
- 8 hot dogs
- 8 hot dog buns, split
  Optional toppings: Shredded cheddar cheese, relish and chopped onion

1. In a large skillet, cook beef over medium heat until no longer pink, 6-8 minutes, breaking into crumbles; drain. Stir in tomato sauce, water, Worcestershire sauce, onion and seasonings.

2. Place hot dogs in a 3-qt. slow cooker; top with beef mixture. Cook, covered, on low 4-5 hours or until heated through. Serve on buns with toppings as desired.

1 chili dog: 371 cal., 20g fat (8g sat. fat), 53mg chol., 992mg sod., 26g carb. (5g sugars, 2g fiber), 21g pro.

TEST KITCHEN TIP
Coney Island dogs originated at the Coney Island boardwalk in Brooklyn, New York, where Nathan Handwerker (yes, that famous Nathan) first sold the meat-topped dogs.

SNAKEWICH WITH VENOM SAUCE

Our Halloween party is so big, I hold it in the street. This sandwich shaped like a snake is tasty and a scary-good centerpiece.

—Suzanne Clark, Phoenix, AZ

- -

Prep: 45 min. + rising
Bake: 20 min. + cooling
Makes: 20 servings

- 2 loaves (1 lb. each) frozen bread dough
- 3 Tbsp. butter, melted
- 2 Tbsp. sesame seeds or poppy seeds
- ¾ cup roasted sweet red peppers, drained
- 1 cup mayonnaise
- ½ cup finely chopped pepperoncini
- 2 garlic cloves, minced
- 1 lb. sliced deli smoked turkey
- 1 lb. sliced deli ham
- ¾ lb. sliced provolone cheese
- 2 large tomatoes, thinly sliced
- 1 medium head iceberg lettuce, thinly sliced
- 2 pretzel sticks or toothpicks
- 2 pickle slices
- 2 ripe olive slices

1. Thaw dough according to package directions. Roll each loaf into a 2-in.-thick log, shaping 1 end of 1 log into a snake head and 1 end of the second log into a rattle.

2. Transfer to greased baking sheets, curving slightly to resemble a snake. Cover with kitchen towels; let rise in a warm place until doubled, about 45 minutes. Preheat oven to 350°.

3. Brush dough with melted butter; sprinkle with sesame seeds. Bake 20-25 minutes or until golden brown. Remove from pans to wire racks to cool completely.

4. Cut a red pepper into a 3-in.-long strip to make a snake tongue; set aside. Finely chop remaining peppers; place in a bowl; stir in mayonnaise, pepperoncini and garlic.

5. On a large cutting board, trim off the plain end of each loaf, leaving head and rattle ends intact. Cut each loaf horizontally in half. Connect bottom halves to make a snake; layer with meat, cheese, tomatoes and 4 cups sliced lettuce. Spread top halves with 1 cup sauce; place tops over lettuce. Insert snake tongue.

6. For grass, arrange remaining lettuce around sandwich. Insert pretzel sticks to attach pickle slices and olives for eyes. Using a serrated knife, cut sandwich into 20 slices; serve with remaining sauce.

1 slice: 346 cal., 18g fat (5g sat. fat), 39mg chol., 897mg sod., 25g carb. (4g sugars, 2g fiber), 18g pro.

★ ★ ★ ★ ★ **READER REVIEW**

"I love to make something special for our Halloween dinner. This sandwich was easy to put together, looked great, and was super delicious. I cut the recipe in half and the snake was still a decent size. Adults and kids all loved it."

EBRAMKAMP TASTEOFHOME.COM

GOBBLER GOODIES

The kids and I had a ball making these tasty turkeys for Thanksgiving one year. The treats would make a fun favor at each place setting on your Thanksgiving table—if your family doesn't gobble them up first!
—Sue Gronholz, Beaver Dam, WI

Prep: 30 min. • **Cook:** 5 min. + cooling
Makes: 28 servings

¼	cup butter, cubed
4	cups miniature marshmallows
6	cups crisp rice cereal
28	chocolate sandwich cookies
1½	cups chocolate frosting
1	pkg. (11 oz.) candy corn
28	malted milk balls
	White candy coating, optional

1. In a large saucepan, melt butter. Add marshmallows; stir over low heat until melted. Stir in cereal. Cool for 10 minutes.

With buttered hands, form cereal mixture into 1½-in. balls. Twist apart sandwich cookies. If desired, remove filling and save for another use. Spread frosting over each cookie half.

2. Place 28 cookie halves under cereal balls to form a base for each turkey. Place 5 pieces of candy corn in a fan pattern on each remaining cookie half; press each half onto a cereal ball to form the tail. Attach remaining candy corn with frosting to form turkey wings. For each head, attach a malted milk ball with frosting; cut white tip off additional candy corn and attach to head with frosting to form beak. If desired, place melted white candy coating in a piping bag fitted with a #1 round tip; pipe onto head to form eyes. Allow to stand until the frosting has set. Store, tightly covered, at room temperature.

1 turkey: 222 cal., 6g fat (2g sat. fat), 0 chol., 125mg sod., 43g carb. (31g sugars, 1g fiber), 1g pro.

MAC & CHEESE SOUP

I came across this recipe a few years ago and made some changes to suit my family's tastes. Because it starts with packaged macaroni and cheese, it's ready in a jiffy.
—Nancy Daugherty, Cortland, OH

Takes: 30 min. • **Makes:** 8 servings (2 qt.)

1	pkg. (14 oz.) deluxe macaroni and cheese dinner mix
9	cups water, divided
1	cup fresh broccoli florets
2	Tbsp. finely chopped onion
1	can (10¾ oz.) condensed cheddar cheese soup, undiluted
2½	cups 2% milk
1	cup chopped fully cooked ham

1. Set aside cheese sauce packet from macaroni and cheese mix. In a large saucepan, bring 8 cups water to a boil. Add macaroni; cook for 8-10 minutes or until tender.

2. Meanwhile, in another large saucepan, bring remaining water to a boil. Add broccoli and onion; cook, uncovered, for 3 minutes. Stir in the soup, milk, ham and contents of cheese sauce packet; heat through. Drain macaroni; stir into soup.

1 cup: 263 cal., 9g fat (4g sat. fat), 28mg chol., 976mg sod., 32g carb. (6g sugars, 2g fiber), 13g pro.

Broccoli Mac & Cheese Soup: Double the broccoli and omit the ham for a meatless option.

WATERMELON SHARK

Take a bite out of summer boredom with this kid-friendly food project.
—*Taste of Home* Test Kitchen

Prep: 1 hour • **Makes:** 32 servings

- 1   large watermelon
- 2   cups seedless red grapes
- 1   medium cantaloupe, peeled, seeded and cubed
- 2   cups fresh blueberries
- 2   medium oranges
- 1   jar (12 oz.) pineapple preserves
      Swedish Fish candies, optional

1. Using a large sharp knife, cut off 1 end of the watermelon so that it stands at an angle. Using a razor blade or small knife, score an opening for the mouth. With knife, cut out and remove mouth. Cut out triangles for teeth; remove rind from the teeth.

2. For shark fin, cut a triangle from removed rind; attach to shark with toothpicks. For eyes, attach 2 grapes with toothpicks.

3. Remove fruit from inside watermelon; cut into cubes. In a large bowl, combine watermelon, cantaloupe, blueberries and remaining grapes. Finely grate peel from oranges and squeeze juice. In a small bowl, mix preserves, orange juice and peel; add to fruit and toss gently.

4. Stand shark on a platter. Fill opening with some of the fruit mixture; add a few Swedish Fish if desired. Serve with remaining fruit.

¾ cup: 129 cal., 1g fat (0 sat. fat), 0 chol., 7mg sod., 30g carb. (28g sugars, 2g fiber), 2g pro. **Diabetic exchanges:** 1½ fruit, ½ starch.

KICKIN' HAWAIIAN PIZZA

Pineapple adds pizazz and honey lends a touch of sweetness to the sauce in this wonderful pepperoni pizza recipe.
—*John Weakland, Lacey, WA*

Prep: 30 min. • **Bake:** 15 min.
Makes: 12 pieces

- 4   plum tomatoes, coarsely chopped
- 1   can (6 oz.) tomato paste
- ¼   cup water
- ¼   cup roasted sweet red peppers
- 1   Tbsp. dried oregano
- 1   Tbsp. honey
- 2   tsp. dried minced garlic
- 2   tsp. paprika
- 1   tsp. salt
- ¼   tsp. crushed red pepper flakes
- 2   tubes (13.8 oz. each) refrigerated pizza crust
- 2   cups shredded part-skim mozzarella cheese, divided
- 1   cup shredded Romano cheese, divided
- 1   pkg. (3½ oz.) sliced pepperoni
- 1   cup pineapple tidbits, drained

1. For sauce, place the first 10 ingredients in a food processor; cover and process until blended. Transfer to a small saucepan; heat through.

2. Meanwhile, press pizza dough into a greased 15x10x1-in. baking pan; build up edges slightly and seal seam. Bake at 425° for 6-8 minutes or until lightly browned.

3. Spread 1¾ cups sauce over crust (refrigerate remaining sauce for another use). Sprinkle with 1 cup mozzarella and ½ cup Romano; top with pepperoni, pineapple and remaining cheeses.

4. Bake 14-18 minutes or until cheese is melted and crust is golden brown.

1 piece: 294 cal., 10g fat (4g sat. fat), 20mg chol., 860mg sod., 38g carb. (9g sugars, 2g fiber), 14g pro.

CANDY CORN & PEANUT POPCORN BALLS

My daughter and I enjoy baking and cooking together, and this recipe is one my daughter can help make and then share at school. We enjoy making them every fall.
—Kim Shireman, Searcy, AR

- -

Prep: 15 min. • **Cook:** 5 min. + standing
Makes: 1 dozen

- 3   pkg. (3.3 oz. each) butter-flavored microwave popcorn
- 1   pkg. (18½ oz.) candy corn
- 1   jar (16 oz.) dry roasted peanuts, coarsely chopped
- 1   pkg. (10 oz.) miniature marshmallows
- ½   cup butter, cubed
- 2   Tbsp. canola oil
- 1   tsp. vanilla extract

1. Cook popcorn according to package directions; place in a large bowl. Add candy corn and peanuts; mix well.
2. In a large saucepan, combine the marshmallows, butter and oil. Cook and stir over medium-low heat until melted. Stir in vanilla. Pour over popcorn mixture; mix well. Cool slightly.
3. With greased hands, shape mixture into 12 popcorn balls, about 2⅓ cups each. Place on waxed paper; let stand until set.
1 popcorn ball: 663 cal., 36g fat (11g sat. fat), 20mg chol., 607mg sod., 80g carb. (56g sugars, 4g fiber), 11g pro.

MAKE-AHEAD S'MORES

These can be prepared ahead of time and stored. I will often pull out a few for snacks whenever unexpected company stops by.
—Anne Sherman, Orangeburg, SC

- -

Takes: 20 min. • **Makes:** 16 servings

- 8   oz. semisweet chocolate, chopped
- 1   can (14 oz.) sweetened condensed milk
- 1   tsp. vanilla extract
- 16   whole graham crackers, halved
- 2   cups miniature marshmallows

1. In a heavy saucepan, melt chocolate over low heat. Add milk; cook and stir until smooth. Stir in vanilla. Making 1 s'more at a time, spread 1 Tbsp. chocolate mixture over each of 2 graham cracker halves.
2. Place 8 or 9 marshmallows on 1 cracker; gently press the other cracker on top. Repeat. Store in an airtight container at room temperature.
1 serving: 157 cal., 6g fat (3g sat. fat), 0 chol., 100mg sod., 26g carb. (15g sugars, 2g fiber), 2g pro.

CHEESY PEPPERONI BUNS

A pizza version of the sloppy joe, this hot and melty open-faced sandwich is a surefire kid pleaser. The adults will love it, too!
—Tanya Belt, Newcomerstown, OH

- -

Takes: 25 min. • **Makes:** 12 servings

1	lb. lean ground beef (90% lean)
2	cups pizza sauce or pasta sauce
1	pkg. (3½ oz.) sliced pepperoni, chopped
4	slices American cheese, chopped
12	mini buns, split
2	cups shredded part-skim mozzarella cheese

1. Preheat oven to 350°. In a large skillet, cook beef over medium heat until no longer pink, 5-7 minutes, breaking into crumbles; drain. Stir in pizza sauce, pepperoni and American cheese. Cook and stir until cheese is melted, 4-5 minutes.

2. Place buns on a baking sheet, cut sides up. Spoon meat mixture onto buns; top with mozzarella cheese. Bake until cheese is melted, about 5 minutes. If desired, serve with additional warmed pizza sauce.

2 open-faced sandwiches: 280 cal., 14g fat (6g sat. fat), 46mg chol., 612mg sod., 18g carb. (4g sugars, 1g fiber), 18g pro.

★ ★ ★ ★ ★ **READER REVIEW**

"Great quick meal. The kids loved it! And I had time to enjoy visiting with them!"

NIGHTSKYSTAR TASTEOFHOME.COM

JACK-O'-LANTERN SANDWICHES

Be prepared for happy faces when you make these eye-catching jack-o'-lanterns. We loaded the little sandwiches with flavorful fillings, then cut fun faces with cookie cutters.
—*Taste of Home* Test Kitchen

- -

Takes: 15 min. • **Makes:** 8 servings

½	cup mayonnaise
2	tsp. Italian salad dressing mix
16	slices whole wheat or white bread
8	slices American cheese
1	lb. shaved deli chicken or turkey
8	lettuce leaves

1. In a bowl, combine the mayonnaise and salad dressing mix; spread over 1 side of each slice of bread. Top half the slices with cheese, chicken and lettuce. Top with remaining bread.
2. Cut sandwiches with a 4-in. pumpkin-shaped cutter. Remove top slice; using a small triangular cutter and a knife, decorate as desired. Replace slice.
1 sandwich: 357 cal., 18g fat (5g sat. fat), 50mg chol., 1139mg sod., 27g carb. (4g sugars, 4g fiber), 21g pro.

APPLE CARTWHEELS

Stuff apples with a yummy filling, and then slice the fruit into rings to make eye-appealing after-school snacks. The filling is an irresistible combination of creamy peanut butter, sweet honey, miniature chocolate chips and raisins.
—Miriam Miller, Thorp, WI

- -

Prep: 20 min. + chilling
Makes: about 2 dozen

¼	cup peanut butter
1½	tsp. honey
½	cup miniature semisweet chocolate chips
2	Tbsp. raisins
4	medium unpeeled Red Delicious apples, cored

1. In a small bowl, combine peanut butter and honey; fold in chocolate chips and raisins.
2. Fill centers of apples with peanut butter mixture; refrigerate for at least 1 hour. Cut into ¼-in. rings.
1 piece: 50 cal., 3g fat (1g sat. fat), 0 chol., 13mg sod., 7g carb. (6g sugars, 1g fiber), 1g pro.

KIDDIE CRUNCH MIX

This no-bake snack mix is a delightful treat for kids, and you can easily increase the amount to fit your needs. Place in individual bags, or pour some into colored ice cream cones for a fun presentation.
—Kara de la Vega, Santa Rosa, CA

Takes: 10 min. • **Makes:** 6 cups

- 1 cup plain or frosted animal crackers
- 1 cup bear-shaped crackers
- 1 cup miniature pretzels
- 1 cup salted peanuts
- 1 cup M&M's
- 1 cup yogurt- or chocolate-covered raisins

In a bowl, combine all ingredients. Store in an airtight container.

½ cup: 266 cal., 14g fat (5g sat. fat), 4mg chol., 159mg sod., 33g carb. (23g sugars, 3g fiber), 6g pro.

MUMMY CUPCAKES

These Halloween mummies are not scary at all! Their bright eyes and cute little smiles will enchant your party guests.
—*Taste of Home* Test Kitchen

Takes: 25 min. • **Makes:** varies

   Cupcakes of your choice
- 1 can (16 oz.) chocolate frosting
   Pastry tip—basket weave tip #48
- 1 can (16 oz.) vanilla frosting
   Candy eyes

1. Frost cupcakes with chocolate frosting.
2. Insert tip #48 into a pastry bag; fill with vanilla frosting. Pipe long bands across each cupcake, leaving a small gap for the eyes. Attach 2 eyes per cupcake.

STRAWBERRY CREAM FLOATS

When it starts warming up in Colorado, my children ask for ice-cold treats. This rosy pink cream float is one of our household favorites.
—Crystal Jo Bruns, Iliff, CO

Takes: 25 min. • **Makes:** 8 servings

  1 cup heavy whipping cream
  2 Tbsp. confectioners' sugar
STRAWBERRY SODA
  2 pkg. (14 oz. each) frozen unsweetened sliced strawberries (about 6 cups), thawed
  1 cup sugar
  ⅓ cup lime juice
  2 cups chilled carbonated water
ASSEMBLY
  4 cups vanilla ice cream
     Sliced fresh strawberries, optional

1. In a small bowl, beat cream until it begins to thicken. Add confectioners' sugar; beat until soft peaks form. Refrigerate until serving.

2. Place the strawberries, sugar and lime juice in a blender; cover and process until pureed. Press through a fine-mesh strainer into a pitcher; discard seeds. Stir in the carbonated water.

3. Divide the ice cream among 8 glasses. Pour strawberry soda over ice cream. Top with whipped cream and, if desired, fresh strawberries; serve immediately.

1 serving: 383 cal., 18g fat (11g sat. fat), 70mg chol., 65mg sod., 54g carb. (46g sugars, 3g fiber), 3g pro.

PUPPY CHOW

This snack mix is perfect for a late-night treat or a pick-me-up any time of the day. I sometimes take a batch to work, and it's always eaten up quickly.
—Mary Obeilin, Selinsgrove, PA

Takes: 15 min. • **Makes:** about 6 cups

  1 cup semisweet chocolate chips
  ¼ cup creamy peanut butter
  6 cups Corn or Rice Chex
  1 cup confectioners' sugar

1. In a large microwave-safe bowl, melt chocolate chips on high for 30 seconds. Stir; microwave until the chips are melted, 30 seconds longer. Stir in the peanut butter. Gently stir in cereal until well coated; set aside.

2. Place confectioners' sugar in a large airtight container. Add cereal mixture and shake until well coated. Store in an airtight container in the refrigerator.

Note: This recipe was tested in a 1,100-watt microwave.

½ cup: 194 cal., 7g fat (3g sat. fat), 0 chol., 170mg sod., 33g carb. (19g sugars, 1g fiber), 3g pro.

SWEET & SALTY PEANUT BUTTER BITES

My son Micah and I love peanut butter cups, so we made them into a new treat. We entered them in a creative baking contest and won first place!
—Autumn Emigh, Gahanna, OH

Prep: 20 min. • **Cook:** 5 min. + standing
Makes: about 5 dozen

- ½ cup semisweet chocolate chips
- 4 peanut butter cups (¾ oz. each), chopped
- 1⅓ cups creamy peanut butter
- 1 cup sugar
- 1 cup light corn syrup
- ⅛ tsp. salt
- 4 cups Rice Krispies
- 1 cup broken pretzels

1. Freeze chocolate chips and peanut butter cups until partially frozen, about 15 minutes. Meanwhile, in a large saucepan, combine the peanut butter, sugar, corn syrup and salt. Cook and stir over low heat until blended.
2. Remove from heat; stir in Rice Krispies and pretzels until coated. Let stand for 5 minutes; gently fold in chocolate chips and peanut butter cups until just combined. Drop by tablespoonfuls onto waxed paper; let stand until set.

1 cookie: 86 cal., 4g fat (1g sat. fat), 0 chol., 67mg sod., 13g carb. (10g sugars, 0 fiber), 2g pro.

RAVIOLI CASSEROLE

The whole family will love this yummy dish that tastes like lasagna without all the fuss. Timesaving ingredients such as prepared spaghetti sauce and frozen ravioli make it a cinch to fix. Children can help you assemble this one.
—Mary Ann Rothert, Austin, TX

Prep: 10 min. • **Bake:** 30 min.
Makes: 8 servings

- 1 pkg. (20 oz.) refrigerated cheese ravioli
- 3½ cups pasta sauce
- 2 cups small-curd 4% cottage cheese
- 4 cups shredded mozzarella cheese
- ¼ cup grated Parmesan cheese
  Minced fresh parsley, optional

1. Preheat oven to 350°. Prepare ravioli according to package directions; drain. Spread 1 cup pasta sauce in an ungreased 13x9-in. baking dish. Layer with half the ravioli, 1¼ cups sauce, 1 cup cottage cheese and 2 cups mozzarella cheese. Repeat the layers. Sprinkle with Parmesan cheese.
2. Bake casserole, uncovered, until bubbly, 30-40 minutes. Let stand 5-10 minutes before serving. If desired, sprinkle with fresh parsley.
1 cup: 518 cal., 25g fat (12g sat. fat), 88mg chol., 1411mg sod., 44g carb. (13g sugars, 5g fiber), 30g pro.

DIRT DESSERT

My mom used to serve this yummy dessert, and I just loved it. It's so fun to eat and a snap to make. Add some gummy worms on top for the kids if you'd like.
—Kristi Linton, Bay City, MI

- -

Prep: 30 min. + chilling • **Makes:** 20 servings

  1 **pkg. (8 oz.) cream cheese, softened**
 ¼ **cup butter, softened**
  1 **cup confectioners' sugar**
3½ **cups cold 2% milk**
  2 **pkg. (3.4 oz. each) instant vanilla pudding mix**
  1 **carton (12 oz.) frozen whipped topping, thawed**
  1 **pkg. (15½ oz.) Oreo cookies, crushed**

1. In a large bowl, beat the cream cheese, butter and confectioners' sugar until smooth. In a large bowl, whisk milk and pudding mixes for 2 minutes; let stand for 2 minutes or until soft-set. Gradually stir into cream cheese mixture. Fold in whipped topping.

2. Spread 1⅓ cups crushed cookies into an ungreased 13x9-in. dish. Layer with half the pudding mixture and half the remaining cookies. Repeat layers. Refrigerate for at least 1 hour before serving.

½ cup: 278 cal., 13g fat (7g sat. fat), 16mg chol., 316mg sod., 38g carb. (26g sugars, 1g fiber), 3g pro.

BRING IT
For a punchy treat sure to thrill the under-12 set, sneak some slithery gummy worms into the crumb topping just before serving.

CHOCOLATE SPOONS

My daughter adores decorating spoons with drizzles and candies. She then likes to stir them into hot chocolate.
—January Brylow, Milwaukee, WI

- -

Prep: 15 min. + standing • **Makes:** 1 dozen

- ½ cup Nutella
- 12 metal or plastic spoons
- ¾ lb. white candy coating, melted
  Optional toppings: Assorted colored sugars, small candies and sprinkles

1. Place 2 tsp. Nutella onto each spoon. Dip spoons quickly in melted candy coating; allow excess to drip off. Decorate with toppings if desired. Place on waxed paper; let stand until set.
2. Use to stir servings of hot cocoa.
1 serving: 212 cal., 12g fat (8g sat. fat), 0 chol., 5mg sod., 28g carb. (26g sugars, 0 fiber), 1g pro.

MAKE AHEAD
DIY HOT COCOA MIX

Because we have long, cold winters in Idaho, hot chocolate is a staple.
—Tracy Dalin, Gooding, ID

- -

Takes: 10 min.
Makes: 21 servings (7 cups hot cocoa mix)

- 2¾ cups nonfat dry milk powder
- 2 cups powdered nondairy creamer
- 1 cup confectioners' sugar
- ¾ cup baking cocoa
- 1 pkg. (3.9 oz.) instant chocolate pudding mix
- 1 cup miniature marshmallows, optional
- ½ cup miniature semisweet chocolate chips, optional

EACH SERVING
- ¾ cup hot 2% milk

In a large airtight container, mix the first 5 ingredients. If desired, stir in the marshmallows and chocolate chips. Store in a cool, dry place up to 6 months.
To prepare hot cocoa: Place ⅓ cup mix in a mug. Stir in hot milk until blended.
¾ cup prepared hot cocoa: 246 cal., 8g fat (5g sat. fat), 16mg chol., 163mg sod., 35g carb. (25g sugars, 1g fiber), 10g pro.

BIRD NESTS

This is a fun, kid-friendly recipe I pulled together a few years ago. My kids love helping me make these.
—Jessica Boivin, Nekoosa, WI

- -

Prep: 40 min. • **Makes:** 2 dozen

- 2 pkg. (10 to 12 oz. each) white baking chips
- 1 pkg. (10 oz.) pretzel sticks
- 24 yellow chicks Peeps candy
- 1 pkg. (12 oz.) M&M's eggs or other egg-shaped candy

1. In a large metal bowl over simmering water, melt baking chips; stir until smooth. Reserve ½ cup melted chips for the decorations; keep warm.
2. Add pretzel sticks to remaining chips; stir to coat evenly. Drop the mixture into 24 mounds on waxed paper; shape into bird nests using 2 forks.
3. Dip bottoms of Peeps in reserved melted chips; place in nests. Attach the eggs with remaining melted chips. Let stand until set.
1 nest: 276 cal., 11g fat (7g sat. fat), 7mg chol., 215mg sod., 41g carb. (30g sugars, 1g fiber), 4g pro.

BACON BREAKFAST PIZZA

Pizza for breakfast? Yes, please! I used to make this rise-and-shine recipe for my morning drivers when I worked at a pizza delivery place. It's a quick and easy eye-opener that became a quick hit!
—Cathy Shortall, Easton, MD

- -

Takes: 30 min. • **Makes:** 8 servings

- 1   tube (13.8 oz.) refrigerated pizza crust
- 2   Tbsp. olive oil, divided
- 6   large eggs
- 2   Tbsp. water
- 1   pkg. (3 oz.) bacon bits
- 1   cup shredded Monterey Jack cheese
- 1   cup shredded cheddar cheese

1. Preheat oven to 400°. Unroll and press dough onto bottom and ½ in. up sides of a greased 15x10x1-in. pan. Prick thoroughly with a fork; brush with 1 Tbsp. oil. Bake until lightly browned, 7-8 minutes.
2. Meanwhile, whisk together eggs and water. In a nonstick skillet, heat remaining oil over medium heat. Add eggs; cook and stir just until thickened and no liquid egg remains. Spoon over crust. Sprinkle with bacon bits and cheeses.
3. Bake until cheese is melted, 5-7 minutes.
1 piece: 352 cal., 20g fat (8g sat. fat), 169mg chol., 842mg sod., 24g carb. (3g sugars, 1g fiber), 20g pro.

> **TEST KITCHEN TIP**
> Casey's, a convenience store chain from Iowa, is famous for breakfast pizza, which was introduced by the store in 2001. The popularity of breakfast pizzas has spread across the country, and they are enjoyed any time of day!

ORANGE TAFFY

This taffy has the perfect blend of tart and sweet. It takes time to wrap all the little candies, but the kids can help. It's a terrific way to involve them in the kitchen.
—Christine Olson, Horse Creek, CA

- -

Prep: 20 min. • **Cook:** 1 hour + cooling
Makes: about 6 dozen

- 2   cups sugar
- 2   cups light corn syrup
- 1   can (6 oz.) frozen orange juice concentrate, undiluted
       Pinch salt
- 1   cup half-and-half cream
- ½   cup butter, cubed

1. In a heavy saucepan, combine first 4 ingredients. Cook and stir over medium heat until sugar is dissolved. Bring to a rapid boil and cook until a candy thermometer reads 245° (firm-ball stage). Remove from the heat; gradually add cream and butter. Return to the heat; cook and stir until mixture reaches 245° again.
2. Pour into a greased 15x10x1-in. pan; cool. When cool enough to handle, roll into ½-in. logs or 1-in. balls. Wrap individually in foil or waxed paper; twist ends.
1 piece: 67 cal., 2g fat (1g sat. fat), 5mg chol., 28mg sod., 14g carb. (11g sugars, 0 fiber), 0 pro.

Recipe Index